Praise for *Mistakes Were Made (but not by me)*

"This book casts a bright and penetrating light on how and why nation-states, organizations, and individuals get into malignant messes. Tavris and Aronson don't let any of us off the hook but they do teach us how to avoid hanging ourselves on that hook again and again. One of the most needed and important books for our time."

—Warren Bennis, author of *On Becoming a Leader*

"This book is indispensable reading for all psychotherapists. It explains not only why many clients cannot break out of the self-justifications that keep them stuck, but also how we can learn to discover and correct errors in our own clinical practice."

—Harriet Lerner, author of *The Dance of Anger*

"To err is human, to rationalize even more so. Now, thanks to this brilliant book, we can finally see how and why even the best-meaning people may justify terrible behavior. *Mistakes Were Made* will not turn us into angels, but it is hard to think of a better—or more readable—guide to the mind's most devilish tricks."

—David Callahan, author of *The Cheating Culture*

"Please, somebody, get a copy of this book to the president and his cabinet right away. Read it aloud into the Congressional Record. If this book doesn't change the way we think about our mistakes, then we're all doomed."

—Michael Shermer, contributing editor and columnist, *Scientific American*, author of *Why People Believe Weird Things*

"This book is charming and delightful. But mainly it's just damn smart. Armed with reams of scientific data and loads of real-world anecdotes, Tavris and Aronson explain how politicians, pundits, doctors, lawyers, psychotherapists—and, oh yes, the rest of us—come to believe that we are right and reasonable . . . and why we maintain that dangerous self-deception in the face of glaring evidence to the contrary. Every page sparkles with sharp insight and keen observation. Mistakes were made—but not in this book!"

—Daniel Gilbert, author of *Stumbling on Happiness*

"Tavris and Aronson—a dream team of two of psychology's greatest communicators—investigate our self-serving explanations and malleable memories, explaining how well-meaning people stay the course when pursuing ill-fated ventures, then shuck responsibility when failure arrives. This is a fascinating exploration of our astonishing powers of self-justification."

—David Myers, author of *Intuition: Its Powers and Perils*

"This eye-opener of a book is essential reading, not because we've all made mistakes—certainly not!—but because we've all been victims of mistakes made by others. Why do these people behave so badly? Tavris and Aronson's explanation is illuminating, entertaining, based on solid science, and highly relevant to our public and private lives."

—Judith Rich Harris, author of
The Nurture Assumption and *No Two Alike*

"Tavris and Aronson have combined their formidable skills to produce a gleaming model of social insight and scientific engagement. Make no mistake, you need to read this book."

—Robert B. Cialdini, author of *Influence: Science and Practice*

"Carol Tavris and Elliot Aronson have made a genuinely illuminating contribution to the study of human nature, one positively brimming with intelligence and insight . . . They are to be congratulated for this immensely engaging and intelligent volume, for shedding some illumination on that dark side of human behavior when it starts to go wrong and then gets horribly worse."

—*Metapsychology Online Reviews*

ALSO BY CAROL TAVRIS

Anger: The Misunderstood Emotion

The Mismeasure of Woman

Psychology (with Carole Wade)

Invitation to Psychology (with Carole Wade)

ALSO BY ELLIOT ARONSON

The Social Animal

Nobody Left to Hate

Age of Propaganda (with Anthony Pratkanis)

Social Psychology (with Timothy Wilson and Robin Akert)

Mistakes Were Made
(but not by *me*)

Why We Justify

Foolish Beliefs, Bad Decisions,

and Hurtful Acts

o o o

CAROL TAVRIS *and* ELLIOT ARONSON

A HARVEST BOOK ∘ HARCOURT, INC.

Orlando   Austin   New York   San Diego   London

For information about permission to reproduce selections from this book,
write to Permissions, Houghton Mifflin Harcourt Publishing Company,
215 Park Avenue South, New York, New York 10003.

www.hmhco.com

"Frank and Debra" extract from Andrew Christensen and Neil S. Jacobson's *Reconcilable
Differences* is © 2000 Guilford Press and is reprinted with permission of Guilford Press.

The Library of Congress has cataloged the hardcover edition as follows:
Tavris, Carol.
Mistakes were made (but not by me): why we justify foolish beliefs,
bad decisions, and hurtful acts/Carol Tavris & Elliot Aronson.—1st ed.
p.   cm.
Includes bibliographical references and index.
1. Cognitive dissonance.   2. Self-deception.   I. Aronson, Elliot.   II. Title.
BF337.C63T38   2007
153—dc22   2006026953
ISBN 978-0-15-101098-1
ISBN 978-0-15-603390-9 (pbk.)

Text set in Adobe Garamond

Printed in the United States of America
First Harvest edition 2008
DOC   20   19   18   17   16   15   14   13

To Ronan, my Wonderful O'
—Carol Tavris

o   o   o

To Vera, of course
—Elliot Aronson

We are all capable of believing things which we know to be untrue, and then, when we are finally proved wrong, impudently twisting the facts so as to show that we were right. Intellectually, it is possible to carry on this process for an indefinite time: the only check on it is that sooner or later a false belief bumps up against solid reality, usually on a battlefield.

—George Orwell (1946)

A great nation is like a great man:
When he makes a mistake, he realizes it.
Having realized it, he admits it.
Having admitted it, he corrects it.
He considers those who point out his faults as his most benevolent
    teachers.

—Lao Tzu

CONTENTS

o   o   o

INTRODUCTION

o   o   o

Knaves, Fools, Villains, and Hypocrites:
How Do They Live with Themselves?

Mistakes were quite possibly made by the administrations in which I served.

> —Henry Kissinger, responding to charges that he committed
> war crimes in his role in the United States' actions in
> Vietnam, Cambodia, and South America in the 1970s

If, in hindsight, we also discover that mistakes may have been made . . . I am deeply sorry.

> —Cardinal Edward Egan of New York, referring to the bishops
> who failed to deal with child molesters among the Catholic clergy

Mistakes were made in communicating to the public and customers about the ingredients in our French fries and hash browns.

> —McDonald's, apologizing to Hindus and other vegetarians
> for failing to inform them that the "natural flavoring"
> in their potatoes contained beef by-products

This week's question: How can you tell when a presidential scandal is serious?

   A. The president's poll numbers drop.

   B. The press goes after him.

   C. The opposition calls for his impeachment.

   D. His own party members turn on him.

   E. Or the White House says, "mistakes were made."

—Bill Schneider on CNN's *Inside Politics*

[AS FALLIBLE HUMAN BEINGS, all of us share the impulse to justify ourselves and avoid taking responsibility for any actions that turn out to be harmful, immoral, or stupid.]Most of us will never be in a position to make decisions affecting the lives and deaths of millions of people, but whether the consequences of our mistakes are trivial or tragic, on a small scale or a national canvas, most of us find it difficult, if not impossible, to say, "I was wrong; I made a terrible mistake." The higher the stakes—emotional, financial, moral—the greater the difficulty.

It goes further than that: Most people, when directly confronted with proof that they are wrong, do not change their point of view or course of action but justify it even more tenaciously. Politicians, of course, offer the most visible, and often tragic, examples of this practice. Throughout his presidency, George W. Bush was the epitome of a man for whom even irrefutable evidence could not pierce his mental armor of self-justification. Bush was wrong in his claim that Saddam Hussein had weapons of mass destruction, he was wrong in claiming that Saddam was linked with Al Qaeda, he was wrong in predicting that Iraqis would be dancing joyfully in the streets to receive American soldiers, he was wrong in his gross underestimate of the human and financial costs of the war, and he was most famously wrong in his speech six weeks after the invasion began, when he announced (under a banner reading MISSION ACCOMPLISHED) that "major combat operations in Iraq have ended."

Even as commentators from the right and left called on Bush to admit he had been mistaken, Bush merely found new justifications for the war: getting rid of a "very bad guy," fighting terrorists, promoting peace in the Middle East, bringing democracy to Iraq, increasing American security, and finishing "the task [our troops] gave their lives for." In the midterm election of 2006, which most political observers regarded as a referendum on the war, the Republican party lost both houses of Congress; a report issued shortly thereafter by sixteen American intelligence agencies announced that the occupation of Iraq had actually *increased* Islamic radicalism and the risk of terrorism. Yet Bush said to a delegation of conservative columnists, "I've never been more convinced that the decisions I made are the right decisions."[1]

Of course, George Bush was not the first, nor will he be the last, politician to justify decisions that turned out to have been based on incorrect premises or have disastrous consequences. Lyndon Johnson would not heed the advisers who repeatedly told him the war in Vietnam was unwinnable, and he sacrificed his presidency because of his self-justifying certainty that all of Asia would "go Communist" if America withdrew. When politicians' backs are nailed to the wall, they may reluctantly acknowledge *error,* but not responsibility. They have refined the art of speaking in the passive voice: Oh, all right, mistakes were made, but not by me; by someone else, who shall remain nameless.[2] When Henry Kissinger said that the "administration" may have made mistakes, he was sidestepping the fact that as national security adviser and secretary of state (simultaneously) he, in effect, *was* the administration. This self-justification allowed him to accept the Nobel Peace Prize with a straight face and a clear conscience.

We look at the behavior of politicians with amusement or alarm or horror, but, psychologically, what they do is no different in kind, though certainly in consequence, from what most of us have done at one time or another in our private lives. We stay in an unhappy relationship or merely one that is going nowhere because, after all, we invested so much time in making it work. We stay in a deadening job way too long because we look for all the reasons to justify staying and are unable to clearly assess the benefits of leaving. We buy a lemon of a car because it looks gorgeous, spend thousands of dollars to keep the damn thing running, and then we spend even more to justify that investment. We self-righteously create a rift with a friend or relative over some real or imagined slight, yet see ourselves as the pursuers of peace—if only the other side would apologize and make amends.

Self-justification is not the same thing as lying or making excuses. Obviously, people will lie or invent fanciful stories to duck the fury of a lover, parent, or employer; to keep from being sued or sent to prison; to avoid losing face; to avoid losing a job; to stay in power. But there is a big difference between what a guilty man says to the public to convince them of something he knows is untrue ("I did not have sex with that woman"; "I am not a crook"), and the process of persuading himself that he did a good thing. In the former situation, he is lying and knows he is lying to save his own skin. In the latter, he is lying to himself. That is why self-justification is more powerful and more dangerous than the explicit lie. It allows people to convince themselves that what they did was the best thing they could have done. In fact, come to think of it, it was the right thing. "There was nothing else I could have done." "Actually, it was a brilliant solution to the problem." "I was doing the best for the nation." "Those bastards deserved what they got." "I'm entitled."

Self-justification not only minimizes our mistakes and bad decisions; it is also the reason that everyone can see a hypocrite in action except the hypocrite. It allows us to create a distinction between our moral lapses and someone else's, and to blur the discrepancy between our actions and our moral convictions. Aldous Huxley was right when he said, "There is probably no such thing as a conscious hypocrite." It seems unlikely that Newt Gingrich said to himself, "My, what a hypocrite I am. There I was, all riled up about Bill Clinton's sexual affair, while I was having an extramarital affair of my own right here in town." Similarly, the prominent evangelist Ted Haggard seemed oblivious to the hypocrisy of publicly fulminating against homosexuality while enjoying his own sexual relationship with a male prostitute.

In the same way, we each draw our own moral lines and justify them. For example, have you ever done a little finessing of expenses on income taxes? That probably compensates for the legitimate expenses you forgot about, and besides, you'd be a fool not to, considering that everybody else does. Did you fail to report some extra cash income? You're entitled, given all the money that the government wastes on pork-barrel projects and programs you detest. Have you been writing personal e-mails and surfing the Net at your office when you should have been tending to business? Those are perks of the job, and besides, it's your own protest against those stupid company rules, and besides, your boss doesn't appreciate all the extra work you do.

Gordon Marino, a professor of philosophy and ethics, was staying in a hotel when his pen slipped out of his jacket and left an ink spot on the silk bedspread. He decided he would tell the manager, but he was tired and did not want to pay for the damage. That evening he went out with some friends and asked their advice. "One of them told me to stop with the moral fanaticism," Marino said. "He argued, 'The management expects such accidents and builds their cost into the price of the rooms.' It did not take long to persuade me that there was no need to trouble the manager. I reasoned that if I had spilled this ink in a family-owned bed-and-breakfast, then I would have immediately reported the accident, but that this was a chain hotel, and yadda yadda yadda went the hoodwinking process. I did leave a note at the front desk about the spot when I checked out."[3]

But, you say, all those justifications are true! Hotel room charges do include the costs of repairs caused by clumsy guests! The government does waste money! My company probably wouldn't mind if I spend a little time on e-mail and I do get my work done (eventually)! Whether those claims are true or false is irrelevant. When we cross these lines, we are justifying behavior that we know is wrong precisely so that we can continue to see ourselves as honest people and not criminals or thieves. Whether the behavior in question is a small thing like spilling ink on a hotel bedspread, or a big thing like embezzlement, the mechanism of self-justification is the same.

Now, between the conscious lie to fool others and unconscious self-justification to fool ourselves lies a fascinating gray area, patrolled by that unreliable, self-serving historian—memory. Memories are often pruned and shaped by an ego-enhancing bias that blurs the edges of past events, softens culpability, and distorts what really happened. When researchers ask husbands and wives what percentage of the housework they do, the wives say, "Are you kidding? I do almost everything, at least 90 percent." And the husbands say, "I do a lot, actually, about 40 percent." Although the specific numbers differ from couple to couple, the total always exceeds 100 percent by a large margin.[4] It's tempting to conclude that one spouse is lying, but it is more likely that each is remembering in a way that enhances his or her contribution.

Over time, as the self-serving distortions of memory kick in and we forget or distort past events, we may come to believe our own lies, little by little. We know we did something wrong, but gradually we begin to think it wasn't all our fault, and after all the situation was complex. We start underestimating our own responsibility, whittling away at it until it is a mere shadow of its former hulking self. Before long, we have persuaded ourselves, believing privately what we originally said publicly. John Dean, Richard Nixon's White House counsel, the man who blew the whistle on the conspiracy to cover up the illegal activities of the Watergate scandal, explained how this process works:

Interviewer: You mean those who made up the stories were believing their own lies?

Dean: That's right. If you said it often enough, it would become true. When the press learned of the wire taps on news-
men and White House staffers, for example, and flat denials
failed, it was claimed that this was a national-security matter.
I'm sure many people believed that the taps *were* for national
security; they weren't. That was concocted as a justification
after the fact. But when they said it, you understand, they
really *believed* it.[5]

Like Nixon, Lyndon Johnson was a master of self-justification.
According to his biographer Robert Caro, when Johnson came to believe in something, he would believe in it "totally, with absolute conviction, regardless of previous beliefs, or of the facts in the matter."
George Reedy, one of Johnson's aides, said that he "had a remarkable
capacity to convince himself that he held the principles he should
hold at any given time, and there was something charming about the
air of injured innocence with which he would treat anyone who
brought forth evidence that he had held other views in the past. It
was not an act. . . . He had a fantastic capacity to persuade himself
that the 'truth' which was convenient for the present was *the truth*
and anything that conflicted with it was the prevarication of enemies. He literally willed what was in his mind to become reality."[6]
Although Johnson's supporters found this to be a rather charming aspect of the man's character, it might well have been one of the major
reasons that Johnson could not extricate the country from the quag-
mire of Vietnam. A president who justifies his actions only to the
public might be induced to change them. A president who has justified his actions to himself, believing that he has *the truth*, becomes
impervious to self-correction.

o   o   o

The Dinka and Nuer tribes of the Sudan have a curious tradition.
They extract the permanent front teeth of their children—as many

as six bottom teeth and two top teeth—which produces a sunken chin, a collapsed lower lip, and speech impediments. This practice apparently began during a period when tetanus (lockjaw, which causes the jaws to clench together) was widespread. Villagers began pulling out their front teeth and those of their children to make it possible to drink liquids through the gap. The lockjaw epidemic is long past, yet the Dinka and Nuer are still pulling out their children's front teeth.[7] How come?

In 1847, Ignac Semmelweiss famously exhorted his fellow physicians to wash their hands before delivering babies. He realized that they must have acquired some kind of "morbid poison" on their hands from doing autopsies on women who had died of childbed fever, then transferred the poison to women in labor. (He didn't know the exact mechanism, but he had the right idea.) Semmelweiss ordered his own medical students to wash their hands in a chlorine antiseptic solution, and death rates from childbed fever dropped rapidly thereafter. Yet his colleagues refused to accept Semmelweiss's concrete evidence, the lower death rate among his own patients.[8] Why didn't they embrace Semmelweiss's discovery immediately, thanking him effusively for finding the reason for so many unnecessary deaths?

After World War II, Ferdinand Lundberg and Marynia Farnham published the bestseller *Modern Woman: The Lost Sex,* in which they claimed that a woman who achieves in "male spheres of action" may seem to be successful in the "big league," but she pays a big price: "sacrifice of her most fundamental instinctual strivings. She is not, in sober reality, temperamentally suited to this sort of rough and tumble competition, and it damages her, particularly in her own feelings." And it makes her frigid, besides: "Challenging men on every hand, refusing any longer to play even a relatively submissive role, multitudes of women found their capacity for sexual gratification dwindling."[9] In the ensuing decade, Dr. Farnham, who earned her MD from the University of Minnesota and did postgraduate work at Harvard Medical School, made a career out of telling women not to have careers. Wasn't she worried about becoming frigid and damaging her fundamental instinctual strivings?

The sheriff's department in Kern County, California, arrested a retired high-school principal, Patrick Dunn, on suspicion of the murder of his wife. They interviewed two people who told conflicting stories. One was a woman who had no criminal record and no personal incentive to lie about the suspect, and who had calendars and her boss to back up her account of events. The other was a career criminal facing six years in prison, who had offered to incriminate Dunn as part of a deal with prosecutors, and who offered nothing to support his story except his word for it. The detectives had to choose between believing the woman (and in Dunn's innocence), or the criminal (and in Dunn's guilt). They chose to believe the criminal.[10] Why?

By understanding the inner workings of self-justification, we can answer these questions and make sense of dozens of other things that people do that would otherwise seem unfathomable or crazy. We can answer the question so many people ask when they look at ruthless dictators, greedy corporate CEOs, religious zealots who murder in the name of God, priests who molest children, or people who cheat their siblings out of a family inheritance: How in the world can they *live* with themselves? The answer is: exactly the way the rest of us do.

Self-justification has costs and benefits. By itself, it's not necessarily a bad thing. It lets us sleep at night. Without it, we would prolong the awful pangs of embarrassment. We would torture ourselves with regret over the road not taken or over how badly we navigated the road we did take. We would agonize in the aftermath of almost every decision: Did we do the right thing, marry the right perso? buy the right house, choose the best car, enter the right career? mindless self-justification, like quicksand, can draw us dee? disaster. It blocks our ability to even see our errors, let al? them. It distorts reality, keeping us from getting all the i? need and assessing issues clearly. It prolongs and wi?

lovers, friends, and nations. It keeps us from letting go of unhealthy habits. It permits the guilty to avoid taking responsibility for their deeds. And it keeps many professionals from changing outdated attitudes and procedures that can be harmful to the public.

None of us can live without making blunders. But we do have the ability to say: "This is not working out here. This is not making sense." To err is human, but humans then have a choice between covering up or fessing up. The choice we make is crucial to what we do next. We are forever being told that we should learn from our mistakes, but how can we learn unless we first admit that we made any? To do that, we have to recognize the siren song of self-justification. In the next chapter, we will discuss cognitive dissonance, the hard-wired psychological mechanism that creates self-justification and protects our certainties, self-esteem, and tribal affiliations. In the chapters that follow, we will elaborate on the most harmful consequences of self-justification: how it exacerbates prejudice and corruption, distorts memory, turns professional confidence into arrogance, creates and perpetuates injustice, warps love, and generates feuds and rifts.

The good news is that by understanding how this mechanism works, we can defeat the wiring. Accordingly, in the final chapter, we will step back and see what solutions emerge for ourselves as individuals, for our relationships, for society. Understanding is the first step toward finding solutions that will lead to change and redemption. That is why we wrote this book.

CHAPTER 1

o   o   o

Cognitive Dissonance:
The Engine of Self-justification

Press release date: November 1, 1993
WE DIDN'T MAKE A MISTAKE when we wrote in our previous releases that New York would be destroyed on September 4 and October 14, 1993. We didn't make a mistake, not even a teeny eeny one!

Press release date: April 4, 1994
All the dates we have given in our past releases are correct dates given by God as contained in Holy Scriptures. Not one of these dates was wrong . . . Ezekiel gives a total of 430 days for the siege of the city . . . [which] brings us exactly to May 2, 1994. By now, all the people have been forewarned. We have done our job. . . .

We are the only ones in the entire world guiding the people to their safety, security, and salvation!

We have a 100 percent track record![1]

IT'S FASCINATING, AND SOMETIMES funny, to read dooms-day predictions, but it's even more fascinating to watch what happens to the reasoning of true believers when the prediction flops and the world keeps muddling along. Notice that hardly anyone ever says, "I blew it! I can't believe how stupid I was to believe that non-sense"? On the contrary, most of the time they become even more deeply convinced of their powers of prediction. The people who believe that the Bible's book of Revelation or the writings of the sixteenth-century self-proclaimed prophet Nostradamus have predicted every disaster from the bubonic plague to 9/11 cling to their convictions, unfazed by the small problem that their vague and murky predictions were intelligible only after the event occurred.

Half a century ago, a young social psychologist named Leon Festinger and two associates infiltrated a group of people who believed the world would end on December 21.[2] They wanted to know what would happen to the group when (they hoped!) the prophecy failed. The group's leader, whom the researchers called Marian Keech, promised that the faithful would be picked up by a flying saucer and elevated to safety at midnight on December 20. Many of her followers quit their jobs, gave away their homes, and dispersed their savings, waiting for the end. Who needs money in outer space? Others waited in fear or resignation in their homes. (Mrs. Keech's own husband, a nonbeliever, went to bed early and slept soundly through the night as his wife and her followers prayed in the living room.) Festinger made his own prediction: The believers who had not made a strong commitment to the prophecy—who awaited the end of the world by themselves at home, hoping they weren't going to die at midnight— would quietly lose their faith in Mrs. Keech. But those who had given away their possessions and were waiting with the others for the space-ship would increase their belief in her mystical abilities. In fact, they would now do everything they could to get others to join them.

At midnight, with no sign of a spaceship in the yard, the group felt a little nervous. By 2 A.M., they were getting seriously worried.

At 4:45 A.M., Mrs. Keech had a new vision: The world had been spared, she said, because of the impressive faith of her little band. "And mighty is the word of God," she told her followers, "and by his word have ye been saved—for from the mouth of death have ye been delivered and at no time has there been such a force loosed upon the Earth. Not since the beginning of time upon this Earth has there been such a force of Good and light as now floods this room."

The group's mood shifted from despair to exhilaration. Many of the group's members, who had not felt the need to proselytize before December 21, began calling the press to report the miracle, and soon they were out on the streets, buttonholing passersby, trying to convert them. Mrs. Keech's prediction had failed, but not Leon Festinger's.

o   o   o

The engine that drives self-justification, the energy that produces the need to justify our actions and decisions—especially the wrong ones—is an unpleasant feeling that Festinger called "cognitive dissonance." Cognitive dissonance is a state of tension that occurs whenever a person holds two cognitions (ideas, attitudes, beliefs, opinions) that are psychologically inconsistent, such as "Smoking is a dumb thing to do because it could kill me" and "I smoke two packs a day." Dissonance produces mental discomfort, ranging from minor pangs to deep anguish; people don't rest easy until they find a way to reduce it. In this example, the most direct way for a smoker to reduce dissonance is by quitting. But if she has tried to quit and failed, now she must reduce dissonance by convincing herself that smoking isn't really so harmful, or that smoking is worth the risk because it helps her relax or prevents her from gaining weight (and after all, obesity is a health risk, too), and so on. Most smokers manage to reduce dissonance in many such ingenious, if self-deluding, ways.

Dissonance is disquieting because to hold two ideas that contradict each other is to flirt with absurdity and, as Albert Camus observed, we humans are creatures who spend our lives trying to convince ourselves that our existence is not absurd. At the heart of it, Festinger's theory is about how people strive to make sense out of contradictory ideas and lead lives that are, at least in their own minds, consistent and meaningful. The theory inspired more than 3,000 experiments that, taken together, have transformed psychologists' understanding of how the human mind works. Cognitive dissonance has even escaped academia and entered popular culture. The term is everywhere. The two of us have heard it in TV newscasts, political columns, magazine articles, bumper stickers, even on a soap opera. Alex Trebek used it on *Jeopardy,* Jon Stewart on *The Daily Show,* and President Bartlet on *The West Wing.* Although the expression has been thrown around a lot, few people fully understand its meaning or appreciate its enormous motivational power.

In 1956, one of us (Elliot) arrived at Stanford University as a graduate student in psychology. Festinger had arrived that same year as a young professor, and they immediately began working together, designing experiments to test and expand dissonance theory.[3] Their thinking challenged many notions that were gospel in psychology and among the general public, such as the behaviorist's view that people do things primarily for the rewards they bring, the economist's view that human beings generally make rational decisions, and the psychoanalyst's view that acting aggressively gets rid of aggressive impulses.

Consider how dissonance theory challenged behaviorism. At the time, most scientific psychologists were convinced that people's actions are governed by reward and punishment. It is certainly true that if you feed a rat at the end of a maze, he will learn the maze faster than if you don't feed him; if you give your dog a biscuit when she gives you her paw, she will learn that trick faster than if you sit around hoping she will do it on her own. Conversely, if you punish your pup when you catch her peeing on the carpet, she will soon stop doing it. Behaviorists further argued that anything that was merely associated with reward would become more attractive—your puppy will like you because you give her biscuits—and anything associated with pain would become noxious and undesirable.

Behavioral laws do apply to human beings, too, of course; no one would stay in a boring job without pay, and if you give your toddler a cookie to stop him from having a tantrum, you have taught him to have another tantrum when he wants a cookie. But, for better or worse, the human mind is more complex than the brain of a rat or a puppy. A dog may appear contrite for having been caught peeing on the carpet, but she will not try to think up justifications for her misbehavior. Humans think; and because we think, dissonance theory demonstrated that our behavior transcends the effects of rewards and punishments and often contradicts them.

For example, Elliot predicted that if people go through a great deal of pain, discomfort, effort, or embarrassment to get something, they will be happier with that "something" than if it came to them easily. For behaviorists, this was a preposterous prediction. Why would people like anything associated with pain? But for Elliot, the answer was obvious: self-justification. The cognition that I am a sensible, competent person is dissonant with the cognition that I went through a painful procedure to achieve something—say, joining a group that turned out to be boring and worthless. Therefore, I would distort my perceptions of the group in a positive direction, trying to find good things about them and ignoring the downside.

It might seem that the easiest way to test this hypothesis would be to rate a number of college fraternities on the basis of how severe their initiations are, and then interview members and ask them how much they like their fraternity. If the members of severe-initiation fraternities like their frat brothers more than do members of mild-initiation fraternities, does this prove that severity produces the liking? It does not. It may be just the reverse. If the members of a fraternity regard themselves as being a highly desirable, elite group, they may require a severe initiation to prevent the riffraff from joining. Only those who are highly attracted to the severe-initiation group to begin with would be willing to go through the initiation to get into it. Those who are not excited by a particular fraternity but just want to be in one, any one, will choose fraternities that require mild initiations.

That is why it is essential to conduct a controlled experiment. The beauty of an experiment is the random assignment of people to conditions. Regardless of a person's degree of interest at the outset in joining the group, each participant would be randomly assigned to either the severe-initiation or the mild-initiation condition. If people who go through a tough time to get into a group later find that group to be more attractive than those who get in with no effort, then we know that it was the effort that caused it, not differences in initial levels of interest.

And so Elliot and his colleague Judson Mills conducted just such an experiment.[4] Stanford students were invited to join a group that would be discussing the psychology of sex, but before they could qualify for admission, they would first have to pass an entrance requirement. Some of the students were randomly assigned to a severely embarrassing initiation procedure: They had to recite, out loud to the experimenter, lurid, sexually explicit passages from *Lady Chatterley's Lover* and other racy novels. (For conventional 1950s students, this was a painfully embarrassing thing to do.) Others were randomly assigned to a mildly embarrassing initiation procedure: reading aloud sexual words from the dictionary.

After the initiation, each of the students listened to an identical tape recording of a discussion allegedly being held by the group of people they had just joined. Actually, the audiotape was prepared in advance so that the discussion was as boring and worthless as it could be. The discussants talked haltingly, with long pauses, about the secondary sex characteristics of birds—changes in plumage during courtship, that sort of thing. The taped discussants hemmed and hawed, frequently interrupted one another, and left sentences unfinished.

Finally, the students rated the discussion on a number of dimensions. Those who had undergone only a mild initiation saw the discussion for what it was, worthless and dull, and they correctly rated the group members as being unappealing and boring. One guy on the tape, stammering and muttering, admitted that he hadn't done the required reading on the courtship practices of some rare bird, and the mild-initiation listeners were annoyed by him. What an irresponsible idiot! He didn't even do the basic reading! He let the group down! Who'd want to be in a group with him? But those who had gone through a severe initiation rated the discussion as interesting and exciting and the group members as attractive and sharp. They forgave the irresponsible idiot. His candor was refreshing! Who wouldn't want to be in a group with such an honest guy? It was hard to believe that they were listening to the same tape recording. Such is the power of dissonance.

This experiment has been replicated several times by other scientists who have used a variety of initiation techniques, from electric shock to excessive physical exertion.[5] The results are always the same: Severe initiations increase a member's liking for the group. These findings do not mean that people enjoy painful experiences, such as filling out their income-tax forms, or that people enjoy things because they are associated with pain. What they do show is that if a person voluntarily goes through a difficult or a painful experience *in order* to attain some goal or object, that goal or object becomes more attractive. If, on your way to join a discussion group, a flowerpot fell from the open window of an apartment building and hit you on the head, you would not like that discussion group any better. But if you volunteered to get hit on the head by a flowerpot to become a member of the group, you would definitely like the group more.

Believing Is Seeing

> I will look at any additional evidence to confirm the opinion to which
> I have already come.
>
> —Lord Molson, British politician (1903–1991)

Dissonance theory also exploded the self-flattering idea that we humans, being *Homo sapiens,* process information logically. On the contrary: If the new information is consonant with our beliefs, we think it is well founded and useful: "Just what I always said!" But if the new information is dissonant, then we consider it biased or foolish: "What a dumb argument!" So powerful is the need for consonance that when people are forced to look at disconfirming evidence, they will find a way to criticize, distort, or dismiss it so that they can maintain or even strengthen their existing belief. This mental contortion is called the "confirmation bias." Lenny Bruce, the legendary American humorist and social commentator, described it vividly as he watched the famous 1960 confrontation between Richard Nixon and John Kennedy, in the nation's very first televised presidential debate:

> I would be with a bunch of Kennedy fans watching the debate and their comment would be, "He's really slaughtering Nixon." Then we would all go to another apartment, and the Nixon fans would say, "How do you like the shellacking he gave Kennedy?" And then I realized that each group loved their candidate so that a guy would have to be this blatant—he would have to look into the camera and say: "I am a thief, a crook, do you hear me, I am the worst choice you could ever make for the Presidency!" And even then his following would say, "Now there's an honest man for you. It takes a big guy to admit that. There's the kind of guy we need for President."[7]

In 2003, after it had become abundantly clear that there were no weapons of mass destruction in Iraq, Americans who had supported the war and President Bush's reason for launching it were thrown into dissonance: We believed the president, and we (and he) were wrong. How to resolve this? For Democrats who had thought Saddam Hussein had WMDs, the resolution was relatively easy: The Republicans were wrong again; the president lied, or at least was too eager to listen to faulty information; how foolish of me to believe him. For Republicans, however, the dissonance was sharper. More than half of them resolved it by refusing to accept the evidence, telling a Knowledge Networks poll that they believed the weapons *had* been found. The survey's director said, "For some Americans, their desire to support the war may be leading them to screen out information that weapons of mass destruction have not been found. Given the intensive news coverage and high levels of public attention to the topic, this level of misinformation suggests that some Americans may be avoiding having an experience of cognitive dissonance." You bet.[8]

Neuroscientists have recently shown that these biases in thinking are built into the very way the brain processes information—all brains, regardless of their owners' political affiliation. For example, in a study of people who were being monitored by magnetic resonance imaging (MRI) while they were trying to process dissonant or consonant information about George Bush or John Kerry, Drew Westen and his colleagues found that[the reasoning areas of the brain virtually shut down when participants were confronted with dissonant information, and the emotion circuits of the brain lit up happily when consonance was restored.[9] These mechanisms provide a neurological basis for the observation that once our minds are made up, it is hard to change them.]

Indeed, even reading information that goes against your point of view can make you all the more convinced you are right. In one experiment, researchers selected people who either favored or opposed capital punishment and asked them to read two scholarly, well-documented articles on the emotionally charged issue of whether the death penalty deters violent crimes. One article concluded that it did; the other that it didn't. If the readers were processing information rationally, they would at least realize that the issue is more complex than they had previously believed and would therefore move a bit closer to each other in their beliefs about capital punishment as a deterrence. But dissonance theory predicts that the readers would find a way to distort the two articles. They would find reasons to clasp the confirming article to their bosoms, hailing it as a highly competent piece of work. And they would be supercritical of the disconfirming article, finding minor flaws and magnifying them into major reasons why they need not be influenced by it. This is precisely what happened. Not only did each side discredit the other's arguments; each side became even more committed to its own.[10]

The confirmation bias even sees to it that no evidence—the absence of evidence—is evidence for what we believe. When the FBI and other investigators failed to find any evidence whatsoever for the belief that the nation had been infiltrated by Satanic cults that were ritually slaughtering babies, believers in these cults were unfazed. The absence of evidence, they said, was confirmation of how clever and evil the cult leaders were: They were eating those babies, bones and all. It's not just fringe cultists and proponents of pop psychology who fall prey to this reasoning. When Franklin D. Roosevelt made the terrible decision to uproot thousands of Japanese Americans and put them in incarceration camps for the duration of World War II, he did so entirely on the basis of rumors that Japanese Americans were planning to sabotage the war effort. There was no proof then or later to support this rumor. Indeed, the Army's West Coast commander, General John DeWitt, admitted that they had no evidence of sabotage or treason against a single Japanese-American citizen. "The very fact that no sabotage has taken place," he said, "is a disturbing and confirming indication that such action *will* be taken."[11]

Ingrid's Choice, Nick's Mercedes, and Elliot's Canoe

Dissonance theory came to explain far more than the reasonable notion that people are unreasonable at processing information. It also showed why they continue to be biased after they have made important decisions.[12] Social psychologist Dan Gilbert, in his illuminating book *Stumbling on Happiness,* asks us to consider what would have happened at the end of *Casablanca* if Ingrid Bergman did not patriotically rejoin her Nazi-fighting husband but instead remained with Humphrey Bogart in Morocco.[13] Would she, as Bogart tells her in a heart-wrenching speech, have regretted it—"maybe not today, maybe not tomorrow, but soon, and for the rest of your life"? Or did she forever regret leaving Bogart? Gilbert marshals a wealth of data to show that the answer to both questions is no, that either decision would have made her happy in the long run. Bogart was eloquent but wrong, and dissonance theory tells us why: Ingrid would have found reasons to justify either choice, along with reasons to be glad she did not make the other.

Once we make a decision, we have all kinds of tools at our disposal to bolster it. When our frugal, unflashy friend Nick traded in his eight-year-old Honda Civic on a sudden impulse and bought a new, fully loaded Mercedes, he began behaving oddly (for Nick). He started criticizing his friends' cars, saying things like "Isn't it about time you traded in that wreck? Don't you think you deserve the pleasure of driving a well-engineered machine?" and "You know, it's really unsafe to drive little cars. If you got in an accident, you could be killed. Isn't your life worth an extra few thousand dollars? You have no idea how much peace of mind it brings me to know that my family is safe because I'm driving a solid automobile."

It's possible that Nick simply got bitten by the safety bug and decided, coolly and rationally, that it would be wonderful if everyone drove a great car like the Mercedes. But we don't think so. His behavior, both in spending all that money on a luxury car and in nagging his friends to do the same, was so uncharacteristic that we suspected that he was reducing the dissonance he must have felt over impulsively spending a big chunk of his life's savings on what he would once have referred to as "just a car." Besides, he was doing this just when his kids were about to go to college, an event that would put a strain on his bank account. So Nick began marshalling arguments to justify his decision: "The Mercedes is a wonderful machine; I've worked hard all my life and I deserve it; besides, it's so safe." And if he could persuade his cheapskate friends to buy one too, he would feel doubly justified. Like Mrs. Keech's converts, he began to proselytize.

Nick's need to reduce dissonance (like Ingrid's) was increased by the irrevocability of his decision; he could not unmake that decision without losing a lot of money. Some scientific evidence for the power of irrevocability comes from a clever study of the mental maneuverings of gamblers at a racetrack. The racetrack is an ideal place to study irrevocability because once you've placed your bet, you can't go back and tell the nice man behind the window you've changed your mind. In this study, the researchers simply intercepted people who were standing in line to place two-dollar bets and other people who had just left the window. The investigators asked everyone how certain they were that their horses would win. The bettors who had placed their bets were far more certain about their choice than were the folks waiting in line.[14] But, of course, nothing had changed except the finality of placing the bet. [People become more certain they are right about something they just did if they can't undo it.]

You can see one immediate benefit of understanding how dissonance works: Don't listen to Nick. The more costly a decision, in terms of time, money, effort, or inconvenience, and the more irrevocable its consequences, the greater the dissonance and the greater the need to reduce it by overemphasizing the good things about the choice made. Therefore, when you are about to make a big purchase or an important decision—which car or computer to buy, whether to undergo plastic surgery, or whether to sign up for a costly self-help program—don't ask someone who has just done it. That person will be highly motivated to convince you that it is the right thing to do. Ask people who have spent twelve years and $50,000 on a particular therapy if it helped, and most will say, "Dr. Weltschmerz is wonderful! I would *never* have found true love [got a new job] [lost weight] if it hadn't been for him." After all that time and money, they aren't likely to say, "Yeah, I saw Dr. Weltschmerz for twelve years, and boy, was it ever a waste." If you want advice on what product to buy, ask someone who is still gathering information and is still open-minded. And if you want to know whether a program will help you, don't rely on testimonials: Get the data from controlled experiments.

Self-justification is complicated enough when it follows our conscious choices; at least we know we can expect it. But it also occurs in the aftermath of things we do for unconscious reasons, when we haven't a clue about why we hold some belief or cling to some custom but are too proud to admit it. For example, in the introduction we described the custom of the Dinka and Nuer tribes of the Sudan, who extract several of the permanent front teeth of their children— a painful procedure, done with a fish hook. Anthropologists suggest that this tradition originated during an epidemic of lockjaw; missing front teeth would enable sufferers to get some nourishment. But if that were the reason, why in the world would the villagers continue this custom once the danger had passed?

[A practice that makes no sense at all to outsiders makes perfect sense when seen through the lens of dissonance theory.]During the epidemic, the villagers would have begun extracting the front teeth of all their children, so that if any later contracted tetanus, the adults would be able to feed them. But this is a painful thing to do to children, especially since only some would become afflicted. To further justify their actions, to themselves and their children, the villagers would need to bolster the decision by adding benefits to the procedure after the fact. For example, they might convince themselves that pulling teeth has aesthetic value—say, that sunken-chin look is really quite attractive—and they might even turn the surgical ordeal into a rite of passage into adulthood. And, indeed, that is just what happened. "The toothless look is beautiful," the villagers say. "People who have all their teeth are ugly: They look like cannibals who would eat a person. A full set of teeth makes a man look like a donkey." The toothless look has other aesthetic advantages: "We like the hissing sound it creates when we speak." And adults reassure frightened children by saying, "This ritual is a sign of maturity."[15] The original medical justification for the practice is long gone. The psychological self-justification remains.

People want to believe that, as smart and rational individuals, they know why they made the choices they did, so they are not always happy when you tell them the actual reason for their actions. Elliot learned this firsthand after that initiation experiment. "After each participant had finished," he recalls, "I explained the study in detail and went over the theory carefully. Although everyone who went through the severe initiation said that they found the hypothesis intriguing and that they could see how most people would be affected in the way I predicted, they all took pains to assure me that their preference for the group had nothing to do with the severity of the initiation. They each claimed that they liked the group because that's the way they really felt. Yet almost all of them liked the group more than any of the people in the mild-initiation condition did."

No one is immune to the need to reduce dissonance, even those who know the theory inside out. Elliot tells this story: "When I was a young professor at the University of Minnesota, my wife and I tired of renting apartments; so, in December, we set out to buy our first home. We could find only two reasonable houses in our price range. One was older, charming, and within walking distance from the campus. I liked it a lot, primarily because it meant that I could have my students over for research meetings, serve beer, and play the role of the hip professor. But that house was in an industrial area, without a lot of space for our children to play. The other choice was a tract house, newer but totally without distinction. It was in the suburbs, a thirty-minute drive from campus but only a mile from a lake. After going back and forth on that decision for a few weeks, we decided on the house in the suburbs.

"Shortly after moving in, I noticed an ad in the newspaper for a used canoe and immediately bought it as a surprise for my wife and kids. When I drove home on a freezing, bleak January day with the canoe lashed to the roof of my car, my wife took one look and burst into laughter. 'What's so funny?' I asked. She said, 'Ask Leon Festinger!' Of course! I had felt so much dissonance about buying the house in the suburbs that I needed to do something right away to justify that purchase. I somehow managed to forget that it was the middle of winter and that, in Minneapolis, it would be months before the frozen lake would thaw out enough for the canoe to be usable. But, in a sense, without my quite realizing it, I used that canoe anyway. All winter, even as it sat in the garage, its presence made me feel better about our decision."

Spirals of Violence—and Virtue

Feeling stressed? One Internet source teaches you how to make your own little Damn It Doll, which "can be thrown, jabbed, stomped and even strangled till all the frustration leaves you." A little poem goes with it:

> When you want to kick the desk or throw the phone and
> shout
> Here's a little damnit doll you cannot do without.
> Just grasp it firmly by the legs, and find a place to slam it.
> And as you whack its stuffing out, yell, "damnit, damnit,
> damnit!"

The Damn It Doll reflects one of the most entrenched convictions in our culture, fostered by the psychoanalytic belief in the benefits of catharsis: that expressing anger or behaving aggressively gets rid of anger. Throw that doll, hit a punching bag, shout at your spouse;

you'll feel better afterward. Actually, decades of experimental research have found exactly the opposite: [that when people vent their feelings aggressively they often feel worse, pump up their blood pressure, and make themselves even angrier.[6]]

Venting is especially likely to backfire if a person commits an aggressive act against another person directly, which is exactly what cognitive dissonance theory would predict. When you do anything that harms someone else—get them in trouble, verbally abuse them, or punch them out—a powerful new factor comes into play: the need to justify what you did. Take a boy who goes along with a group of his fellow seventh graders who are taunting and bullying a weaker kid who did them no harm. The boy likes being part of the gang but his heart really isn't in the bullying. Later, he feels some dissonance about what he did. "How can a decent kid like me," he wonders, "have done such a cruel thing to a nice, innocent little kid like him?" To reduce dissonance, he will try to convince himself that the victim is neither nice nor innocent: "He is such a nerd and crybaby. Besides, he would have done the same to me if he had the chance." Once the boy starts down the path of blaming the victim, he becomes more likely to beat up on the victim with even greater ferocity the next chance he gets. Justifying his first hurtful act sets the stage for more aggression. That's why the catharsis hypothesis is wrong.

The first experiment that demonstrated this actually came as a complete surprise to the investigator. Michael Kahn, then a graduate student in clinical psychology at Harvard, designed an ingenious experiment that he was sure would demonstrate the benefits of catharsis. Posing as a medical technician, Kahn took polygraph and blood pressure measurements from college students, one at a time, allegedly as part of a medical experiment. As he was taking these measurements, Kahn feigned annoyance and made some insulting remarks to the students (having to do with their mothers). The students got angry; their blood pressure soared. In the experimental

condition, the students were allowed to vent their anger by inform-
ing Kahn's supervisor of his insults; thus, they believed they were getting him into big trouble. In the control condition, the students did
not get a chance to express their anger.

Kahn, a good Freudian, was astonished by the results: Catharsis
was a total flop. The people who were allowed to express their anger
about Kahn felt far greater animosity toward him than did those
who were not given that opportunity. In addition, expressing their
anger increased their already heightened blood pressure; the high
blood pressure of those who were not allowed to express their anger
soon returned to normal.[17] Seeking an explanation for this unexpected pattern, Kahn discovered dissonance theory, which was just
getting attention at the time, and realized it could beautifully account for his results. Because the students thought they had gotten
him into serious trouble, they had to justify their action by convincing themselves that he deserved it, thus increasing their anger against
him—and their blood pressure.

Children learn to justify their aggressive actions early: They hit a
younger sibling, who starts to cry, and immediately claim, "But he
started it! He deserved it!" Most parents find these childish self-
justifications to be of no great consequence, and usually they aren't.
But it is sobering to realize that the same mechanism underlies the
behavior of gangs who bully weaker children, employers who mis-
treat workers, lovers who abuse each other, police officers who continue beating a suspect who has surrendered, tyrants who imprison
and torture ethnic minorities, and soldiers who commit atrocities
against civilians. In all these cases, a vicious circle is created: Aggression begets self-justification, which begets more aggression. Fyodor
Dostoevsky understood perfectly how this process works. In *The
Brothers Karamazov,* he has Fyodor Pavlovitch, the brothers'
scoundrel of a father, recall "how he had once in the past been asked,
'Why do you hate so and so, so much?' And he had answered them,
with his shameless impudence, 'I'll tell you. He has done me no

harm. But I played him a dirty trick, and ever since I have hated him.'"

Fortunately, dissonance theory also shows us how a person's generous actions can create a spiral of benevolence and compassion, a "virtuous circle." When people do a good deed, particularly when they do it on a whim or by chance, they will come to see the beneficiary of their generosity in a warmer light. Their cognition that they went out of their way to do a favor for this person is dissonant with any negative feelings they might have had about him. In effect, after doing the favor, they ask themselves: "Why would I do something nice for a jerk? Therefore, he's not as big a jerk as I thought he was— as a matter of fact, he is a pretty nice guy who deserves a break."

Several experiments have supported this prediction. In one, college students participated in a contest where they won a substantial sum of money. Afterward, the experimenter approached one third of them and explained that he was using his own funds for the experiment and was running short, which meant he might be forced to close down the experiment prematurely. He asked, "As a special favor to me, would you mind returning the money you won?" (They all agreed.) A second group was also asked to return the money, but this time it was the departmental secretary who made the request, explaining that the psychology department's research fund was running low. (They still all agreed.) The remaining participants were not asked to return their winnings at all. Finally, everyone filled out a questionnaire that included an opportunity to rate the experimenter. Participants who had been cajoled into doing a special favor for him liked him the best; they convinced themselves he was a particularly fine, deserving fellow. The others thought he was pretty nice but not anywhere near as wonderful as the people who had done him a personal favor believed.[18]

Although scientific research on the virtuous circle is new, the general idea may have been discovered in the eighteenth century by Benjamin Franklin, a serious student of human nature as well as science and politics. While serving in the Pennsylvania legislature, Franklin was disturbed by the opposition and animosity of a fellow legislator. So he set out to win him over. He didn't do it, he wrote, by "paying any servile respect to him"—that is, by doing the other man a favor—but by inducing his target to do a favor for *him*— loaning him a rare book from his library:

> He sent it immediately and I returned it in about a week with another note, expressing strongly my sense of the favor. When we next met in the House, he spoke to me (which he had never done before), and with great civility; and he ever after manifested a readiness to serve me on all occasions, so that we became great friends, and our friendship continued to his death. This is another instance of the truth of an old maxim I had learned, which says, "He that has once done you a kindness will be more ready to do you another than he whom you yourself have obliged."[19]

o   o   o

Dissonance is bothersome under any circumstance, but it is most painful to people when an important element of their self-concept is threatened—typically when they do something that is inconsistent with their view of themselves.[20] If an athlete or celebrity you admire is accused of rape, child molestation, or murder, you will feel a pang of dissonance. The more you identify with this person, the greater the dissonance, because more of yourself would be involved. But you would feel a much more devastating rush of dissonance if you regarded yourself as a person of high integrity and you did something criminal. After all, you can always change your allegiance to a celebrity and find another hero. But if you violated your own values, you would feel much greater dissonance because, at the end of the day, you have to go on living with yourself.

Because most people have a reasonably positive self-concept, believing themselves to be competent, moral, and smart, their efforts at reducing dissonance will be designed to preserve their positive self-images.[21] When Mrs. Keech's doomsday predictions failed, for example, imagine the excruciating dissonance her committed followers felt: "I am a smart person" clashed with "I just did an incredibly stupid thing: I gave away my house and possessions and quit my job because I believed a crazy woman." To reduce that dissonance, her followers could either have modified their opinion of their intelligence or justified the "incredibly stupid" thing they did. It's not a close contest; it's justification by three lengths. Mrs. Keech's true believers saved their self-esteem by deciding they hadn't done anything stupid; in fact, they had been really smart to join this group because their faith saved the world from destruction. In fact, if everyone else were smart, they would join, too. Where's that busy street corner?

None of us is off the hook on this one. *We* might feel amused at *them,* those foolish people who believe fervently in doomsday predictions; but, as political scientist Philip Tetlock shows in his book *Expert Political Judgment: How Good Is It? How Can We Know?,* even professional "experts" who are in the business of economic and political forecasting are usually no more accurate than us untrained folks—or than Mrs. Keech, for that matter.[22] Hundreds of studies have shown that predictions based on an expert's "personal experience" or "years of training" are rarely better than chance, in contrast to predictions based on actuarial data. But when experts are wrong, the centerpiece of their professional identity is threatened. Therefore, as dissonance theory would predict, the more self-confident and famous they are, the less likely they will be to admit mistakes. And that is just what Tetlock found. Experts reduce the dissonance caused by their failed forecasts by coming up with explanations of why they would have been right "if only"—if only that improbable calamity had not intervened; if only the timing of events had been different; if only blah blah blah.

[Dissonance reduction] operates like a thermostat, keeping our self-esteem bubbling along on high. That is why we are usually oblivious to the self-justifications, the little lies to ourselves that prevent us from even acknowledging that we made mistakes or foolish decisions. But dissonance theory applies to people with low self-esteem, too, to people who consider themselves to be schnooks, crooks, or incompetents. They are not surprised when their behavior confirms their negative self-image. When they make a wrongheaded prediction or go through a severe initiation to get into a dull group, they merely say, "Yup, I screwed up again; that's just like me." A used-car salesman who knows that he is dishonest does not feel dissonance when he conceals the dismal repair record of the car he is trying to unload; a woman who believes she is unlovable does not feel dissonance when men reject her; a con man does not experience dissonance when he cheats an old man out of his life's savings.

Our convictions about who we are carry us through the day, and we are constantly interpreting the things that happen to us through the filter of those core beliefs. When they are violated, even by a good experience, it causes us discomfort. An appreciation of the power of self-justification helps us understand, therefore, why people who have low self-esteem, or who simply believe that they are incompetent in some domain, are not totally overjoyed when they do something well; why, on the contrary, they often feel like frauds. If the woman who believes she is unlovable meets a terrific guy who starts pursuing her seriously, she will feel momentarily pleased, but that pleasure is likely to be tarnished by a rush of dissonance: "What does he see in me?" Her resolution is unlikely to be "How nice; I must be more appealing than I thought I was." More likely, it will be "As soon as he discovers the real me, he'll dump me." She will pay a high psychological price to have that consonance restored.

⌈Indeed, several experiments find that most people who have low self-esteem or a low estimate of their abilities do feel uncomfortable with their dissonant successes and dismiss them as accidents or anomalies.[23] This is why they seem so stubborn to friends and family members who try to cheer them up⌋ "Look, you just won the Pulitzer

Prize for literature! Doesn't *that* mean you're good?" "Yeah, it's nice, but just a fluke. I'll never be able to write another word, you'll see." Self-justification, therefore, is not only about protecting high self-esteem; it's also about protecting low self-esteem if that is how a person sees himself.

The Pyramid of Choice

Imagine two young men who are identical in terms of attitudes, abilities, and psychological health. They are reasonably honest and have the same middling attitude toward, say, cheating: They think it is not a good thing to do, but there are worse crimes in the world. Now they are both in the midst of taking an exam that will determine whether they will get into graduate school. They each draw a blank on a crucial essay question. Failure looms . . . at which point each one gets an easy opportunity to cheat, by reading another student's answers. The two young men struggle with the temptation. After a long moment of anguish, one yields and the other resists. Their decisions are a hair's breadth apart; it could easily have gone the other way for each of them. Each gains something important, but at a cost: One gives up integrity for a good grade, the other gives up a good grade to preserve his integrity.

Now the question is: How do they feel about cheating a week later? Each student has had ample time to justify the course of action he took. The one who yielded to temptation will decide that cheating is not so great a crime. He will say to himself: "Hey, everyone cheats. It's no big deal. And I really needed to do this for my future career." But the one who resisted the temptation will decide that cheating is far more immoral than he originally thought: "In fact, people who cheat are disgraceful. In fact, people who cheat should be permanently expelled from school. We have to make an example of them."

By the time the students are through with their increasingly intense levels of self-justification, two things have happened: One, they are now very far apart from one another; and two, they have internalized their beliefs and are convinced that they have always felt that way.[24] It is as if they had started off at the top of a pyramid, a millimeter apart; but by the time they have finished justifying their individual actions, they have slid to the bottom and now stand at opposite corners of its base. The one who didn't cheat considers the other to be totally immoral, and the one who cheated thinks the other is hopelessly puritanical. This process illustrates how people who have been sorely tempted, battled temptation, and almost given in to it—but resisted at the eleventh hour—come to dislike, even despise, those who did not succeed in the same effort. It's the people who *almost* decide to live in glass houses who throw the first stones.

The metaphor of the pyramid applies to most important decisions involving moral choices or life options. Instead of cheating on an exam, for example, now substitute: deciding to begin a casual affair (or not), sample an illegal drug (or not), take steroids to improve your athletic ability (or not), stay in a troubled marriage (or not), name names to the House Un-American Activities Committee (or not), lie to protect your employer and job (or not), have children (or not), pursue a demanding career (or stay home with the kids). [When the person at the top of the pyramid is uncertain, when there are benefits and costs of both choices, then he or she will feel a particular urgency to justify the choice made. But by the time the person is at the bottom of the pyramid, ambivalence will have morphed into certainty, and he or she will be miles away from anyone who took a different route.]

This process blurs the distinction that people like to draw between "us good guys" and "those bad guys." Often, standing at the top of the pyramid, we are faced not with a black-and-white, go/no-go decision, but with a gray choice whose consequences are shrouded. The first steps along the path are morally ambiguous, and the right decision is not always clear. We make an early, apparently inconsequential decision, and then we justify it to reduce the ambiguity of the choice. This starts a process of entrapment—action, justification, further action—that increases our intensity and commitment, and may end up taking us far from our original intentions or principles.

It certainly worked that way for Jeb Stuart Magruder, Richard Nixon's special assistant, who was a key player in the plot to burglarize the Democratic National Committee headquarters in the Watergate complex, concealed the White House's involvement, and lied under oath to protect himself and others responsible. When Magruder was first hired, Nixon's adviser Bob Haldeman did not tell him that perjury, cheating, and breaking the law were part of the job description. If he had, Magruder almost certainly would have refused. How, then, did he end up as a central player in the Watergate scandal? It is easy, in hindsight, to say "He should have known" or "He should have drawn the line the first time they asked him to do something illegal."

In his autobiography, Magruder describes his first meeting with Bob Haldeman at San Clemente. Haldeman flattered and charmed him. "Here you're working for something more than just to make money for your company," Haldeman told him. "You're working to solve the problems of the country and the world. Jeb, I sat with the President on the night the first astronauts stepped onto the moon . . . I'm part of history being made." At the end of a day of meetings, Haldeman and Magruder left the compound to go to the president's house. Haldeman was enraged that his golf cart was not right there awaiting him, and he gave his assistant a "brutal chewing out," threatening to fire the guy if he couldn't do his job. Magruder couldn't believe what he was hearing, especially since it was a beautiful evening and a short walk to their destination. At first Magruder thought Haldeman's tirade was rude and excessive. But before long, wanting the job as much as he did, Magruder was justifying Haldeman's behavior: "In just a few hours at San Clemente I had been struck by the sheer *perfection* of life there . . . After you have been spoiled like that for a while, something as minor as a missing golf cart can seem a major affront."[25]

And so, before dinner and even before having been offered a job, Magruder is hooked. It is a tiny first step, but he is on the road to Watergate. Once in the White House, he went along with all of the small ethical compromises that just about all politicians justify in the goal of serving their party. Then, when Magruder and others were working to reelect Nixon, G. Gordon Liddy entered the picture, hired by Attorney General John Mitchell to be Magruder's general counsel. Liddy was a wild card, a James Bond wannabe. His first plan to ensure Nixon's reelection was to spend one million dollars to hire "mugging squads" that would rough up demonstrators; kidnap activists who might disrupt the Republican convention; sabotage the Democratic convention; use "high-class" prostitutes to entice and then blackmail leading Democrats; break into Democratic offices; and use electronic surveillance and wiretapping on their perceived enemies.

Mitchell disapproved of the more extreme aspects of this plan; besides, he said, it was too expensive. So Liddy returned with a proposal merely to break into the DNC offices at the Watergate complex and install wiretaps. This time Mitchell approved, and everyone went along. How did they justify breaking the law? "If [Liddy] had come to us at the outset and said, 'I have a plan to burglarize and wiretap Larry O'Brien's office,' we might have rejected the idea out of hand," wrote Magruder. "Instead, he came to us with his elaborate call girl/kidnapping/mugging/sabotage/wiretapping scheme, and we began to tone it down, always with a feeling that we should leave Liddy a little something—we felt we needed him, and we were reluctant to send him away with nothing." Finally, Magruder added, Liddy's plan was approved because of the paranoid climate in the White House: "Decisions that now seem insane seemed at the time to be rational. . . . We were past the point of halfway measures or gentlemanly tactics."[26]

When Magruder first entered the White House, he was a decent man. But, one small step at a time, he went along with dishonest actions, justifying each one as he did. He was entrapped in pretty much the same way as were the 3,000 people who took part in the famous experiment created by social psychologist Stanley Milgram.[27] In Milgram's original version, two-thirds of the participants administered what they thought were life-threatening levels of electric shock to another person, simply because the experimenter kept saying, "The experiment requires that you continue." This experiment is almost always described as a study of obedience to authority. Indeed it is. But it is more than that: It is also a demonstration of long-term results of self-justification.[28]

Imagine that a distinguished-looking man in a white lab coat walks up to you and offers you twenty dollars to participate in a scientific experiment. He says, "I want you to inflict 500 volts of incredibly painful shock to another person to help us understand the role of punishment in learning." Chances are you would refuse; the money isn't worth it to harm another person, even for science. Of course, a few people would do it for twenty bucks and some would not do it for twenty thousand, but most would tell the scientist where he could stick his money.

Now suppose the scientist lures you along more gradually. Suppose he offers you twenty dollars to administer a minuscule amount of shock, say 10 volts, to a fellow in the adjoining room, to see if this zap will improve the man's ability to learn. The experimenter even tries the 10 volts on you, and you can barely feel it. So you agree. It's harmless and the study seems pretty interesting. (Besides, you've always wanted to know whether spanking your kids will get them to shape up.) You go along for the moment, and now the experimenter tells you that if the learner gets the wrong answer, you must move to the next toggle switch, which delivers a shock of 20 volts. Again, it's a small and harmless jolt. Because you just gave the learner 10, you see no reason why you shouldn't give him 20. And because you just gave him 20, you say to yourself, 30 isn't much more than 20, so I'll go to 30. He makes another mistake, and the scientist says, "Please administer the next level—40 volts."

Where do you draw the line? When do you decide enough is enough? Will you keep going to 450 volts, or even beyond that, to a switch marked XXX DANGER? When people are asked in advance how far they imagine they would go, almost no one says they would go to 450. But when they are actually in the situation, two-thirds of them go all the way to the maximum level they believe is dangerous. They do this by justifying each step as they went along: This small shock doesn't hurt; 20 isn't much worse than 10; if I've given 20, why not 30? As they justified each step, they committed themselves further. By the time people were administering what they believed were strong shocks, most found it difficult to justify a sudden decision to quit. Participants who resisted early in the study, questioning the very validity of the procedure, were less likely to become entrapped by it and more likely to walk out.

The Milgram experiment shows us how ordinary people can end up doing immoral and harmful things through a chain reaction of behavior and subsequent self-justification. When we, as observers, look at them in puzzlement or dismay, we fail to realize that we are often looking at the end of a long, slow process down that pyramid. At his sentencing, Magruder said to Judge John Sirica: "I know what I have done, and Your Honor knows what I have done. Somewhere between my ambition and my ideals, I lost my ethical compass." How do you get an honest man to lose his ethical compass? You get him to take one step at a time, and self-justification will do the rest.

o   o   o

Knowing how dissonance works won't make any of us automatically immune to the allure of self-justification, as Elliot learned when he bought that canoe in January. You can't just say to people, as he did after the initiation experiments, "See how you reduced dissonance? Isn't that interesting?" and expect them to reply, "Oh, thank you for showing me the real reason I like the group. That sure makes me feel smart!" All of us, to preserve our belief that we are smart, will occasionally do dumb things. We can't help it. We are wired that way.

But this does not mean that we are doomed to keep striving to justify our actions after the fact—like Sisyphus, never reaching the top of the hill of self-acceptance. A richer understanding of how and why our minds work as they do is the first step toward breaking the self-justification habit. And that, in turn, requires us to be more mindful of our behavior and the reasons for our choices. It takes time, self-reflection, and willingness.

The conservative columnist William Safire once described the "psychopolitical challenge" that voters face: "how to deal with cognitive dissonance."[29] He began with a story of his own such challenge. During the Clinton administration, Safire recounted, he had criticized Hillary Clinton for trying to conceal the identity of the members of her health-care task force. He wrote a column castigating her efforts at secrecy, which he said were toxic to democracy. No dissonance there; those bad Democrats are always doing bad things. Six years later, however, he found that he was "afflicted" by cognitive dissonance when Vice President Dick Cheney, a fellow conservative Republican whom Safire admires, insisted on keeping the identity of his energy-policy task force a secret. What did Safire do? Because of his awareness of dissonance and how it works, he took a deep breath, hitched up his trousers, and did the tough but virtuous thing: He wrote a column publicly criticizing Cheney's actions. The irony is that because of his criticism of Cheney, Safire received several laudatory letters from liberals—which, he admitted, produced enormous dissonance. Oh, Lord, he did something *those* people approved of?

Safire's ability to recognize his own dissonance, and resolve it by doing the fair thing, is rare. As we will see, his willingness to concede that his own side made a mistake is something that few are prepared to share. Instead, people will bend over backward to reduce dissonance in a way that is favorable to them and their team. The specific ways vary, but our efforts at self-justification are all designed to serve our need to feel good about what we have done, what we believe, and who we are.

CHAPTER 2

o   o   o

Pride and Prejudice . . . and Other Blind Spots

And why do you look at the speck in your brother's eye, but do not
consider the plank in your own eye?

                                          —Matthew 7:3 (New King James version)

WHEN THE PUBLIC LEARNED that Supreme Court Justice An-
tonin Scalia was flying to Louisiana on a government plane to go
duck hunting with Vice President Dick Cheney, despite Cheney's
having a pending case before the Supreme Court, there was a flurry
of protest at Scalia's apparent conflict of interest. Scalia himself was
indignant at the suggestion that his ability to assess the constitution-
ality of Cheney's claim—that the vice president was legally entitled
to keep the details of his energy task force secret—would be tainted
by the ducks and the perks. In a letter to the *Los Angeles Times* explaining why he would not recuse himself, Scalia wrote, "I do not
think my impartiality could reasonably be questioned."

Neuropsychologist Stanley Berent and neurologist James Albers were hired by CSX Transportation Inc. and Dow Chemical to investigate railroad workers' claims that chemical exposure had caused permanent brain damage and other medical problems. More than 600 railroad workers in fifteen states had been diagnosed with a form of brain damage following heavy exposure to chlorinated hydrocarbon solvents. CSX paid more than $170,000 to Berent and Albers' consulting firm for research that eventually disputed a link between exposure to the company's industrial solvents and brain damage. While conducting their study, which involved reviewing the workers' medical files without the workers' informed consent, the two scientists served as expert witnesses for law firms representing CSX in lawsuits filed by workers. Berent saw nothing improper in his research, which he claimed "yielded important information about solvent exposure." Berent and Albers were subsequently reprimanded by the federal Office of Human Research Protections for their conflict of interest in this case.[1]

o   o   o

When you enter the Museum of Tolerance in Los Angeles, you find yourself in a room of interactive exhibits designed to identify the people you can't tolerate. The familiar targets are there (blacks, women, Jews, gays), but also short people, fat people, blond-female people, disabled people, . . . You watch a video on the vast variety of prejudices, designed to convince you that everyone has at least a few, and then you are invited to enter the museum proper through one of two doors: one marked PREJUDICED, the other marked UN-PREJUDICED. The latter door is locked, in case anyone misses the point, but occasionally some people do. When we were visiting the museum one afternoon, we were treated to the sight of four Hasidic Jews pounding angrily on the Unprejudiced door, demanding to be let in.

[The brain is designed with blind spots, optical and psychological, and one of its cleverest tricks is to confer on us the comforting delusion that we, personally, do not have any.] In a sense, dissonance theory is a theory of blind spots—of how and why people unintentionally blind themselves so that they fail to notice vital events and information that might make them question their behavior or their convictions. Along with the [confirmation bias,] the brain comes packaged with other self-serving habits that allow us to justify our own perceptions and beliefs as being accurate, realistic, and unbiased. Social psychologist Lee Ross calls this phenomenon "naïve realism," the inescapable conviction that we perceive objects and events clearly, "as they really are."[2] We assume that other reasonable people see things the same way we do. If they disagree with us, they obviously aren't seeing clearly. Naïve realism creates a logical labyrinth because it presupposes two things: One, people who are open-minded and fair ought to agree with a reasonable opinion. And two, any opinion I hold must be reasonable; if it weren't, I wouldn't hold it. Therefore, if I can just get my opponents to sit down here and listen to me, so I can tell them how things really are, they will agree with me. And if they don't, it must be because they are biased.

Ross knows whereof he speaks, from his laboratory experiments and from his efforts to reduce the bitter conflict between Israelis and Palestinians. Even when each side recognizes that the other side perceives the issues differently, each thinks that the other side is biased while they themselves are objective, and that their own perceptions of reality should provide the basis for settlement. In one experiment, Ross took peace proposals created by Israeli negotiators, labeled them as Palestinian proposals, and asked Israeli citizens to judge them. "The Israelis liked the Palestinian proposal attributed to Israel more than they liked the Israeli proposal attributed to the Palestinians," he says. "If your own proposal isn't going to be attractive to you when it comes from the other side, what chance is there that the *other* side's proposal is going to be attractive when it actually comes from the other side?"[3] Closer to home, social psychologist Geoffrey Cohen found that Democrats will endorse an extremely restrictive welfare proposal, one usually associated with Republicans, if they think it has been proposed by the Democratic Party, and Republicans will support a generous welfare policy if they think it comes from the Republican Party.[4] Label the same proposal as coming from the other side, and you might as well be asking people if they will favor a policy proposed by Osama bin Laden. No one in Cohen's study was aware of their blind spot—that they were being influenced by their party's position. Instead, they all claimed that their beliefs followed logically from their own careful study of the policy at hand, guided by their general philosophy of government.

Ross and his colleagues have found that we believe our own judgments are less biased and more independent than those of others partly because we rely on introspection to tell us what we are thinking and feeling, but we have no way of knowing what others are really thinking.[5] And when we introspect, looking into our souls and hearts, the need to avoid dissonance assures us that we have only the best and most honorable of motives. We take our own involvement in an issue as a source of accuracy and enlightenment—"I've felt strongly about gun control for years; therefore, I know what I'm talking about"—but we regard such personal feelings on the part of others who hold different views as a source of bias—"She can't possibly be impartial about gun control because she's felt strongly about it for years."

All of us are as unaware of our blind spots as fish are unaware of the water they swim in, but those who swim in the waters of privilege have a particular motivation to remain oblivious. When Marynia Farnham achieved fame and fortune during the late 1940s and 1950s by advising women to stay at home and raise children, otherwise risking frigidity, neurosis, and a loss of femininity, she saw no inconsistency (or irony) in the fact that she was privileged to be a physician who was not staying at home raising children, including her own two. When affluent people speak of the underprivileged, they rarely bless their lucky stars that they are privileged, let alone consider that they might be overprivileged. Privilege is their blind spot.[6] It is invisible; they don't think twice about it; they justify their social position as something they are entitled to. In one way or another, all of us are blind to whatever privileges life has handed us, even if those privileges are temporary. Most people who normally fly in what is euphemistically called the "main cabin" regard the privileged people in business and first class as wasteful snobs, if enviable ones. Imagine paying all that extra money for a short, six-hour flight! But as soon as they are the ones paying for a business seat or are upgraded, that attitude vanishes, replaced by a self-justifying mixture of pity and disdain for their fellow passengers, forlornly trooping past them into steerage.

Drivers cannot avoid having blind spots in their field of vision, but good drivers are aware of them; they know they had better be careful backing up and changing lanes if they don't want to crash into fire hydrants and other cars. Our innate biases are, as two legal scholars put it, "like optical illusions in two important respects— they lead us to wrong conclusions from data, and their apparent rightness persists even when we have been shown the trick."[7] We cannot avoid our psychological blind spots, but if we are unaware of them we may become unwittingly reckless, crossing ethical lines and making foolish decisions. Introspection alone will not help our vision, because it will simply confirm our self-justifying beliefs that we, personally, cannot be coopted or corrupted, and that our dislikes or hatreds of other groups are not irrational but reasoned and legitimate. Blind spots enhance our pride and activate our prejudices.

The Road to St. Andrews

The greatest of faults, I should say, is to be conscious of none.

—historian and essayist Thomas Carlyle

The *New York Times* editorial writer Dorothy Samuels summarized the thinking of most of us in the aftermath of learning that Congressman Tom DeLay, former leader of the House Republicans, had accepted a trip to the legendary St. Andrews golf course in Scotland with Jack Abramoff, the corrupt lobbyist-turned-informer in the congressional corruption scandal that ensued. "I've been writing about the foibles of powerful public officials for more years than I care to reveal without a subpoena," she wrote, "and I still don't get it: why would someone risk his or her reputation and career for a lobbyist-bestowed freebie like a vacation at a deluxe resort?"[8]

Dissonance theory gives us the answer: one step at a time. Although there are plenty of unashamedly corrupt politicians who sell their votes to the largest campaign contributor, most politicians, thanks to their blind spots, believe they are incorruptible. When they first enter politics, they accept lunch with a lobbyist, because, after all, that's how politics works and it's an efficient way to get information about a pending bill, isn't it? "Besides," the politician says, "lobbyists, like any other citizens, are exercising their right to free speech. I only have to listen; I'll decide how to vote on the basis of whether my party and constituents support this bill and on whether it is the right thing to do for the American people."

Once you accept the first small inducement and justify it that way, however, you have started your slide down the pyramid. If you had lunch with a lobbyist to talk about that pending legislation, why not talk things over on the local golf course? What's the difference? It's a nicer place to have a conversation. And if you talked things over on the local course, why not accept a friendly offer to go to a better course to play golf with him or her—say, to St. Andrews in Scotland? What's wrong with that? By the time the politician is at the bottom of the pyramid, having accepted and justified ever-larger inducements, the public is screaming, "What's *wrong* with that? Are you kidding?" At one level, the politician is not kidding. Dorothy Samuels is right: Who would jeopardize a career and reputation for a trip to Scotland? The answer is: no one, if that were the first offer he got; but many of us would, if it were an offer preceded by many smaller ones that we had accepted. Pride, followed by self-justification, paves the road to Scotland.

Conflict of interest and politics are synonymous, and everyone understands the cozy collaborations that politicians forge to preserve their own power at the expense of the common welfare. It's harder to see that exactly the same process affects judges, scientists, and physicians, professionals who pride themselves on their ability to be intellectually independent for the sake of justice, scientific advancement, or public health. These are professionals whose training and culture promote the core value of impartiality, so most become indignant at the mere suggestion that financial or personal interests could contaminate their work. Their professional pride makes them see themselves as being above such matters. No doubt, some are; just as, at the other extreme, some judges and scientists are flat-out dishonest, corrupted by ambition or money. (The South Korean scientist Hwang Woo-Suk, who admitted that he had faked his data on cloning, was the scientific equivalent of former congressman Randy "Duke" Cunningham, who went to prison for taking millions in bribes and evading taxes.) In between the extremes of rare integrity and blatant dishonesty are the great majority who, being human, have all the blind spots the rest of us have. Unfortunately, they are also more likely to think they don't, which makes them even more vulnerable to being hooked.

Once upon a time, not so long ago, most scientists ignored the lure of commerce. When Jonas Salk was questioned about patenting his polio vaccine in 1954, he replied, "Could you patent the sun?" How charming, yet how naïve, his remark seems today; imagine, handing over your discovery to the public interest without keeping a few million bucks for yourself. The culture of science valued the separation of research and commerce, and universities maintained a firewall between them. Scientists got their money from the government or independent funding institutions, and were more or less free to spend years investigating a problem that might or might not pay off, either intellectually or practically. A scientist who went public, profiting from his or her discoveries, was regarded with suspicion, even disdain. "It was once considered unseemly for a biologist to be thinking about some kind of commercial enterprise while at the same time doing basic research," says bioethicist and scientist Sheldon Krimsky.[9] "The two didn't seem to mix. But as the leading figures of the field of biology began intensively finding commercial outlets and get-rich-quick schemes, they helped to change the ethos of the field. Now it is the multivested scientists who have the prestige."

The critical event occurred in 1980, when the Supreme Court ruled that patents could be issued on genetically modified bacteria, independent of its process of development. That meant that you could get a patent for discovering a virus, altering a plant, isolating a gene, or modifying any other living organism as a "product of manufacture." The gold rush was on—the scientists' road to St. Andrews. Before long, many professors of molecular biology were serving on the advisory boards of biotechnology corporations and owned stock in companies selling products based on their research. Universities, seeking new sources of revenue, began establishing intellectual property offices and providing incentives for faculty who patented their discoveries. Throughout the 1980s, the ideological climate shifted from one in which science was valued for its own sake, or for the public interest, to one in which science was valued for the profits it could generate in the private interest. Major changes in tax and patent laws were enacted; federal funding of research declined sharply; and tax benefits created a steep rise in funding from industry. The pharmaceutical industry was deregulated, and within a decade it had become one of the most profitable businesses in the United States.[10]

And then scandals involving conflicts of interest on the part of researchers and physicians began to erupt. Big Pharma was producing new, lifesaving drugs but also drugs that were unnecessary at best and risky at worst: More than three-fourths of all drugs approved between 1989 and 2000 were no more than minor improvements over existing medications, cost nearly twice as much, and had higher risks.[11] By 1999, seven major drugs, including Rezulin and Lotronex, had been removed from the market for safety reasons. None had been necessary to save lives (one was for heartburn, one a diet pill, one a painkiller, one an antibiotic) and none was better than older, safer drugs. Yet these seven drugs were responsible for 1,002 deaths and thousands of troubling complications.[12]

The public has reacted to such news not only with the anger they are accustomed to feeling toward dishonest politicians, but also with dismay and surprise: How can scientists and physicians possibly promote a drug they know is harmful? Can't they see that they are selling out? How can they justify what they are doing? Certainly some investigators, like corrupt politicians, know exactly what they are doing. They are doing what they were hired to do—get results that their employers want and suppress results that their employers don't want to hear, as tobacco-company researchers did for decades. But at least public-interest groups, watchdog agencies, and independent scientists can eventually blow the whistle on bad or deceptive research. The greater danger to the public comes from the self-justifications of well-intentioned scientists and physicians who, because of their need to reduce dissonance, truly believe themselves to be above the influence of their corporate funders. Yet, like a plant turning toward the sun, they turn toward the interests of their sponsors without even being aware that they are doing so.

How do we know this? One way is by comparing the results of studies funded independently and those funded by industry, which consistently reveal a funding bias.

- Two investigators selected 161 studies, all published during the same six-year span, of the possible risks to human health of four chemicals. Of the studies funded by industry, only 14 percent found harmful effects on health; of those funded independently, fully 60 percent found harmful effects.[13]

- A researcher examined more than 100 controlled clinical trials designed to determine the effectiveness of a new medication over older ones. Of those favoring the traditional drug, 13 percent had been funded by drug companies and 87 percent by nonprofit institutions.[14]

- Two Danish investigators examined 159 clinical trials that had been published between 1997 and 2001 in the *British Medical Journal,* where authors are required to declare potential conflicts of interest. The researchers could therefore compare studies in which the investigators had declared a conflict of interest with those in which there was none. The findings were "significantly more positive toward the experimental intervention" (i.e., the new drug compared to an older one) when the study had been funded by a for-profit organization.[15]

If most of the scientists funded by industry are not consciously cheating, what is causing the funding bias? Clinical trials of new drugs are complicated by many factors, including length of treatment, severity of the patients' disease, side effects, dosage of new drug, and variability in the patients being treated. The interpretation of results is rarely clear and unambiguous; that is why all scientific studies require replication and refinement and why most findings are open to legitimate differences of interpretation. If you are an impartial scientist and your research turns up an ambiguous but worrisome finding about your new drug, perhaps what seems like a slightly increased risk of heart attack or stroke, you might say, "This is troubling; let's investigate further. Is this increased risk a fluke, was it due to the drug, or were the patients unusually vulnerable?"

However, if you are motivated to show that your new drug is effective and better than older drugs, you will be inclined to downplay your misgivings and resolve the ambiguity in the company's favor. "It's nothing. There's no need to look further." "Those patients were already quite sick, anyway." "Let's assume the drug is safe until proven otherwise." This was the reasoning of the Merck-funded investigators who had been studying the company's multibillion-dollar painkiller drug Vioxx before evidence of the drug's risks was produced by independent scientists.[16]

You will also be motivated to seek only confirming evidence for your hypothesis and your sponsor's wishes. In 1998, a team of scientists reported in the distinguished medical journal the *Lancet* that they had found a positive correlation between autism and childhood vaccines. Naturally, this study generated enormous alarm among parents and caused many to stop vaccinating their children. Six years later, ten of the thirteen scientists involved in this study retracted that particular result and revealed that the lead author, Andrew Wakefield, had had a conflict of interest he had failed to disclose to the journal: He was conducting research on behalf of lawyers representing parents of autistic children. Wakefield had been paid more than $800,000 to determine whether there were grounds for pursuing legal action, and he gave the study's "yes" answer to the lawyers before publication. "We judge that all this information would have been material to our decision-making about the paper's suitability, credibility, and validity for publication," wrote Richard Horton, editor of the *Lancet*.[17]

Wakefield, however, did not sign the retraction and could not see a problem. "Conflict of interest," he wrote in his defense, "is created when involvement in one project potentially could, or actively does, interfere with the objective and dispassionate assessment of the processes or outcomes of another project. We cannot accept that the knowledge that affected children were later to pursue litigation, following their clinical referral and investigation, influenced the content or tone of [our earlier] paper. . . . We emphasise that this was not a scientific paper but a clinical report."[18] Oh. It wasn't a scientific paper, anyway.

Of course we do not know Andrew Wakefield's real motives or thoughts about his research. But we suspect that he, like Stanley Berent in our opening story, convinced himself that he was acting honorably, that he was doing good work, and that he was uninfluenced by having been paid $800,000 by the lawyers. Unlike truly independent scientists, however, he had no incentive to look for disconfirming evidence of a correlation between vaccines and autism, and every incentive to overlook other explanations. In fact, five major studies have found no causal relationship between autism and the preservative in the vaccines (which was discontinued in 2001, with no attendant decrease in autism rates). The correlation is coincidental, a result of the fact that autism is typically diagnosed in children at the same age they are vaccinated.[19]

The Gift that Keeps on Giving

Physicians, like scientists, want to believe their integrity cannot be compromised. Yet every time physicians accept a fee or other incentive for performing certain tests and procedures, for channeling some of their patients into clinical trials, or for prescribing a new, expensive drug that is not better or safer than an older one, they are balancing their patients' welfare against their own financial concerns.

Their blind spot helps them tip the balance in their own favor, and then justify it: "If a pharmaceutical company wants to give us pens, notepads, calendars, lunches, honoraria, or small consulting fees, why not? We can't be bought by trinkets and pizzas." According to surveys, physicians regard small gifts as being ethically more acceptable than large gifts. The American Medical Association agrees, approving of gift-taking from pharmaceutical representatives as long as no single gift is worth much more than $100. The evidence shows, however, that most physicians are influenced even more by small gifts than by big ones.[20] Drug companies know this, which might have something to do with their increased spending on marketing to physicians, from $12.1 billion in 1999 to $22 billion in 2003. That's a lot of trinkets.

The reason Big Pharma spends so much on small gifts is well known to marketers, lobbyists, and social psychologists: Being given a gift evokes an implicit desire to reciprocate. The Fuller Brush salespeople understood this principle decades ago, when they pioneered the [foot-in-the-door technique:] Give a housewife a little brush as a gift, and she won't slam the door in your face. And once she hasn't slammed the door in your face, she will be more inclined to invite you in, and eventually to buy your expensive brushes. Robert Cialdini, who has spent many years studying influence and persuasion techniques, systematically observed Hare Krishna advocates raise money at airports.[21] Asking weary travelers for a donation wasn't working; the Krishnas just made the travelers mad at them. And so the Krishnas came up with a better idea: They would approach target travelers and press a flower into their hands or pin the flower to their jackets. If the target refused the flower and tried to give it back, the Krishna would demur and say, "It is our gift to you." Only then did the Krishna ask for a donation. This time the request was likely to be accepted, because the gift of the flower had established a feeling of indebtedness and obligation in the traveler. How to repay the gift? With a small donation . . . and perhaps the purchase of a charming, overpriced edition of the Bhagavad Gita.

Were the travelers aware of the power of reciprocity to affect their behavior? Not at all. But once reciprocity kicks in, self-justification will follow: "I've always wanted a copy of the Bhagavad Gita; what is it, exactly?" The power of the flower is unconscious. "It's only a flower," the traveler says. "It's only a pizza," the medical resident says. "It's only a small donation that we need to have this educational symposium," the physician says. Yet the power of the flower is one reason that the amount of contact doctors have with pharmaceutical representatives is positively correlated with the cost of the drugs the doctors later prescribe. "That rep has been awfully persuasive about that new drug; I might as well try it; my patients might do well on it." Once you take the gift, no matter how small, the process starts. You will feel the urge to give something back, even if it's only, at first, your attention, your willingness to listen, your sympathy for the giver. Eventually, you will become more willing to give your prescription, your ruling, your vote. Your behavior changes, but, thanks to blind spots and self-justification, your view of your intellectual and professional integrity remains the same.

Carl Elliott, a bioethicist and philosopher who also has an MD, has written extensively about the ways that small gifts entrap their recipients. His brother Hal, a psychiatrist, told him how he ended up on the speakers bureau of a large pharmaceutical company: First they asked him to give a talk about depression to a community group. Why not, he thought; it would be a public service. Next they asked him to speak on the same subject at a hospital. Next they began making suggestions about the content of his talk, urging him to speak not about depression, but about antidepressants. Then they told him they could get him on a national speaking circuit, "where the real money is." Then they asked him to lecture about their own new antidepressant. Looking back, Hal told his brother:

It's kind of like you're a woman at a party, and your boss says to you, "Look, do me a favor: be nice to this guy over there." And you see the guy is not bad-looking, and you're unattached, so you say, "Why not? I can be nice." Soon you find yourself on the way to a Bangkok brothel in the cargo hold of an unmarked plane. And you say, "Whoa, this is not what I agreed to." But then you have to ask yourself: "When did the prostitution actually start? Wasn't it at that party?"[22]

Nowadays, even professional ethicists are going to the party: The watchdogs are being tamed by the foxes they were trained to catch. Pharmaceutical and biotechnology industries are offering consulting fees, contracts, and honoraria to bioethicists, the very people who write about, among other things, the dangers of conflicts of interest between physicians and drug companies. Carl Elliott has described his colleagues' justifications for taking the money. "Defenders of corporate consultation often bristle at the suggestion that accepting money from industry compromises their impartiality or makes them any less objective a moral critic," he writes. "'Objectivity is a myth,' [bioethicist Evan] DeRenzo told me, marshaling arguments from feminist philosophy to bolster her cause. 'I don't think there is a person alive who is engaged in an activity who has absolutely no interest in how it will turn out.'" There's a clever dissonance-reducing claim for you—"perfect objectivity is impossible anyway, so I might as well accept that consulting fee."

Thomas Donaldson, director of the ethics program at the Wharton School, justified this practice by comparing ethics consultants to independent accounting firms that a company might hire to audit their finances. Why not audit their ethics? This stab at self-justification didn't get past Carl Elliott either. "Ethical analysis does not look anything like a financial audit," he says. An accountant's transgression can be detected and verified, but how do you detect the transgressions of an ethics consultant? "How do you tell the differ-

ence between an ethics consultant who has changed her mind for legitimate reasons and one who has changed her mind for money?
How do you distinguish between a consultant who has been hired
for his integrity and one who has been hired because he supports
what the company plans to do?"[23] Still, Elliott says wryly, perhaps we
can be grateful that the AMA's Council on Ethical and Judicial Affairs designed an initiative to educate doctors about the ethical problems involved in accepting gifts from the drug industry. That
initiative was funded by $590,000 in gifts from Eli Lilly and Com-
pany; GlaxoSmithKline, Inc.; Pfizer, Inc.; U. S. Pharmaceutical
Group; AstraZeneca Pharmaceuticals; Bayer Corporation; Procter &
Gamble; and Wyeth-Ayerst Pharmaceutical.

A Slip of the Brain

> Al Campanis was a very nice man, even a sweet man, but also a
> flawed man who made one colossal mistake in his 81 years on
> earth—a mistake that would come to define him forevermore.
>
> —sports writer Mike Littwin, on Campanis's death in 1998

On April 6, 1987, *Nightline* devoted its whole show to the fortieth
anniversary of Jackie Robinson's Major League debut. Ted Koppel
interviewed Al Campanis, general manager of the Los Angeles
Dodgers, who had been part of the Dodger organization since 1943
and who had been Robinson's teammate on the Montreal Royals in
1946. That year, he punched a bigoted player who had insulted
Robinson and, subsequently, championed the admission of black
players into Major League Baseball. And then, in talking with Koppel, Campanis put his brain on automatic drive. Koppel asked him,
as an old friend of Jackie Robinson's, why there were no black managers, general managers, or owners in baseball. Campanis was, at
first, evasive—you have to pay your dues by working in the minors;

there's not much pay while you're working your way up—but Koppel pressed him:

> *Koppel:* Yeah, but you know in your heart of hearts . . . you know that that's a lot of baloney. I mean, there are a lot of black players, there are a lot of great black baseball men who would dearly love to be in managerial positions, and I guess what I'm really asking you is to, you know, peel it away a little bit. Just tell me why you think it is. Is there still that much prejudice in baseball today?
>
> *Campanis:* No, I don't believe it's prejudice. I truly believe that they may not have some of the necessities to be, let's say, a field manager, or perhaps a general manager.
>
> *Koppel:* Do you really believe that?
>
> *Campanis:* Well, I don't say that all of them, but they certainly are short. How many quarterbacks do you have? How many pitchers do you have that are black?

Two days after this interview and the public uproar it caused, the Dodgers fired Campanis. A year later, he said he had been "wiped out" when the interview took place and therefore not entirely himself.

Who was the real Al Campanis? A bigot or a victim of political correctness? Neither. He was a man who liked and respected the black players he knew, who defended Jackie Robinson when doing so was neither fashionable nor expected, and who had a blind spot: He thought that blacks were perfectly able to be great players, merely not smart enough to be managers. And in his heart of hearts, he told Koppel, he didn't see what was wrong with that attitude; "I don't believe it's prejudice," he said. Campanis was not lying or being coy. But, as general manager, he was in a position to recommend the hiring of a black manager, and his blind spot kept him from even considering that possibility.

Just as we can identify hypocrisy in everyone but ourselves, just as it's obvious that others can be influenced by money but not ourselves, so we can see prejudices in everyone else but ourselves. Thanks to our ego-preserving blind spots, we cannot possibly have a prejudice, which is an irrational or mean-spirited feeling about all members of another group. Because we are not irrational or mean spirited, any negative feelings we have about another group are justified; our dislikes are rational and well founded. It's theirs we need to suppress. Like the Hasids pounding on the Unprejudiced door at the Museum of Tolerance, we are blind to our own prejudices.

Prejudices emerge from the disposition of the human mind to perceive and process information in categories. "Categories" is a nicer, more neutral word than "stereotypes," but it's the same thing. Cognitive psychologists consider stereotypes to be energy-saving devices that allow us to make efficient decisions on the basis of past experience; help us quickly process new information and retrieve memories; make sense of real differences between groups; and predict, often with considerable accuracy, how others will behave or how they think.[24] We wisely rely on stereotypes and the quick information they give us to avoid danger, approach possible new friends, choose one school or job over another, or decide that *that* person across this crowded room will be the love of our lives.

That's the upside. The downside is that stereotypes flatten out differences within the category we are looking at and exaggerate differences between categories. Red Staters and Blue Staters often see each other as nonoverlapping categories, but plenty of Kansans do want evolution taught in their schools, and plenty of Californians disapprove of gay marriage. All of us recognize variation within our own gender, party, ethnicity, or nation, but we are inclined to generalize from a few encounters with people of other categories and lump them all together as *them*. This habit starts awfully early. Social psychologist Marilynn Brewer, who has been studying the nature of stereotypes for many years, once reported that her daughter returned from kindergarten complaining that "boys are crybabies."[25] The child's evidence was that she had seen two boys crying on their first day away from home. Brewer, ever the scientist, asked whether there hadn't also been little girls who cried. "Oh yes," said her daughter. "But only *some* girls cry. I didn't cry."

Brewer's little girl was already dividing the world, as everyone does, into us and them. [*Us* is the most fundamental social category in the brain's organizing system, and it's hardwired. Even the collective pronouns *us* and *them* are powerful emotional signals.] In one experiment, in which participants believed their verbal skills were being tested, nonsense syllables such as *xeh, yof, laj,* or *wuh* were randomly paired with either an in-group word (*us, we,* or *ours*), an out-group word (*them, they,* or *theirs*), or, for a control measure, another pronoun (such as *he, hers,* or *yours*). Everyone then had to rate the syllables on how pleasant or unpleasant they were. You might wonder why anyone would have an emotional feeling toward a nonsense word like *yof* or think *wuh* is cuter than *laj.* Yet participants liked the nonsense syllables more when they had been linked with in-group words than with any other word.[26] Not one of them guessed why; not one was aware of how the words had been paired.

As soon as people have created a category called *us,* however, they invariably perceive everybody else as *not-us.* The specific content of *us* can change in a flash: It's us sensible midwesterners against you flashy coastal types; it's us Prius owners against the rest of you gas guzzlers; it's us Boston Red Sox fans against you Los Angeles Angels fans (to pick a random example that happens to describe the two of us during baseball season). "Us-ness" can be manufactured in a minute in the laboratory, as Henri Tajfel and his colleagues demonstrated in a classic experiment with British schoolboys.[27] Tajfel showed the boys slides with varying numbers of dots on them and asked the boys to guess how many dots there were. He arbitrarily told some of them that they were overestimators and others that they were underestimators, and then asked all the boys to work on another task. In this phase, they had a chance to give points to other boys identified as overestimators or underestimators. Although each boy worked alone in his cubicle, almost every single one assigned more points to boys he thought were like him, an overestimator or an underestimator. As the boys emerged from their rooms, the other kids asked them "Which were you?" The answers received cheers from those like them and boos from the others.

Obviously, certain categories of *us* are more crucial to our identities than the kind of car we drive or the number of dots we can guess on a slide—gender, sexuality, religion, politics, ethnicity, and nationality, for starters. Without feeling attached to groups that give our lives meaning, identity, and purpose, we would suffer the intolerable sensation that we were loose marbles floating in a random universe. Therefore, we will do what it takes to preserve these attachments. Evolutionary psychologists argue that ethnocentrism—the belief that our own culture, nation, or religion is superior to all others—aids survival by strengthening our bonds to our primary social groups and thus increasing our willingness to work, fight, and occasionally die for them. When things are going well, people feel pretty tolerant of other cultures and religions—they even feel pretty tolerant of the other sex!—but when they are angry, anxious, or threatened, the default position is to activate their blind spots. *We* have the human qualities of intelligence and deep emotions, but *they* are dumb, *they* are crybabies, *they* don't know the meaning of love, shame, grief, or remorse.[28]

The very act of thinking that *they* are not as smart or reasonable as we are makes us feel closer to others who are like us. But, just as crucially, it allows us to justify how we treat *them*. The usual way of thinking is that stereotyping causes discrimination: Al Campanis, believing that blacks lack the "necessities" to be managers, refuses to hire one. But the theory of cognitive dissonance shows that the path between attitudes and action runs in both directions. Often it is discrimination that evokes the self-justifying stereotype. Al Campanis, lacking the will or guts to make the case to the Dodger organization for being the first to hire a black manager, justifies his failure to act by convincing himself that blacks couldn't do the job anyway. In the same way, if we have enslaved members of another group, deprived them of decent educations or jobs, kept them from encroaching on our professional turfs, or denied them their human rights, then we evoke stereotypes about them to justify our actions. [By convincing ourselves that they are unworthy, unteachable, incompetent, inherently math-challenged, immoral, sinful, stupid, or even subhuman, we avoid feeling guilty or unethical about how we treat them. And we certainly avoid feeling that we are prejudiced.] Why, we even like some of those people, as long as they know their place, which, by the way, is not here, in our club, our university, our job, our neighborhood. In short, we invoke stereotypes to justify behavior that would otherwise make us feel bad about the kind of person we are or the kind of country we live in.

Why, though, given that everyone thinks in categories, do only some people hold bitter, passionate prejudices toward other groups? Al Campanis was not prejudiced in terms of having a strong emotional antipathy toward blacks; we suspect he could have been argued out of his notion that black players could not be good managers. A stereotype might bend or even shatter under the weight of disconfirming information, but the hallmark of prejudice is that it is impervious to reason, experience, and counterexample. In his brilliant book *The Nature of Prejudice,* written more than fifty years ago, social psychologist Gordon Allport described the responses characteristic of a prejudiced man when confronted with evidence contradicting his beliefs:

> *Mr. X:* The trouble with Jews is that they only take care of their own group.
> *Mr. Y:* But the record of the Community Chest campaign shows that they give more generously, in proportion to their

numbers, to the general charities of the community, than do non-Jews.

Mr. X: That shows they are always trying to buy favor and intrude into Christian affairs. They think of nothing but money; that is why there are so many Jewish bankers.

Mr. Y: But a recent study shows that the percentage of Jews in the banking business is negligible, far smaller than the percentage of non-Jews.

Mr. X: That's just it; they don't go in for respectable business; they are only in the movie business or run night clubs.[29]

Allport nailed Mr. X's reasoning perfectly: Mr. X doesn't even try to respond to Mr. Y's evidence; he just slides along to another reason for his dislike of Jews. Once people have a prejudice, just as once they have a political ideology, they do not easily drop it, even if the evidence indisputably contradicts a core justification for it. Rather, they come up with another justification to preserve their belief or course of action. Suppose our reasonable Mr. Y told you that insects were a great source of protein and that the sensational new chef at the Slugs & Bugs Diner is offering delicious entrees involving puréed caterpillars. Will you rush out to try this culinary adventure? If you have a prejudice against eating insects, probably not, even if this chef has made the front page of the *New York Times* Dining Out section. You will, like the bigoted Mr. X, find another reason to justify it. "Ugh," you would tell Mr. Y, "insects are ugly and squishy." "Sure," he says. "Tell me again why you eat lobster and raw oysters?"

⌈Once people acquire a prejudice, therefore, it's hard to dislodge.⌉ As the great jurist Oliver Wendell Holmes Jr. said, "Trying to educate a bigot is like shining light into the pupil of an eye—it constricts." Most people will put a lot of mental energy into preserving their prejudice rather than having to change it, often by waving away disconfirming evidence as "exceptions that prove the rule." (What would disprove the rule, we wonder?) The line "But some of my best friends are . . . ," well deserving of the taunts it now gets, has persisted because it is such an efficient way of resolving the dissonance created when a prejudice runs headlong into an exception. When Elliot moved to Minneapolis years ago to teach at the University of Minnesota, a neighbor said to him, "You're Jewish? But you're so much nicer than . . ." She stopped. "Than what?" he asked. "Than what I expected," she finished lamely. By admitting that Elliot didn't fit her stereotype, she was able to feel open-minded and generous, while maintaining her basic prejudice toward the whole category of Jews. In her mind she was even paying him a compliment; he's so much nicer than all those others of his . . . race.

Jeffrey Sherman and his colleagues have done a series of experiments that demonstrate the effort that highly prejudiced people are prepared to put into maintaining consonance between their prejudice and information that is inconsistent with it. They actually pay more attention to this inconsistent information than to consistent information, because, like Mr. X and the Minnesota neighbor, they need to figure out how to explain away the dissonant evidence. In one experiment, (straight) students were asked to evaluate a gay man, "Robert," who was described as doing eight things that were consistent with the gay stereotype (e.g., he had studied interpretive dance) and eight things that were inconsistent (e.g., he had watched a football game one Sunday). Anti-gay participants twisted the evidence about Robert and later described him as being far more "feminine" than unbiased students did, thereby maintaining their prejudice. To resolve the dissonance caused by the inconsistent facts, they explained them away as being an artifact of the situation. Sure, Robert watched a football game, but only because his cousin Fred was visiting.[30]

These days, most Americans who are unashamedly prejudiced know better than to say so, except to a secure, like-minded audience, given that many people live and work in environments where they can be slapped on the wrist, publicly humiliated, or sacked for saying anything that smacks of an "ism." However, just as it takes mental effort to maintain a prejudice despite conflicting information, it takes mental effort to suppress those negative feelings. Social psychologists Chris Crandall and Amy Eshelman, reviewing the huge research literature on prejudice, found that [whenever people are emotionally depleted—when they are sleepy, frustrated, angry, anxious, drunk, or stressed—they become more willing to express their real prejudices toward another group] When Mel Gibson was arrested for drunk driving and launched into an anti-Semitic tirade, he claimed, in his inevitable statement of apology the next day, that "I said things that I do not believe to be true and which are despicable. I am deeply ashamed of everything I said. . . . I apologize for any behavior unbecoming of me in my inebriated state." Translation: It wasn't me, it was the booze. Nice try, but the evidence shows clearly that while inebriation makes it easier for people to reveal their prejudices, it doesn't put those attitudes in their minds in the first place. Therefore, when people apologize by saying, "I don't really believe what I said; I was tired/worried/angry/drunk"—or, as Al Campanis put it, "wiped out"—we can be pretty sure they really do believe it.

But most people are unhappy about believing it, and that creates dissonance: "I dislike those people" collides with an equally strong conviction that it is morally or socially wrong to say so. People who feel this dissonance, Crandall and Eshelman suggest, will eagerly reach for any self-justification that allows them to express their true beliefs yet continue to feel that they are moral and good. "Justification," they explain, "undoes suppression, it provides cover, and it protects a sense of egalitarianism and a nonprejudiced self-image."[31] No wonder it is such a popular dissonance reducer.

For example, in one typical experiment, white students were told they would be inflicting electric shock on another student, the "learner," whom they knew was white or African American, as part of an apparent study of biofeedback. The students initially gave a lower intensity of shock to black learners than to white ones—reflecting a desire, perhaps, to show they were not prejudiced. Then the students overheard the learner making derogatory comments about them, which, naturally, made them angry. Now, given another opportunity to inflict electric shock, the students who were working with a black learner administered higher levels of shock than did students who were working with a white learner. The same result appears in studies of how English-speaking Canadians behave toward French-speaking Canadians, straights toward homosexuals, non-Jewish students toward Jews, and men toward women.[32] Participants successfully control their negative feelings under normal conditions, but as soon as they become angry or frustrated, or their self-esteem wobbles, they express their prejudice directly because now they can justify it: "I'm not a bad or prejudiced person, but hey—he insulted me!"

In this way, prejudice is the energy of ethnocentrism. It lurks there, napping, until ethnocentrism summons it to do its dirty work, justifying the occasional bad things we good people want to do. For example, in the nineteenth-century American West, Chinese immigrants were hired to work in the gold mines, potentially taking jobs from white laborers. The white-run newspapers fomented prejudice against them, describing the Chinese as "depraved and vicious," "gross gluttons," "bloodthirsty and inhuman." Yet only a decade later, when the Chinese were willing to accept the dangerous, arduous work of building the transcontinental railroad—work that white laborers were unwilling to undertake—public prejudice toward them subsided, replaced by the opinion that the Chinese were sober, industrious, and law-abiding. "They are equal to the best white men," said the railroad tycoon Charles Crocker. "They are very trusty, very intelligent and they live up to their contracts." After the completion of the railroad, jobs again became scarce, and the end of the Civil War brought an influx of war veterans into an already tight job market. Anti-Chinese prejudice returned, with the press now describing the Chinese as "criminal," "conniving," "crafty," and "stupid."[33]

Prejudice justifies the ill treatment we want to inflict on others, and we want to inflict ill treatment on others because we don't like them. And why don't we like them? Because they are competing with us for jobs in a scarce job market. Because their presence makes us doubt that we have the one true religion. Because we want to preserve our positions of status, power, and privilege. Because we need to feel we are better than *somebody*. Because our country is waging war against them. Because we are uncomfortable with their customs, especially their sexual customs, those promiscuous perverts. Because they refuse to assimilate into our culture. Because they are trying too hard to assimilate into our culture.

By understanding prejudice as our self-justifying servant, we can better see why some prejudices are so hard to eradicate: They allow people to justify and defend their most important social identities—their race, their religion, their sexuality—while reducing the dissonance between "I am a good person" and "I really don't like those people." Fortunately, we can also better understand the conditions under which prejudices diminish: when the economic competition subsides, when the truce is signed, when the profession is integrated, when *they* become more familiar and comfortable, when we are in a position to realize that they aren't so different from us.

o   o   o

"In normal circumstances," wrote Hitler's henchman Albert Speer in his memoirs, "people who turn their backs on reality are soon set straight by the mockery and criticism of those around them, which makes them aware they have lost credibility. In the Third Reich there were no such correctives, especially for those who belonged to the upper stratum. On the contrary, every self-deception was multiplied as in a hall of distorting mirrors, becoming a repeatedly confirmed picture of a fantastical dream world which no longer bore any relationship to the grim outside world. In those mirrors I could see nothing but my own face reproduced many times over."[34]

Given that everyone has some blind spots, our greatest hope of self-correction lies in making sure we are not operating in a hall of mirrors, in which all we see are distorted reflections of our own desires and convictions. We need a few trusted naysayers in our lives, critics who are willing to puncture our protective bubble of self-justifications and yank us back to reality if we veer too far off. This is especially important for people in positions of power.

According to historian Doris Kearns Goodwin, [Abraham Lincoln was one of the rare presidents who understood the importance of surrounding himself with people willing to disagree with him. Lincoln created a cabinet that included four of his political opponents,] three of whom had run against him for the Republican nomination in 1860 and who felt humiliated, shaken, and angry to have lost to a relatively unknown backwoods lawyer: William H. Seward (whom Lincoln made secretary of state), Salmon P. Chase (secretary of the treasury), and Edward Bates (attorney general). Although all shared Lincoln's goal of preserving the Union and ending slavery, this "team of rivals" (as Goodwin calls them) disagreed with one another furiously on how to do it. Early in the Civil War, Lincoln was in deep trouble politically. He had to placate not only the Northern abolitionists who wanted escaped slaves emancipated, but also the slave owners from border states like Missouri and Kentucky who could have joined the Confederacy at any time, which would have been a disaster for the Union. As a result of the ensuing debates with his advisers, who had differing ideas about how to keep both sides in line, Lincoln avoided the illusion that he had group consensus on every decision. He was able to consider alternatives and eventually enlist the respect and support of his erstwhile competitors.[35]

As long as we are convinced that we are completely objective, above corruption, and immune to prejudice, most of us from time to time will find ourselves on our own personal road to St. Andrews—and some of us will be on that plane to Bangkok. Jeb Stuart Magruder, whose entrapment into the political corruption of the

Watergate scandal we described in the previous chapter, was blinded by his belief in the importance of doing whatever it took, even if that involved illegal actions, to defeat "them," Nixon's political enemies. But, when caught, Magruder had the guts to face himself. It's a shocking, excruciating moment for anyone, like catching sight of yourself in the mirror and suddenly realizing that a huge purple growth has appeared on your forehead. Magruder could have done what most of us would be inclined to do: Get some heavy makeup and say, "What purple growth?" But he resisted the impulse. In the final analysis, Magruder said, no one forced him or the others to break the law. "We could have objected to what was happening or resigned in protest," he wrote.[36] "Instead, we convinced ourselves that wrong was right, and plunged ahead.

"There is no way to justify burglary, wiretapping, perjury, and all the other elements of the cover-up. . . . I and others rationalized illegal actions on the grounds of 'politics as usual' or 'intelligence gathering' or 'national security.' We were completely wrong, and only when we have admitted that and paid the public price of our mistakes can we expect the public at large to have much faith in our government or our political system."

CHAPTER 3

o   o   o

Memory, the Self-justifying Historian

What we ... refer to confidently as memory ... is really a form of storytelling that goes on continually in the mind and often changes with the telling.

—memoirist and editor William Maxwell

MANY YEARS AGO, DURING the Jimmy Carter administration, Gore Vidal was on the *Today* show being interviewed by Tom Brokaw, the host. According to Vidal, Brokaw started by saying, "You've written a lot about bisexuality . . ." but Vidal cut him off, saying, "Tom, let me tell you about these morning shows. It's too early to talk about sex. Nobody wants to hear about it at this hour, or if they do, they are doing it. Don't bring it up." "Yeah, uh, but Gore, uh, you have written a lot about bisex . . ." Vidal interrupted, saying that his new book had nothing to do with bisexuality and he'd rather talk about politics. Brokaw tried once more, and Vidal again declined, saying, "Now let's talk about Carter. . . . What is he doing with these Brazilian dictators pretending they are freedom-loving, democratic leaders?" And so the conversation turned to Carter for the rest of the interview. Several years later, when Brokaw had become anchor of the *Nightly News, Time* did a feature on him, asking him about any especially difficult interviews he had conducted. Brokaw singled out the conversation with Gore Vidal: "I wanted to talk politics," Brokaw recalled, "and he wanted to talk about bisexuality."

It was a "total reversal," Vidal said, "to make me the villain of the story."[1]

Was it Tom Brokaw's intention to turn Gore Vidal into the villain of the story? Was Brokaw lying, as Vidal implied? That is unlikely. After all, Brokaw chose the story to tell the *Time* reporter; he could have selected any difficult interview in his long career to talk about, rather than one that required him to embellish or lie; indeed, for all he knew, the reporter would check the original transcript. [Brokaw made the reversal of who-said-what unconsciously, not to make Vidal look bad, but to make himself look good.] As the new anchor of the *Nightly News,* it would have been unseemly for him to have been asking questions about bisexuality; better to believe (and remember) that he had always chosen the intellectual high road of politics.

When two people produce entirely different memories of the same event, observers usually assume that one of them is lying. Of course, some people do invent or embellish stories to manipulate or deceive their audiences, as James Frey notably did with his bestseller *A Million Little Pieces.* [But most of us, most of the time, are neither telling the whole truth nor intentionally deceiving. We aren't lying; we are self-justifying. All of us, as we tell our stories, add details and omit inconvenient facts; we give the tale a small, self-enhancing spin; that spin goes over so well that the next time we add a slightly more dramatic embellishment; we justify that little white lie as making the story better and clearer—until what we remember may not have happened that way, or even may not have happened at all.]

In this way, memory becomes our personal, live-in, self-justifying historian. Social psychologist Anthony Greenwald once described the self as being ruled by a "totalitarian ego" that ruthlessly destroys information it doesn't want to hear and, like all fascist leaders, rewrites history from the standpoint of the victor.[2] But whereas a totalitarian ruler rewrites history to put one over on future generations, the totalitarian ego rewrites history to put one over on itself. History is written by the victors, and when we write our own histories, we do so just as the conquerors of nations do: to justify our actions and make us look and feel good about ourselves and what we did or what we failed to do. If mistakes were made, memory helps us remember that they were made by someone else. If we were there, we were just innocent bystanders.

At the simplest level, memory smoothes out the wrinkles of dissonance by enabling the confirmation bias to hum along, selectively causing us to forget discrepant, disconfirming information about beliefs we hold dear. For example, if we were perfectly rational beings, we would try to remember smart, sensible ideas and not bother taxing our minds by remembering foolish ones. But dissonance theory predicts that we will conveniently forget good arguments made by an opponent just as we forget foolish arguments made by our own side. A silly argument in favor of our own position arouses dissonance because it raises doubts about the wisdom of that position or the intelligence of the people who agree with it. Likewise, a sensible argument by an opponent also arouses dissonance because it raises the possibility that the other side, God forbid, may be right or have a point to take seriously. Because a silly argument on our side and a good argument on the other guy's side both arouse dissonance, the theory predicts that we will either not learn these arguments very well or will forget them quickly. And that is just what Edward Jones and Rika Kohler showed in a classic experiment on attitudes toward desegregation in North Carolina in 1958.[3] Each side tended to remember the plausible arguments agreeing with their own position and the implausible arguments agreeing with the opposing position; each side forgot the implausible arguments for their view and the plausible arguments for the opposition.

Of course, our memories can be remarkably detailed and accurate, too. We remember first kisses and favorite teachers. We remember family stories, movies, dates, baseball stats, childhood humiliations and triumphs. We remember the central events of our life stories. But when we do misremember, our mistakes aren't random. [The everyday, dissonance-reducing distortions of memory help us make sense of the world and our place in it, protecting our decisions and beliefs. The distortion is even more powerful when it is motivated by the need to keep our self-concept consistent; by the wish to be right; by the need to preserve self-esteem; by the need to excuse failures or bad decisions; or by the need to find an explanation, preferably one safely in the past, of current problems.[4] Confabulation, distortion, and plain forgetting are the foot soldiers of memory, and they are summoned to the front lines when the totalitarian ego wants to protect us from the pain and embarrassment of actions we took that are dissonant with our core self-images: "I did *that*?" That is why memory researchers love to quote Nietzsche: " 'I have done that,' says my memory. 'I cannot have done that,' says my pride, and remains inexorable. Eventually—memory yields."

The Biases of Memory

One of us (Carol) had a favorite children's book, James Thurber's *The Wonderful O*, which she remembers her father giving her when she was a child. "A band of pirates takes over an island and forbids the locals to speak any word or use any object containing the letter *O*," Carol recalls. "I have a vivid memory of my father reading *The Wonderful O* and our laughing together at the thought of shy Ophelia Oliver saying her name without its *O*'s. I remember trying valiantly, along with the invaded islanders, to guess the fourth *O* word that must never be lost (after love, hope, and valor), and my father's teasing guesses: Oregon? Orangutan? Ophthalmologist? And then, not long ago, I found my first edition of *The Wonderful O*. It had been published in 1957, one year after my father's death. I stared at that date in disbelief and shock. Obviously, someone else gave me that book, someone else read it to me, someone else laughed with me about Phelia Liver, someone else wanted me to understand that the fourth *O* was freedom. Someone lost to my recollection."

⟦This small story illustrates three important things about memory: how disorienting it is to realize that a vivid memory, one full of emotion and detail, is indisputably wrong; that even being absolutely, positively sure a memory is accurate does not mean that it is; and how errors in memory support our current feelings and beliefs.⟧ "I have a set of beliefs about my father," Carol observes, "the warm man he was, the funny and devoted dad who loved to read to me and take me rummaging through libraries, the lover of wordplay. So it was logical for me to assume—no, to *remember*—that he was the one who read me *The Wonderful O*."

The metaphors of memory fit our times and technology. Centuries ago, philosophers compared memory to a soft wax tablet that would preserve anything imprinted on it. With the advent of the printing press, people began to think of memory as a library that stores events and facts for later retrieval. (Those of us of a certain age still think of it that way, muttering about where we "filed" information in our cluttered mental cabinets.) With the inventions of movies and tape recorders, people started thinking of memory as a video camera, clicking on at the moment of birth and automatically recording every moment thereafter. Nowadays we think of memory in computer terms, and although some of us wish for more RAM, we assume that just about everything that happens to us is "saved." Your brain might not choose to screen all those memories, but they are in there, just waiting for you to retrieve them, bring out the pop-corn, and watch.

These metaphors of memory are popular, reassuring, and wrong. Memories are not buried somewhere in the brain, as if they were bones at an archeological site; nor can we uproot them, as if they were radishes; nor, when they are dug up, are they perfectly pre-served. We do not remember everything that happens to us; we se-lect only highlights. (If we didn't forget, our minds could not work efficiently, because they would be cluttered with mental junk—the temperature last Wednesday, a boring conversation on the bus, every phone number we ever dialed.) Moreover, recovering a memory is not at all like retrieving a file or replaying a tape; it is like watching a few unconnected frames of a film and then figuring out what the rest of the scene must have been like. We may reproduce poetry, jokes, and other kinds of information by rote, but when we remem-ber complex information we shape it to fit it into a story line.

Because memory is reconstructive, it is subject to confabula-tion—confusing an event that happened to someone else with one that happened to you, or coming to believe that you remember something that never happened at all. In reconstructing a memory, people draw on many sources. When you remember your fifth birth-day party, you may have a direct recollection of your younger brother putting his finger in the cake and spoiling it for you, but you will also incorporate information that you got later from family sto-ries, photographs, home videos, and birthday parties you've seen on television. You weave all these elements together into one integrated account. If someone hypnotizes you and regresses you to your fifth birthday party, you'll tell a lively story about it that will feel terribly real to you, but it will include many of those postparty details that never actually happened. After a while, you won't be able to distin-guish your actual memory from subsequent information that crept in from elsewhere. That phenomenon is called "source confusion," otherwise known as the "where did I hear that?" problem.⁵ Did I read it, see it, or did someone tell me about it?

Mary McCarthy made brilliant use of her understanding of confabulation in *Memories of a Catholic Girlhood,* which is a rare exception to the way most of us tell our stories. At the end of every chapter, McCarthy subjected her memories to the evidence for or against them, even when the evidence killed a good story. In "A Tin Butterfly," McCarthy vividly recalls the time her punitive Uncle Myers and Aunt Margaret, the relatives who took her and her brothers in when their parents died, accused her of stealing her younger brother's Cracker Jack prize, a tin butterfly. She hadn't, and a thorough household search failed to uncover it. But one night after dinner the butterfly was discovered under the tablecloth on the dining table, near Mary's place. Her uncle and aunt whipped Mary furiously for this alleged theft, he with a strop, she with a hairbrush, but the question of what had happened to the toy remained a mystery. Years later, when the siblings were grown and reminiscing together, they got to talking about the dreaded Uncle Myers. "It was then my brother Preston told me," McCarthy writes, "that on the famous night of the butterfly, he had seen Uncle Myers steal into the dining room from the den and lift the tablecloth, with the tin butterfly in his hand."

End of chapter. Fabulous! A dramatic ending, brilliantly told. And then McCarthy adds a postscript. As she was writing the story, she says, "I suddenly remembered that in college I had started writing a play on the subject. Could the idea that Uncle Myers put the butterfly at my place have been suggested to me by my teacher? I can almost hear her voice saying to me, excitedly: 'Your uncle must have done it!'" McCarthy called her brothers, but none of them recalled her version of events, including Preston, who did not remember either seeing Uncle Myers with the butterfly (he was only seven at the time) or claiming that he had said so the night of the family visit. "The most likely thing, I fear," McCarthy concludes, "is that I fused two memories"—the tale of the missing butterfly and the teacher's subsequent explanation of what might have happened.[6] And it made psychological sense: Uncle Myers's planting of the butterfly under the tablecloth was consonant with McCarthy's feelings about his overall malevolence and further justified her righteous indignation about being unfairly punished.

When most people write their memoirs or describe their past experiences, however, they don't do it the way Mary McCarthy did. They do it the way they would tell their stories to a therapist: "Doctor, here's what happened." They count on the listener not to say, "Oh, yeah? Are you sure it happened that way? Are you positive your mother hated you? Are you certain your father was such a brute? And while we're at it, let's examine those memories you have of your horrible ex. Any chance you have forgotten anything *you* did that might have been a tad annoying—say, that little affair you justified having with the lawyer from Bug Tussle, Oklahoma?" On the contrary, we tell our stories in the confidence that the listener will not dispute them or ask for contradictory evidence, which means we rarely have an incentive to scrutinize them for accuracy. You have memories about your father that are salient to you and that represent the man he was and the relationship you had with him. What have you forgotten? You remember that time when you were disobedient and he swatted you, and you are still angry that he didn't explain why he was disciplining you. But could you have been the kind of kid a father couldn't explain things to, because you were impatient and impulsive and didn't listen? When we tell a story, we tend to leave ourselves out: My father did thus-and-such because of who he was, not because of the kind of kid I was. That's the self-justification of memory. And it is why, when we learn that a memory is wrong, we feel stunned, disoriented, as if the ground under us has shifted. In a sense, it has. It has made us rethink our own role in the story.

Every parent has been an unwilling player in the you-can't-win game. Require your daughter to take piano lessons, and later she will complain that you wrecked her love of the piano. Let your daughter give up lessons because she didn't want to practice, and later she will complain that you should have forced her to keep going—why, now she can't play the piano at all. Require your son to go to Hebrew school in the afternoon, and he will blame you for having kept him from becoming another Hank Greenberg. Allow your son to skip Hebrew school, and he will later blame you for his not feeling more connected to his heritage. Betsy Petersen produced a full-bodied whine in her memoir *Dancing With Daddy,* blaming her parents for only giving her swimming lessons, trampoline lessons, horseback-riding lessons, and tennis lessons, but not ballet lessons. "The only thing I wanted, they would not give me," she wrote. [Parent blaming is a popular and convenient form of self-justification because it al-lows people to live less uncomfortably with their regrets and im-perfections. Mistakes were made, by them. Never mind that I raised hell about those lessons or stubbornly refused to take advantage of them. Memory thus minimizes our own responsibility and exagger-ates theirs.]

By far, the most important distortions and confabulations of memory are those that serve to justify and explain our own lives. The mind, sense-making organ that it is, does not interpret our experi-ences as if they were shattered shards of glass; it assembles them into a mosaic. From the distance of years, we see the mosaic's pattern. It seems tangible, unchangeable; we can't imagine how we could recon-figure those pieces into another design. But it is a result of years of telling our story, shaping it into a life narrative that is complete with heroes and villains, an account of how we came to be the way we are. Because that narrative is the way we understand the world and our place in it, it is bigger than the sum of its parts. If one part, one memory, is shown to be wrong, people have to reduce the resulting dissonance and even rethink the basic mental category: You mean Dad (Mom) wasn't such a bad (good) person after all? You mean Dad (Mom) was a complex human being? The life narrative may be fundamentally true; your father or mother might really have been hateful, or saintly. The problem is that when the narrative becomes a major source of self-justification, one the storyteller relies on to excuse mistakes and failings, memory becomes warped in its service. The storyteller remembers only the confirming examples of the parent's malevolence and forgets dissonant instances of the parent's good qualities. Over time, as the story hardens, it becomes more difficult to see the whole parent—the mixture of good and bad, strengths and flaws, good intentions and unfortunate blunders.

Memories create our stories, but our stories also create our memories. Once we have a narrative, we shape our memories to fit into it. In a series of experiments, Barbara Tversky and Elizabeth Marsh showed how we "spin the stories of our lives." In one, people read a story about two roommates, each of whom did an annoying thing and a sociable thing. Then they wrote a letter about one of them, either a letter of complaint to a housing authority or a letter of recommendation to a social club. As they wrote, the study participants added elaborations and details to their letters that had not been part of the original story; for example, if they were writing a recommendation, they might add, "Rachel is bubbly." Later, when they were asked to recall the original story as accurately as possible, their memories had become biased in the direction of the letter they had written.[7] They remembered the false details they had added and forgot the dissonant information they had not written about.

To show how memory changes to fit our story, psychologists study how memories evolve over time: If your memories of the same people change, becoming positive or negative depending on what is happening in your life now, then it's all about you, not them. This process happens so gradually that it can be a jolt to realize you ever felt differently. "A few years back I found a diary that I wrote as a teen," a woman wrote to the advice columnist Dear Amy. "It was filled with insecurity and anger. I was shocked to read that I had ever felt that way. I consider my relationship with my mom to be very close, and I don't remember any major problems, though the diary would suggest otherwise."

The reason this letter writer doesn't "remember any major problems" was identified in two experiments by Brooke Feeney and Jude Cassidy, who showed how teenagers (mis)remember quarrels with each of their parents. Adolescents and their parents came into the lab and filled out forms listing typical topics of disagreement—personal appearance, curfews, fighting with siblings, the usual. Next, each adolescent had a ten-minute session with each parent separately to discuss and try to resolve their greatest areas of disagreement. Finally, the teenagers rated how they felt about the conflict, how intense their emotions were, their attitudes toward their parents, and so on. Six weeks later, they were asked to recall and rate again the conflict and their reactions to it. The teenagers who felt close to their parents remembered the quarrel as having been less intense and conflicted than they reported at the time. The teenagers who felt ambivalent and remote from their parents remembered the conflict as having been angrier and more bitter than they rated it at the time.[8]

Just as our current feelings about our parents shape our memories of how they treated us, our current self-concepts affect memories of our own lives. In 1962, Daniel Offer, then a young resident in psychiatry, and his colleagues interviewed 73 fourteen-year-old boys about their home lives, sexuality, religion, parents, parental discipline, and other emotionally charged topics. Offer and his colleagues were able to reinterview almost all these fellows thirty-four years later, when they were forty-eight years old, to ask them what they remembered of their adolescence. "Remarkably," the researchers concluded, "the men's ability to guess what they had said about themselves in adolescence was no better than chance." Most of those who remembered themselves as having been bold, outgoing teenagers, had, at age fourteen, described themselves as shy. Having lived through the sexual revolution of the 1970s and 1980s, the men recalled themselves as having been much more liberal and adventurous sexually as teenagers than they really had been. Nearly half remembered that as teenagers they believed that having sexual intercourse as high-school students was okay, but only 15 percent of them actually felt that way when they were fourteen. The men's current self-concepts blurred their memories, bringing their past selves into harmony with their present ones.[9]

[Memories are distorted in a self-enhancing direction in all sorts of ways. Men and women alike remember having had fewer sexual partners than they really did, they remember having far more sex with those partners than they actually had, and they remember using condoms more often than they actually did. People also remember voting in elections they didn't vote in, they remember voting for the winning candidate rather than the politician they did vote for, they remember giving more to charity than they really did, they remember that their children walked and talked at an earlier age than they really did . . . You get the idea.[10]]

If a memory is a central part of your identity, a self-serving distortion is even more likely. Ralph Haber, a distinguished cognitive psychologist, likes to tell the story of how he chose to go to graduate school at Stanford over his mother's objections. She wanted him to continue his education at the University of Michigan, he remembered, where he would be close to home; but he wanted to get far away and become more independent. "My memory has always been that when Stanford offered me admission and a fellowship, I leapt for joy, accepted with enthusiasm, and prepared to head west. A done deal!" Twenty-five years later, when Haber went back to Michigan for his mother's eightieth birthday, she handed him a shoebox of letters they had written to each other over the years. In the very first letters he pulled out, he learned that he had clearly decided to stay at Michigan and reject all his other offers. "It was my mother," he told us, "who pleaded passionately for me to change my mind" and leave. "I must have rewritten the entire history of this conflicted choice so my memory came out consistent," Haber now says, "consistent with what I actually did in leaving the shelter of home; consistent with how I wanted to see myself—being able to leave home; and consistent with my need for a loving mother who wanted me nearby." Haber's professional specialty, by the way, is autobiographical memory.

In Ralph Haber's case, the distortions of memory preserved his self-concept of always having been an independent spirit. But for most people, the self-concept is based on a belief in change, improvement, and growth. For some of us, it's based on a belief that we have changed completely; indeed, the past self seems like an entirely different person. When people have had a religious conversion, survived a disaster, suffered through cancer, or recovered from an addiction, they often feel transformed; the former self, they say, is "not me." For people who have experienced such transformations, memory helps resolve the inconsistency between their past and current selves by literally changing their perspectives. [When people recall actions that are dissonant with their current view of themselves— for example, when religious people are asked to remember times they did not attend religious services when they felt they should have, or when antireligious people remember attending services— they visualize the memory from a third-person perspective, as if they were an impartial observer. But when they remember actions that are consonant with their current identities, they tell a first-person story, as if they were looking at their former selves through their own eyes.[11]]

What happens, though, if we only think we have improved but actually haven't changed at all? Again, memory to the rescue. In one experiment, Michael Conway and Michael Ross had 106 undergraduates take a study-skills improvement program that, like many such programs, promised more than it delivered. At the start, the students rated their study skills and then were randomly assigned to take the course or be put on a waiting list. The training had absolutely no ef-

fect on their study habits or grades. How, then, did the students justify the waste of time and effort? Three weeks later, when asked to
recall as accurately as possible their own initial skills evaluation, they
misremembered their skills as being far worse than they had stated at
the outset, which allowed them to believe they had improved when
they actually had not changed at all. Six months later, when asked to
recall their grades in that course, they misremembered that, too, believing their grades to have been higher than they were. The students
who stayed on the waiting list for the skills program, having ex-
pended no effort, energy, or time, felt no cognitive dissonance and
had nothing to justify. Having no need to distort their memories,
they remembered their abilities and recent grades accurately.[12]

Conway and Ross called this self-serving memory distortion "getting what you want by revising what you had." On the larger stage
of the life cycle, many of us do just that: [We misremember our history as being worse than it was, thus distorting our perception of
how much we have improved, to feel better about ourselves now.[13]
Of course, all of us do grow and mature, but generally not as much
as we think we have. This bias in memory explains why each of us
feels that we have changed profoundly, but our friends, enemies, and
loved ones are the same old friends, enemies, and loved ones they
ever were.] We run into Harry at the high-school reunion, and while
Harry is describing how much he's learned and grown since gradua-
tion, we're nodding and saying to ourselves, "Same old Harry; a little
fatter, a little balder."

The self-justifying mechanisms of memory would be just another
charming, and often exasperating, aspect of human nature were it
not for the fact that we live our lives, we make decisions about
people, we form guiding philosophies, and we construct entire narratives on the basis of memories that are often right but also often
dead wrong. It's frustrating enough that things happened that we
don't remember; it is scary when we remember things that never

happened. Many of our mistaken memories are benign, on the level of who read us *The Wonderful O,* but sometimes they have more profound consequences, not only for ourselves but for our families, our friends, and society at large.

True Stories of False Memories

In Germany in 1995, Binjamin Wilkomirski published *Fragments,* a memoir of his horrifying childhood experiences in the concentration camps of Majdanek and Birkenau. An account of a small child's observations of Nazi atrocities and his eventual rescue and move to Switzerland, *Fragments* received extravagant praise. Reviewers compared it to the works of Primo Levi and Anne Frank. The *New York Times* said the book was "stunning" and the *Los Angeles Times* called it a "classic first-hand account of the Holocaust." In the United States, *Fragments* received the 1996 National Jewish Book Award for autobiography and memoir, and the American Orthopsychiatric Association gave Wilkomirski its Hayman Award for Holocaust and genocide study. In Britain, the book won the Jewish Quarterly Literary Prize; in France, it won the Prix Mémoire de la Shoah. The Holocaust Memorial Museum in Washington sent Wilkomirski on a six-city United States fund-raising tour.

Then it turned out that *Fragments* was a confabulation from start to finish. Its author, whose real name was Bruno Grosjean, was not Jewish and had no Jewish ancestry. He was a Swiss musician who had been born in 1941 to an unmarried woman named Yvonne Grosjean and been adopted several years later by a childless Swiss couple, the Dössekkers. Nor had he ever stepped foot in a concentration camp. His story was drawn from history books he had read, films he had seen, and Jerzy Kosinski's *The Painted Bird,* a surrealistic novel about a boy's brutal treatment during the Holocaust.[14] (Ironically, Kosinski's claim that his novel was autobiographical was later revealed to be fraudulent.)

Let's shift from Switzerland to a wealthy suburb of Boston, where Will Andrews lives. (This was the name given him by the psychologist who interviewed him.) Will is a handsome, articulate man in his forties, happily married. Will believes that he was abducted by aliens, and he has vivid memories of having been experimented on medically, psychologically, and sexually for at least ten years. In fact, he says, his alien guide became pregnant by him, producing twin boys, now eight years old, whom, he says sadly, he will never see but who play a large emotional role in his life. The abductions, he said, were terrifying and painful, but overall he is happy that he was "chosen."[15]

Are these two men guilty of fraud? Did Bruno-Binjamin Grosjean-Dössekker-Wilkomirski make up his story to become world famous, and did Will Andrews concoct memories of having been abducted by aliens to get on *Oprah*? We don't think so, and we don't think that they were lying, either, any more than Tom Brokaw was lying, if on a smaller scale. Well, then, are these men mentally ill? Not at all. They have led perfectly reasonable lives, functioning normally, holding good jobs, having relationships, paying their bills. In fact, they are representative of the many thousands of people who have come to remember accounts of terrible suffering in their childhoods or adulthoods, experiences that were later proved beyond reasonable doubt to have never happened to them. Psychologists who have tested many of these individuals report that they do not suffer from schizophrenia or other psychotic disorders. Their mental problems, if they have any, fall within the usual range of human miseries, such as depression, anxiety, eating disorders, loneliness, or existential anomie.

So, no, Wilkomirski and Andrews are not crazy or deceitful, but their memories are false, and false for particular, self-justifying reasons. Their stories, so different on the face of it, are linked by common psychological and neurological mechanisms that can create false memories that nonetheless feel vividly, emotionally real. These memories do not develop overnight, in a blinding flash. They take months, sometimes years, to develop, and the stages by which they emerge are now well known to psychological scientists.

According to the Swiss historian Stefan Maechler, who interviewed Wilkomirski, his friends, his relatives, his ex-wife, and just about everyone else connected with the story, Bruno Grosjean's motivation was not calculated self-interest but self-persuasion. Grosjean spent more than twenty years transforming himself into Wilkomirski; writing *Fragments* was the last step of his metamorphosis into a new identity, not the first step of a calculated lie. "Videotapes and eyewitness reports of Wilkomirski's presentations give the impression of a man made euphoric by his own narrative," Maechler wrote. "He truly blossomed in his role as concentration-camp victim, for it was in it that he finally found himself."[16] Wilkomirski's new identity as a survivor of the Holocaust gave him a powerful sense of meaning and purpose, along with the adoration and support of countless others. How else was he going to get medals and speaking invitations? Not as a second-rate clarinetist.

Binjamin Wilkomirski, a.k.a. Bruno Grosjean, spent his first four years being bounced around from place to place. His mother saw him only intermittently and finally abandoned him completely, placing him in a children's home, where he lived until he was adopted by the Dössekkers. In adulthood, Wilkomirski decided that his early years were the source of his present problems, and perhaps they were. Apparently, however, an all-too-common story of being born to a single mother who couldn't care for him, and being eventually adopted by a kindly but formal couple, couldn't explain his difficulties dramatically enough. But what if he had not been adopted but rescued after the war, and exchanged for a child named Bruno Grosjean in the orphanage? "Why else," his biographer says Wilkomirski felt, "would he have the panic attacks that suddenly overwhelm him?

Or the misshapen bump at the back of his head and the scar on his forehead? Or the nightmares that constantly plague him?"[17]

Why else? Panic attacks are a normal response to stress by those vulnerable to them. Just about everyone has bumps and scars of one kind or another; in fact, Wilkomirski's own son has the same misshapen bump in the same place, suggesting a genetic answer to that mystery. Nightmares are common in the general population and, surprisingly, they do not necessarily reflect actual experience. Many traumatized adults and children do not have nightmares, and many nontraumatized people do.

But Wilkomirski was not interested in these explanations. On a quest for meaning in his life, he stepped off his pyramid by deciding he would find the true reason for his symptoms in his first four lost years. At first, he didn't actually remember any early traumatic experiences, and the more he obsessed about his memories, the more elusive his early years felt. He started reading about the Holocaust, including survivors' accounts. He began to identify with Jews, putting a mezuzah on his door and wearing a Star of David. At the age of thirty-eight, he met Elitsur Bernstein, an Israeli psychologist who was living in Zurich, a man who would become his closest friend and adviser on his journeys into his past.

Hunting down his memories, Wilkomirski traveled to Majdanek with a group of friends, including the Bernsteins. When they arrived, Wilkomirski wept: "This was my home! This was where the children were quarantined!" The group visited the historians at the camp's archive, but when Wilkomirski asked them about the children's quarantine, they laughed at him. Very young children died or were killed, they said; the Nazis didn't run a nursery for them in a special barracks. By this time, however, Wilkomirski was too far along on his identity quest to turn back because of evidence that he was wrong, so his reaction was to reduce dissonance by dismissing the historians: "They made me look really stupid. It was a very rotten thing to do," he told Maechler. "From that moment on, I knew that I could depend more on my memory than on what is said by the so-called historians, who never gave a thought to children in their research."[18]

The next step for Wilkomirski was to go into therapy to get help for his nightmares, fearfulness, and panic attacks. He found a psychodynamically oriented analyst named Monika Matta, who analyzed his dreams and worked with nonverbal techniques, such as drawing and other methods of increasing "awareness of the body's emotions." Matta urged him to write down his memories. For people who always have remembered a traumatic or secret experience, writing can indeed be beneficial, often enabling sufferers to see their experience in a new light and to begin to put it behind them.[19] But for those who are trying to remember something that never happened, writing, analyzing dreams, and drawing pictures—techniques that are the staples of many psychotherapists—are all methods that quickly conflate imagination with reality.

Elizabeth Loftus, a leading scientist in the field of memory, calls this process ["imagination inflation,"] because the more you imagine something, the more likely you are to inflate it into an actual memory, adding details as you go.[20] (Scientists have even tracked imagination inflation into the brain, using functional MRI to show how it works at a neural level.[21]) For example, Giuliana Mazzoni and her colleagues asked their study participants to tell them a dream, and in return gave them a (false) "personalized" dream analysis. They told half the participants the dream meant that they had been harassed by a bully before the age of three, been lost in a public place, or been through a similar upsetting early event. Compared with control subjects who were given no such interpretations, the dream subjects were more likely to come to believe the dream explanation had really occurred, and about half of them eventually produced detailed memories of the experience. In another experiment, people were asked to remember when their school nurse took a skin sample from their little finger to carry out a national health test. (No such test existed.) Simply imagining this unlikely scenario caused the participants to become more confident that it had happened to them. And the more confident they became, the more sensory details they added to their false memories ("the place smelled horrible").[22] Researchers have created imagination inflation indirectly, too, merely by asking people to explain how an unlikely event *might* have happened. Cognitive psychologist Maryanne Garry finds that as people tell you how an event might have happened, it starts to feel real to them. Children are especially vulnerable to this suggestion.[23]

Writing turns a fleeting thought into a fact of history, and for Wilkomirski, writing down his memories confirmed his memories. "My illness showed me that it was time for me to write it all down for myself," said Wilkomirski, "just as it was held in my memory, to trace every hint all the way back."[24] Just as he rejected the historians at Majdanek who challenged his recall, he rejected the scientists who told him memory doesn't work that way.

While *Fragments* was in production, the publisher received a letter from a man alleging that Wilkomirski's story was untrue. The publisher, alarmed, contacted Wilkomirski for confirmation. Elitsur Bernstein and Monika Matta sent letters of support. "In reading Bruno's manuscript I never had any doubt as to its so-called 'authenticity,'" Bernstein wrote to the publisher. "I shall take the liberty of saying that in my judgment only someone who has experienced such things can write about them in such a way." Monika Matta, doing a little self-justification dance of her own, likewise had no doubts about the authenticity of Wilkomirski's memories or identity. Wilkomirski, she wrote, was a gifted, honest man who had "an extraordinarily precisely functioning memory" and had been profoundly shaped by his childhood experience. She wrote that she hoped that any "absurd doubts can be dispelled," because the publication of the book was very important for Wilkomirski's mental health. It was her wish, she wrote, that fate not overtake him in such a perfidious way, "*demonstrating to him yet again that he is a 'no-body.'*"[25] The publisher, convinced by the testimonials and reassurances of the experts, brought the book out on schedule. The "nobody" was somebody at last.

o   o   o

On August 8, 1983, while he was riding his bike across rural Nebraska, Michael Shermer was abducted by aliens. A large spaceship landed, forcing Shermer to the side of the road. Aliens descended from the ship and abducted him for ninety minutes, after which he had no memory of what had happened. Shermer's experience was not unusual; millions of Americans believe they have had some kind of encounter with UFOs or aliens. For some it happens while they are driving long, boring miles with little change of scenery, usually at night; they "gray out," losing track of time and distance, and then wonder what happened during the minutes or hours they were out of it. Some people, professional pilots among them, see mysterious lights they can't explain hovering in the sky. For most, the experience occurs in the weird mental haze between sleeping and waking, when they wake with a jolt to see ghosts, aliens, shadows, or spirits on their bed. Often they feel physically paralyzed, unable to move.

The bicycle racer, the driver, and the sleeper are at the top of the pyramid: Something mysterious and alarming has happened, but what? You can live with not knowing why you woke up in a grumpy mood today, but you can't live with not knowing why you woke up with a goblin sitting on your bed. If you are a scientist or other stripe of skeptic, you will make some inquiries and learn that the explanation of this frightening event is reassuring: During the deepest stage of sleep, when dreaming is most likely to occur, a part of the brain shuts down body movements, so you won't go hurling yourself around the bed as you dream of chasing tigers. If you awaken from this stage before your body does, you will actually be momentarily paralyzed; if your brain is still generating dream images, you will, for a few seconds, have a waking dream. That's why those figures on the bed are dreamlike, nightmarish—you *are* dreaming, but with your eyes open. [Sleep paralysis,] says Richard J. McNally, a Harvard psychological scientist and clinician who studies memory and trauma, is "no more pathological than a hiccup." It is quite common, he says, "especially for people whose sleep patterns have been disrupted by jet lag, shift work, or fatigue." About 30 percent of the population has had the sensation of sleep paralysis, but only about 5 percent have had the waking hallucinations as well. Just about everyone who has experienced sleep paralysis plus waking dreams reports that the feeling this combination evokes is terror.[26] It is, dare we say, an alien sensation.

Michael Shermer, a skeptic by disposition and profession, understood almost immediately what had happened to him: "My abduction experience was triggered by extreme sleep deprivation and physical exhaustion," he later wrote.[27] "I had just ridden a bicycle 83 straight hours and 1,259 miles in the opening days of the 3,100-mile nonstop transcontinental Race Across America. I was sleepily weaving down the road when my support motor home flashed its high beams and pulled alongside, and my crew entreated me to take a sleep break. At that moment a distant memory of the 1960s television series *The Invaders* was inculcated into my waking dream. . . . Suddenly the members of my support team were transmogrified into aliens."

People like Shermer react to this otherworldly experience by saying, in effect, "My, what a weird and scary waking dream; isn't the brain fascinating?" But Will Andrews, and the more than three million other Americans who believe they have had some kind of encounter with extraterrestrials, step off the pyramid in a different direction. Clinical psychologist Susan Clancy, who interviewed hundreds of believers, found that the process moves along steadily as the possibility of alien abduction comes to seem more and more believable. "All of the subjects I interviewed," she writes, "followed the same trajectory: once they started to suspect they'd been abducted by aliens, there was no going back. . . . Once the seed of belief was planted, once alien abduction was even suspected, the abductees began to search for confirmatory evidence. And once the search had begun, the evidence almost always turned up."[28]

The trigger is the frightening experience. "One night I woke up in the middle of the night and couldn't move," said one of her interviewees. "I was filled with terror and thought there was an intruder in the house. I wanted to scream, but I couldn't get any sound to come out. The whole thing lasted only an instant, but that was enough for me to be afraid to go back to sleep." Understandably, the person wants to make sense of what happened, and looks for an explanation that might also account for other ongoing problems. "I've been depressed since as long as I can remember," said one of the people in Clancy's study. "Something is seriously wrong with me, and I want to know what it is." Others reported sexual dysfunctions, battles with weight, and odd experiences or symptoms that baffled and worried them: "I wondered why my pajamas were on the floor when I woke up"; "I've been having so many nosebleeds—I never have nosebleeds"; "I wondered where I got these coin-shaped bruises on my back."[29]

Why do these people choose alien abduction as an explanation for these symptoms and concerns? Why don't they consider more reasonable explanations, such as "because I was hot in the middle of the night and took off my PJs" or "I'm getting paunchy—I need more exercise" or "Maybe it's time for Prozac or couples counseling"? Given all the available explanations for sleep problems, depression, sexual dysfunction, and routine physical symptoms, Clancy wondered, why would anyone choose the most implausible one, alien abduction? How can people claim to remember events that most of us would consider impossible, unless they really happened? The answers lie partly in American culture and partly in the needs and personalities of the "experiencers," the term that many who believe they have been abducted call themselves.

Experiencers come to believe that alien abduction is a reasonable explanation for their symptoms first by hearing and reading stories about it, along with testimonials by believers. When a story is repeated often enough, it becomes so familiar that it chips away at a person's initial skepticism, even a story as unlikely as persuading people that they witnessed a demonic possession when they were children.[30] Certainly, the alien-abduction story is everywhere in American popular culture, in books, in movies, on television, on talk shows. In turn, the story fits the needs of the experiencers. Clancy found that most had grown up with, but rejected, traditional religious beliefs, replacing them with a New Age emphasis on channeling and alternative healing practices. They are more prone to fantasy and suggestion than other people, and they have more trouble with source confusion, tending to confuse things that they have thought about or experienced directly with stories they read or have heard on television. (Shermer, in contrast, recognized his aliens as coming from a 1960s television series.) Perhaps most important, the abduction explanation captures the emotional intensity and dramatic importance of the experiencers' frightening waking dreams. The explanation feels real to them, Clancy says, in a way that mundane old "sleep paralysis" doesn't.

The "eureka!" that experiencers feel at the fit between the alien-abduction explanation and their symptoms is exhilarating, as was the fit Wilkomirski found between the Holocaust-survivor explanation and his own difficulties. The abduction story helps experiencers explain their psychological distress and also avoid responsibility for their mistakes, regrets, and problems. "I couldn't be touched," one woman told Clancy, "not even by my husband, who's a kind and gentle man. Imagine being forty-five and not knowing what good sex was! Now I understand that it's related to what the beings did to me. I was a sexual experiment to them from an early age." Every one of Clancy's interviewees told her they felt changed because of their experiences, that they had become better people, that their lives had improved, and, most of all, that their lives now had meaning. Will Andrews said, "I was ready to just give up. I didn't know what was wrong, but I knew something was missing. Today, things are different. I feel great. I know there's something out there—much bigger, more important than we are—and for some reason they chose to make their presence known to me. I have a connection with them. . . . The beings are learning from us and us from them and ultimately a new world is being created. And I'll have a part in it, either directly or through the twins." Will's wife (the one on this planet) gave us an additional motive for Will's invention of invisible alien progeny when she plaintively wondered to Clancy, "Would things have been different if we had been able to have kids?"[31]

At the final stage, once the experiencers have accepted the alien-abduction theory of their problems and retrieved their memories, they seek out other people like them and read only accounts that confirm their new explanation. They firmly reject any dissonance-creating evidence or any other way of understanding what happened to them. One of Clancy's interviewees said, "I swear to God, if someone brings up sleep paralysis to me one more time I'm going to puke. There was something in the room that night! I was spinning. . . . I wasn't sleeping. I was taken."[32] Every one of the people Clancy interviewed was aware of the scientific explanation and had angrily rejected it. In Boston a few years ago, a debate was held between Mc-Nally and John Mack, a psychiatrist who had accepted the abductees' stories as true.[33] Mack brought an experiencer with him. The woman listened to the debate, including McNally's evidence about how people who believe they were abducted are fantasy prone and have come to misinterpret a common sleep experience as one of seeing aliens. During the ensuing discussion, the woman said to Mc-Nally, "Don't you see, I wouldn't believe I'd been abducted if someone could just give me one reasonable alternative explanation." McNally said, "We just did."

By the end of this process, standing at the bottom of the pyramid at a far distance from skeptics like Michael Shermer, experiencers have internalized their new false memories and cannot now distinguish them from true ones. When they are brought into the laboratory and asked to describe their traumatic abductions by aliens, their heightened physiological reactions (such as heart rate and blood pressure) are as great as those of patients who suffer from posttraumatic stress disorder.[34] They have come to believe their own stories.

o   o   o

False memories allow us to forgive ourselves and justify our mistakes, but sometimes at a high price: an inability to take responsibility for our lives. An appreciation of the distortions of memory, a realization that even deeply felt memories might be wrong, might encourage people to hold their memories more lightly, to drop the certainty that their memories are always accurate, and to let go of the appealing impulse to use the past to justify problems of the present. If we are to be careful about what we wish for because it might come true, we must also be careful which memories we select to justify our lives, because then we will have to live by them.

Certainly one of the most powerful stories that many people wish to live by is the victim narrative. Nobody has actually been abducted by aliens (though experiencers will argue fiercely with us), but millions have survived cruelties as children: neglect, sexual abuse, parental alcoholism, violence, abandonment, the horrors of war. Many people have come forward to tell their stories: how they coped, how they endured, what they learned, how they moved on. Stories of trauma and transcendence are inspiring examples of human resilience.[35]

It is precisely because these accounts are so emotionally powerful that thousands of people have been drawn to construct "me, too" versions of them. A few have claimed to be Holocaust survivors;

thousands have claimed to be survivors of alien abduction; and tens of thousands have claimed to be survivors of incest and other sexual traumas that allegedly were repressed from memory until they entered therapy in adulthood. Why would people claim to remember that they had suffered harrowing experiences if they hadn't, especially when that belief causes rifts with families or friends? By distorting their memories, these people can ["get what they want by revising what they had,"] and what they want is to turn their present lives, no matter how bleak or mundane, into a dazzling victory over adversity. Memories of abuse also help them resolve the dissonance between "I am a smart, capable person" and "My life sure is a mess right now" with an explanation that makes them feel good and removes responsibility: "It's not my fault my life is a mess. Look at the horrible things they did to me." Ellen Bass and Laura Davis made this reasoning explicit in *The Courage to Heal.* They tell readers who have no memory of childhood sexual abuse that "when you first remember your abuse or acknowledge its effects, you may feel tremendous relief. Finally there is a reason for your problems. There is someone, and something, to blame."[36]

It is no wonder, then, that most of the people who have created false memories of early suffering, like those who believe they were abducted by aliens, go to great lengths to justify and preserve their new explanations. Consider the story of a young woman named Holly Ramona, who, after a year in college, went into therapy for treatment of depression and bulimia. The therapist told her that these common problems were usually symptoms of child sexual abuse, which Holly denied had ever happened to her. Yet over time, at the urging of the therapist and then at the hands of a psychiatrist who administered sodium amytal (popularly and mistakenly called "truth serum"), Holly came to remember that between the ages of five and sixteen she had been repeatedly raped by her father, who even forced her to have sex with the family dog. Holly's outraged father sued both therapists for malpractice, for "implanting or reinforcing false memories that [he] had molested her as a child." The jury agreed, exonerating the father and finding the therapists guilty.[37]

This ruling put Holly in a state of dissonance that she could resolve in one of two ways: She could accept the verdict, realize that her memories were false, beg her father's forgiveness, and attempt to reconcile the family that had been torn apart over her accusations. Or she could reject the verdict as a travesty of justice, become more convinced than ever that her father had abused her, and renew her commitment to recovered-memory therapy. By far, the latter was the easier choice because of her need to justify the harm she had caused her father and the rest of her family. To change her mind now would have been like turning a steamship around in a narrow river—not much room to maneuver and hazards in every direction; much easier to stay the course. Indeed, Holly Ramona not only vehemently rejected the verdict; she bolstered that decision by going to graduate school to become a psychotherapist. The last we heard, she was encouraging some of her own clients to recover memories of their childhood sexual abuse.

Yet every once in a while someone steps forward to speak up for truth, even when the truth gets in the way of a good, self-justifying story. It's not easy, because it means taking a fresh, skeptical look at the comforting memory we have lived by, scrutinizing it from every angle for its plausibility, and, no matter how great the ensuing dissonance, letting go of it. For her entire adult life, for example, writer Mary Karr had harbored the memory of how, as an innocent teenager, she had been abandoned by her father. That memory allowed her to feel like a heroic survivor of her father's neglect. But when she sat down to write her memoirs, she faced the realization that the story could not have been true.

"Only by studying actual events and questioning your own motives will the complex inner truths ever emerge from the darkness,"
she wrote.

But how could a memoirist even begin to unearth his life's truths
with fake events? At one point, I wrote a goodbye scene to show
how my hard-drinking, cowboy daddy had bailed out on me when
I hit puberty. When I actually searched for the teenage reminis-
cences to prove this, the facts told a different story: my daddy had
continued to pick me up on time and make me breakfast, to invite
me on hunting and fishing trips. I was the one who said no. I left
him for Mexico and California with a posse of drug dealers, and
then for college.

   This was far sadder than the cartoonish self-portrait I'd started
out with. If I'd hung on to my assumptions, believing my drama
came from obstacles I'd never had to overcome—a portrait of myself as scrappy survivor of unearned cruelties—I wouldn't have
learned what really happened. Which is what I mean when I say
God is in the truth.[38]

CHAPTER 4

o   o   o

Good Intentions, Bad Science:
The Closed Loop of Clinical Judgment

It doesn't matter how beautiful the guess is, or how smart the guesser is, or how famous the guesser is; if the experiment disagrees with the guess, then the guess is wrong. That's all there is to it.

—physicist Richard Feynman

IF HOLLY RAMONA FELT dissonance at the verdict that convicted her therapists of implanting false memories in her, how do you imagine her therapists felt? Would they be inclined to say, "Oh dear, Holly, we apologize for being so dreadfully mistaken in our treatment of your depression and eating disorders. We had better go back to school and learn a little more about memory"? The response of another psychotherapist is, we fear, more typical. A woman we will call Grace went into therapy after having a panic attack. She was not getting along with her male employer, and for the first time in her life she felt she was in a situation she could not control. But instead of treating her for panic attacks or helping her solve the job difficulty, the psychotherapist decided that Grace's symptoms meant that her father had sexually abused her when she was a child. At first, Grace embraced her therapist's interpretation; after all, the therapist was an expert on these matters. Over time, she, like Holly, came to believe that her father had molested her. Grace accused her father directly, cut off relations with her parents and sisters, and temporarily left her husband and son. Yet her new memories never felt right to her, because they contradicted the overall history of her good and loving relationship with her father. One day she told the therapist that she no longer believed her father had ever abused her.

Grace's therapist might have accepted what her client told her and begun working with her on finding a better explanation for her problems. She might have read up on the latest research showing which therapeutic approach is the method of choice for panic attacks. She might have talked over the case with her colleagues, to see if she was overlooking something. Grace's therapist, however, did none of these things. When Grace expressed doubts that her recovered memories were true, the therapist replied: "You're sicker than you ever were."[1]

o   o   o

In the 1980s and 1990s, the newly emerging evidence of the sexual abuse of children and women set off two unintended hysterical epidemics. [One was the phenomenon of recovered-memory therapy, in which adults went into therapy with no memory of childhood trauma and came out believing that they had been sexually molested by their parents or tortured in Satanic cults, sometimes for many years, without ever being aware of it at the time and without any corroboration by siblings, friends, or physicians.] Under hypnosis, they said, their therapists enabled them to remember the horrifying experiences they had suffered as toddlers, as infants in the crib, and sometimes even in previous lives. One woman recalled that her mother put spiders in her vagina. Another said her father had molested her from the ages of five to twenty-three, and even raped her just days before her wedding—memories she repressed until therapy. Others said they had been burned, although their bodies bore no scars. Some said they had been impregnated and forced to have abortions, although their bodies showed no evidence. Those who went to court to sue their alleged perpetrators were able to call on expert witnesses, many with impressive credentials in clinical psychology and psychiatry, who testified that these recovered memories were valid evidence of abuse.[2]

[The second major epidemic was a panic about the sexual abuse of children in daycare centers.] In 1983, teachers at the McMartin Preschool in Manhattan Beach, California, were accused of committing heinous acts on the toddlers in their care, such as torturing them in Satanic rituals in underground chambers, slaughtering pet rabbits in front of them, and forcing them to submit to sexual acts. Some children said the teachers had taken them flying in an airplane. The prosecution was unable to convince the jury that the children had been abused, but the case produced copycat accusations against daycare teachers across the country: the Little Rascals Day Care case in North Carolina, Kelly Michaels in New Jersey, the Amirault family in Massachusetts, Dale Akiki in San Diego, and alleged molestation rings in Jordan, Minnesota; Wenatchee, Washington; Niles, Michigan; Miami, Florida; and dozens of other communities. Everywhere, the children told bizarre stories. Some said they had been attacked by a robot, molested by clowns and lobsters, or forced to eat a frog. One boy said he had been tied naked to a tree in the school yard in front of all the teachers and children, although no passerby noticed it and no other child verified it. Social workers and other psychotherapists were called in to assess the children's stories, do therapy with the children, and help them disclose what had happened. Many later testified in court that, on the basis of their clinical judgment, they were certain the day-care teachers were guilty.[3]

Where do epidemics go when they die? How come celebrities have not been turning up on talk shows lately to reveal their recovered memories of having been tortured as infants? Have all the sadistic pedophiles closed down their day-care centers? Most of the teachers who were convicted in the day-care cases have been freed on appeal, but many teachers and parents remain in prison, or are confined to house arrest, or must live out their lives as registered sex offenders. The heyday of the recovered-memory movement is past, although many lives were shattered and countless families have never been re-united. But cases still occasionally appear in the courts, in the news, in films, and in popular books.[4] Martha Beck's *Leaving the Saints,* which describes how her Mormon father had allegedly subjected her to ritual sexual abuse when she was a child, neglects to tell readers that she had forgotten all about it until she consulted a recovered-memory psychotherapist who taught her self-hypnosis.

Thus while the epidemics have subsided, the assumptions that ignited them remain embedded in popular culture: If you were repeatedly traumatized in childhood, you probably repressed the memory of it. If you repressed the memory of it, hypnosis can retrieve it for you. If you are utterly convinced that your memories are true, they are. If you have no memories but merely suspect that you were abused, you probably were. If you have sudden flashbacks or dreams of abuse, you are uncovering a true memory. Children almost never lie about sexual matters. If your child has nightmares, wets the bed, wants to sleep with a night-light, or masturbates, those might be signs your child has been molested.

These beliefs did not pop up in the cultural landscape overnight, like mushrooms. They came from mental-health professionals who disseminated them at conferences, in clinical journals, in the media, and in bestselling books, and who promoted themselves as experts in diagnosing child sexual abuse and determining the validity of a recovered memory. Their claims were based largely on lingering Freudian (and pseudo-Freudian) ideas about repression, memory, sexual trauma, and the meaning of dreams, and on their own confidence in their clinical powers of insight and diagnosis. All the claims these therapists made have since been scientifically studied. All of them are mistaken.

◦   ◦   ◦

It is painful to admit this, but when the McMartin story first hit the news, the two of us, independently, were inclined to believe that the preschool teachers were guilty. Not knowing the details of the allegations, we mindlessly accepted the "where there's smoke, there's fire" cliché; as scientists, we should have known better. When, months after the trial ended, the full story came out—about the emotionally disturbed mother who made the first accusation and whose charges became crazier and crazier until even the prosecutors stopped paying attention to her; about how the children had been coerced over many months to "tell" by zealous social workers on a moral crusade; about how the children's stories became increasingly outlandish—we felt foolish and embarrassed that we had sacrificed our scientific skepticism on the altar of outrage. Our initial gullibility caused us plenty of dissonance, and it still does. But our dissonance is nothing compared to that of the people who were personally involved or who took a public stand, including the many psychotherapists, psychiatrists, and social workers who considered themselves skilled clinicians and advocates for children's rights.

None of us likes learning that we were wrong, that our memories are distorted or confabulated, or that we made an embarrassing professional mistake. For people in any of the healing professions, the stakes are especially high. If you hold a set of beliefs that guide your practice and you learn that some of them are mistaken, you must either admit you were wrong and change your approach, or reject the new evidence. If the mistakes are not too threatening to your view of your competence and if you have not taken a public stand defending them, you will probably willingly change your approach, grateful to have a better one. But if some of those mistaken beliefs have made your client's problems worse, torn up your client's family, or sent innocent people to prison, then you, like Grace's therapist, will have serious dissonance to resolve.

It's the Semmelweiss dilemma that we described in the introduction. Why didn't his colleagues tell him, "Say, Ignac, thank you so much for finding the reason for the tragic, unnecessary deaths of our patients"? For these physicians to have accepted his simple, life-saving intervention—wash your hands—they would have had to admit that they had been the cause of the deaths of all those women in their care. This was an intolerable realization, for it went straight to the heart of the physicians' view of themselves as medical experts and wise healers; and so, in essence, they told Semmelweiss to get lost and take his stupid ideas with him. Because their stubborn refusal to accept Semmelweiss's evidence—the lower death rate among his own patients—happened long before the era of malpractice suits, we can say with assurance that they were acting out of a need to protect their egos, not their income. Medicine has advanced since their day, but the need for self-justification hasn't budged.

Most occupations are ultimately, if slowly, self-improving and self-correcting. If you are a physician today, you wash your hands and you wear latex gloves, and if you forget, your colleagues, nurses, or patients will remind you. If you run a toy company and make a mistake in predicting that your new doll will outsell Barbie, the market will let you know. If you are a scientist, you can't fake the data on your cloned sheep and then try to pull the wool over your colleagues' eyes; the first lab that cannot replicate your results will race to tell the world. If you are an experimental psychologist and make a mistake in the design of your experiment or analysis of results, your colleagues and critics will be eager to inform you, the rest of the scientific community, and everyone on the ex-planet Pluto. Naturally, not all scientists are scientific, that is, open-minded and willing to give up their strong convictions or admit that conflicts of interest might taint their research. But even when an individual scientist is not self-correcting, science eventually is.

The mental-health professions are different. People who work in these fields have an amalgam of credentials, training, and approaches that often bear little connection to one another. Imagine that the profession of law consisted of people who attended law school, studied every topic within the law, and passed the grueling bar exam; and of people who only paid $78 and took a weekend course in courtroom etiquette. You will have a glimpse of the problem.

In the profession of psychotherapy, clinical psychologists are the closest equivalents of trained lawyers. Most have a Ph.D., and if they earned their degree from a major university rather than from an independent therapy mill, they have a knowledge of basic psychological findings. Some do research themselves, for example on the ingredients of successful therapy or on the origins of emotional disorders. But whether or not they personally do research, they tend to be well versed in psychological science and in knowing which kind of therapy is demonstrably most effective for what problem. For example, [cognitive and behavioral methods are the psychological treatments of choice for panic attacks, depression, eating disorders, insomnia, chronic anger, and other emotional disorders. These methods are often as effective or more effective than medication.[5]]

In contrast, most psychiatrists, who have medical degrees, learn about medicine and medication, but they rarely learn much about the scientific method or even about basic research in psychology. Throughout the twentieth century, they were generally practitioners of Freudian psychoanalysis or one of its offshoots; you needed an MD to be admitted to a psychoanalytic training institute. As the popularity of psychoanalysis declined and the biomedical model of disorder gained the upper hand, most psychiatrists began treating patients with medication rather than any form of talk therapy. Yet while psychiatrists learn about the brain, many still learn almost nothing about psychology or about the questioning, skeptical essence of science. Anthropologist Tanya Luhrmann spent four years studying residents in psychiatry, attending their classes and conventions, observing them in clinics and emergency rooms. She found that residents are not expected to read much; rather, they are expected to absorb the lessons handed them without debate or question. The lectures they attend offer practical skills, not intellectual substance; a lecturer will talk about what to do in therapy rather than why the therapy helps or what kind of therapy might be best for a given problem.[6]

Finally, there are the many people who practice one of the many different forms of psychotherapy. Some have a master's degree in psychology, counseling, or clinical social work; they are licensed in their specialty, such as marriage and family therapy. Some, however, have no training in psychology at all, or even a college degree. The word "psychotherapist" is unregulated; in many states, anyone can say that he or she is a therapist without having any training in anything.

In the past two decades, as the number of mental-health practitioners of all kinds has soared, most psychotherapy-training programs have cut themselves off from their scientifically trained cousins in university departments of psychology.[7] "What do we need to know statistics and research for?" many graduates of these programs ask. "All we need to know is how to do therapy, and for that, I mostly need clinical experience." In some respects, they are right. Therapists are constantly making decisions about the course of treatment: What might be beneficial now? What direction should we go? Is this the right time to risk challenging my client's story, or will I challenge him right out of the room? Making these decisions requires experience with the infinite assortment of quirks and passions of the human psyche, that heart of darkness and love.

Moreover, by its very nature, psychotherapy is a private transaction between the therapist and the client. No one is looking over the therapist's shoulder in the intimacy of the consulting room, eager to pounce if he or she does something wrong. Yet the inherent privacy of the transaction means that therapists who lack training in science and skepticism have no internal corrections to the self-protecting cognitive biases that afflict us all. [What these therapists see confirms what they believe, and what they believe shapes what they see. It's a closed loop. Did my client improve? Excellent; what I did was effective. Did my client remain unchanged or get worse? That's unfortunate, but she *is* resistant to therapy and deeply troubled; besides, sometimes the client has to get worse before she can get better.] Do I believe that repressed rage causes sexual difficulties? My client's erection problem must reflect his repressed rage at his mother or his wife. Do I believe that sexual abuse causes eating disorders? My client's bulimia must mean she was molested as a child.

We want to be clear that most therapists are effective, and that some clients *are* resistant to therapy and *are* deeply troubled. This chapter is not an indictment of therapy, any more than writing about the mistakes of memory means that all memory is unreliable or that writing about the conflicts of interest among scientists means that all scientists do tainted research. Our intention is to examine the kinds of mistakes that can result from the closed loop of clinical practice, and show how self-justification perpetuates them.

For anyone in private practice, skepticism and science are ways out of the closed loop. Skepticism, for example, teaches therapists to be cautious about taking what their clients tell them at face value. If a woman says her mother put spiders in her vagina when she was three, the skeptical therapist can be empathic without believing that this event literally happened. If a child says his teachers took him flying in a plane full of clowns and frogs, the skeptical therapist might be charmed by the story without believing that teachers actually chartered a private jet (on their salary, no less). Scientific research provides therapists with ways of improving their clinical practice and of avoiding mistakes. [If you are going to use hypnosis, for example, you had better know that while hypnosis can help clients learn to relax, manage pain, and quit smoking, you should never use it to help your client retrieve memories, because your willing, vulnerable client will often make up a memory that is unreliable.[8] ⌐

Yet today there are many thousands of psychiatrists, social workers, counselors, and psychotherapists who go into private practice with neither skepticism nor evidence to guide them. Paul Meehl, who achieved great distinction as both a clinician and a scientific researcher, once observed that when he was a student, the common factor in the training of all psychologists was "the general scientific commitment not to be fooled and not to fool anyone else. Some things have happened in the world of clinical practice that worry me in this respect. That skepsis, that passion not to be fooled and not to fool anyone else, does not seem to be as fundamental a part of all psychologists' mental equipment as it was a half century ago. . . . I have heard of some psychological testimony in courtrooms locally in which this critical mentality appears to be largely absent."[9]

An example of the problem Meehl feared can be seen in the deposition of a prominent psychiatrist, Bessel van der Kolk, who has testified frequently on behalf of plaintiffs in repressed-memory cases. Van der Kolk explained that as a psychiatrist, he had had medical training and a psychiatric residency, but had never taken a course in experimental psychology.

> *Q:* Are you aware of any research on the reliability or the validity of clinical judgment or clinical predictions based on interview information?
>
> *A:* No.
>
> *Q:* What's your understanding of the current term "disconfirming evidence"?
>
> *A:* I guess that means evidence that disconfirms treasured notions that people have.
>
> *Q:* What's the most powerful piece of disconfirming evidence that you're aware of for the theory that people can repress memories or that they can block out of their awareness a

series of traumatic events, store those in their memory, and recover those with some accuracy years later?

A: What's the strongest thing against that?

Q: Yes. What's the strongest piece of disconfirming evidence?

A: I really can't think of any good evidence against that . . .

Q: Have you read any literature on the concept of false
memories using hypnosis?

A: No.

Q: Is there research on whether clinicians over a period of
years develop more accurate clinical judgment?

A: I don't know if there is, actually . . .

Q: Is [there] a technique that you use to distinguish true
and false memories?

A: We all, we all as human beings are continuously faced
with whether we believe what somebody feeds us or not, and
we all make judgments all the time. And there is such a thing
as internal consistency, and if people tell you something with
internal consistency and with appropriate affect, you tend to
believe that the stories are true.[10]

At the time of this deposition, van der Kolk had not read any of
the voluminous research literature on false memories or how hypnosis can create them, nor was he aware of the documented unreliability of "clinical predictions based on interview information." He had
not read any of the research disconfirming his belief that traumatic
memories are commonly repressed. Yet he has testified frequently
and confidently on behalf of plaintiffs in repressed-memory cases.
Like many clinicians, he is confident that he knows when a client
is telling the truth, and whether a memory is true or false, based on
his clinical experience; the clues are whether the client's story has
"internal consistency" and whether the client recounts the memory
with appropriate emotion—that is, whether the client really *feels* the
memory is true. The problem with this reasoning, however, is that,

as we saw in the previous chapter, thousands of mentally healthy people believe they were abducted by aliens, telling, with all the appropriate feeling, internally consistent stories of the bizarre experiments they believe they endured. As research psychologist John Kihlstrom has observed, "The weakness of the relationship between accuracy and confidence is one of the best-documented phenomena in the 100-year history of eyewitness memory research,"[11] but van der Kolk was unaware of a finding that just about every undergraduate who has taken psychology 101 would know.

No one is suggesting that U.N. observers disturb the privacy of the therapeutic encounter, or that all therapists should start doing their own research. An understanding of how to think scientifically may not aid therapists in the subjective process of helping a client who is searching for answers to existential questions. But it matters profoundly when therapists claim expertise and certainty in domains in which unverified clinical opinion can ruin lives. The scientific method consists of the use of procedures designed to show not that our predictions and hypotheses are right, *but that they might be wrong.* Scientific reasoning is useful to anyone in any job because it makes us face the possibility, even the dire reality, that we were mistaken. It forces us to confront our self-justifications and put them on public display for others to puncture. At its core, therefore, science is a form of arrogance control.

The Problem of the Benevolent Dolphin

Every so often, a heartwarming news story tells of a shipwrecked sailor who was on the verge of drowning in a turbulent sea. Suddenly, a dolphin popped up at his side and, gently but firmly, nudged the swimmer safely to shore. It is tempting to conclude that dolphins must really like human beings, enough to save us from drowning. But wait—are dolphins aware that humans don't swim as well as they do? Are they actually intending to be helpful? To answer that question, we would need to know how many shipwrecked sailors have been gently nudged further out to sea by dolphins, there to drown and never be heard from again. We don't know about those cases, because the swimmers don't live to tell us about their evil-dolphin experiences. If we had that information, we might conclude that dolphins are neither benevolent nor evil; they are just being playful.

Sigmund Freud himself fell victim to the flawed reasoning of the benevolent-dolphin problem. When his fellow analysts questioned his notion that all men suffer from castration anxiety, he was amused. He wrote: "One hears of analysts who boast that, though they have worked for dozens of years, they have never found a sign of the existence of the castration complex. We must bow our heads in recognition of . . . [this] piece of virtuosity in the art of overlooking and mistaking."[12] So if analysts see castration anxiety in their patients, Freud was right; and if they fail to see it, they are "overlooking" it, and Freud is still right. Men themselves cannot tell you if they feel castration anxiety, because it's unconscious, but if they deny that they feel it, they are, of course, in denial.

What a terrific theory! No way for it to be wrong. But that is the very reason that Freud, for all his illuminating observations about civilization and its discontents, was not doing science. For any theory to be scientific, it must be stated in such a way that it can be shown to be false as well as true. If every outcome confirms your hypotheses that all men unconsciously suffer from castration anxiety; or that intelligent design, rather than evolution, accounts for the diversity of species; or that your favorite psychic would accurately have predicted 9/11 if only she hadn't been taking a shower that morning; or that all dolphins are kind to humans, your beliefs are a matter of faith, not science. Freud, however, saw himself as the consummate scientist. In 1934, the American psychologist Saul Rosenzweig wrote to him, suggesting that Freud subject his psychoanalytic assertions to experimental testing. "The wealth of dependable observations on which these assertions rest make them independent of experimental verification," Freud replied loftily. "Still, [experiments] can do no harm."[13]

Because of the confirmation bias, however, the "dependable observation" is not dependable. Clinical intuition—"I know it when I see it"—is the end of the conversation to many psychiatrists and psychotherapists, but the start of the conversation to the scientist—"a good observation; but what exactly have you seen, and how do you know you are right?" Observation and intuition, without independent verification, are unreliable guides; like roguish locals misdirecting the tourists, they occasionally send everyone off in the wrong direction.

Although there are few orthodox Freudians anymore, there are many psychodynamic schools of therapy, so called because they derive from Freud's emphasis on unconscious mental dynamics. Most of these programs are unconnected to university departments of psychology, and their students learn little to nothing about scientific methods or even about basic psychological findings. And then there are the many unlicensed therapists who don't know much about psychodynamic theories but nonetheless have uncritically absorbed the Freudian language that permeates the culture—notions of regression, denial, and repression. What unites these clinical practitioners is their misplaced reliance on their own powers of observation and the closed loop it creates. Everything they see confirms what they believe.

One danger of the closed loop is that it makes practitioners vulnerable to logical fallacies. Consider the famous syllogism "All men are mortal; Socrates is a man; therefore Socrates is mortal." So far, so good. But just because all men are mortal, it does not follow that all mortals are men, and it certainly does not follow that all men are Socrates. Yet the recovered-memory movement was based from the very beginning on the logical fallacy that if some women who have been sexually abused later develop depression, eating disorders, and panic attacks, then all women who suffer from depression, eating disorders, and panic attacks must have been sexually abused. Accordingly, many psychodynamic clinicians began pushing their unhappy clients to rummage around in their pasts to find supporting evidence for their theory. But their clients, when first asked, denied that they had been abused. What to do with this dissonant response? The answer came in Freud's idea that the unconscious actively represses traumatic experiences, particularly those of a sexual nature. That explains it! That explains how Holly Ramona could forget that her father raped her for eleven years.

Once these clinicians had latched on to repression to explain why their clients were not remembering traumatic sexual abuse, you can see why some felt justified, indeed professionally obligated, to do whatever it took to pry that repressed memory out of there. Because the client's denials are all the more evidence of repression, strong methods are called for. If hypnosis won't do it, let's try sodium amytal ("truth serum"), another intervention that simply relaxes a person and increases the chances of false memories.[14]

Of course, many of us intentionally avoid a painful memory by distracting ourselves or trying not to think about it; and many of us have had the experience of suddenly recalling a painful memory, one we thought long gone, when we are in a situation that evokes it. The situation provides what memory scientists call retrieval cues, familiar signals that reawaken the memory.[15]

Psychodynamic therapists, however, claim that repression is entirely different from the normal mechanisms of forgetting and recall. They think it explains why a person can forget years and years of traumatic experiences, such as repeated rape. Yet in his meticulous review of the experimental research and the clinical evidence, presented in his book *Remembering Trauma,* clinical psychologist Richard McNally concluded: "The notion that the mind protects itself by repressing or dissociating memories of trauma, rendering them inaccessible to awareness, is a piece of psychiatric folklore devoid of convincing empirical support."[16] Overwhelmingly, the evidence shows just the opposite. [The problem for most people who have suffered traumatic experiences is not that they forget them but that they cannot forget them: The memories keep intruding.]

Thus, people do not repress the memory of being tortured, being in combat, or being the victim of a natural disaster (unless they suffered brain damage at the time), although details of even these horrible experiences are subject to distortion over time, as are all memories. "Truly traumatic events—terrifying, life-threatening experiences—are never forgotten, let alone if they are repeated," says McNally. "The basic principle is: if the abuse was traumatic at the time it occurred, it is unlikely to be forgotten. If it was forgotten, then it was unlikely to have been traumatic. And even if it was forgotten, there is no evidence that it was blocked, repressed, sealed behind a mental barrier, inaccessible."

This is obviously disconfirming information for clinicians committed to the belief that people who have been brutalized for years will repress the memory. If they are right, surely Holocaust survivors would be leading candidates for repression. But as far as anyone knows, and as McNally documents, no survivors of the Holocaust have forgotten or repressed what happened to them. Recovered-memory advocates have a response to that evidence, too—they distort it. In one study conducted forty years after the war, survivors of Camp Erika, a Nazi concentration camp, were asked to recall what they had endured there. When their current recollections were compared with depositions they had provided when they were first released, it turned out that the survivors remembered what happened to them with remarkable accuracy. Any neutral observer would read this research and say, "How incredible! They were able to recall all those details after forty years." Yet one team of recovered-memory advocates cited this study as evidence that "amnesia for Nazi Holocaust camp experiences has also been reported." What was reported was nothing remotely like amnesia. Some survivors failed to recall a few violent events, among a great many similar ones, or had forgotten a few details, such as the name of a sadistic guard. This is not repression; it is the normal forgetting of details that all of us experience over the years.[17]

Clinicians who believe in repression, therefore, see it everywhere, even where no one else does. But if everything you observe in your clinical experience is evidence to support your beliefs, what would you consider counterevidence? What if your client has no memory of abuse not because she is repressing, but because it never happened? What could ever break you out of the closed loop? To guard against the bias of our own direct observations, scientists invented the control group: the group that *isn't* getting the new therapeutic method, the people who *aren't* getting the new drug. Most people understand the importance of control groups in the study of a new drug's effectiveness, because without a control group, you can't say if people's positive response is due to the drug or to a placebo effect, the general expectation that the drug will help them. For instance, one study of women who had complained of sexual problems found that 41 percent said that their libido returned when they took Viagra. So, however, did 43 percent of the control group who took a sugar pill.[18] (This study showed conclusively that the organ most involved in sexual excitement is the brain.)

Obviously, if you are a psychotherapist, you can't randomly put some of your clients on a waiting list and give others your serious attention; the former will find another therapist pronto. But if you are not trained to be aware of the benevolent-dolphin problem, and if you are absolutely, positively convinced that your views are right and your clinical skills unassailable, you can make serious errors. A clinical social worker explained why she had decided to remove a child from her mother's custody: The mother had been physically abused as a child, and "we all know," the social worker said to the judge, that that is a major risk factor for the mother's abuse of her own child one day. This assumption of the cycle of abuse came from observations of confirming cases: abusive parents, in jail or in therapy, reporting that they were severely beaten or sexually abused by their own parents. What is missing are the disconfirming cases: the abused children who do not grow up to become abusive parents. They are invisible to social workers and other mental-health professionals because, by definition, they don't end up in prison or treatment. Research psychologists who have done longitudinal studies, following children over time, have found that while being physically abused as a child is associated with an increased chance of becoming an abusive parent, the great majority of abused children—nearly 70 percent—do not repeat their parents' cruelties.[19] If you are doing therapy with a victim of parental abuse or with an abusive parent, this information may not be relevant to you. But if you are in a position to make predictions that will affect whether, say, a parent should lose custody, it most surely is.

Similarly, suppose you are doing therapy with children who have been sexually molested. They touch your heart, and you take careful note of their symptoms: They are fearful, wet the bed, want to sleep with a night-light, have nightmares, masturbate, or expose their genitals to other children. After a while, you will probably become pretty confident of your ability to determine whether a child has been abused, using those symptoms as a checklist to guide you. You may give a very young child anatomically correct dolls to play with, on the grounds that what he or she cannot reveal in words may be revealed in play. One of your young clients pounds a stick into a doll's vagina. Another scrutinizes a doll's penis with alarming concentration for a four-year-old.

Therapists who have not been trained to think scientifically will probably not wonder about the invisible cases—the children they don't see as clients. They probably will not think to ask how common the symptoms of bedwetting, sex play, and fearfulness are in the general population of children. When researchers did ask, they found that children who have not been molested are also likely to masturbate and be sexually curious; temperamentally fearful children are also likely to wet the bed and be scared of the dark.[20] Even children who have been molested show no predictable set of symptoms, something scientists learned only by observing children's reactions over time instead of by assessing them once or twice in a clinical interview. A review of forty-five studies that followed sexually abused children for up to eighteen months found that although these children at first had more symptoms of fearfulness and sexual acting-out than nonabused children, "no one symptom characterized a majority of sexually abused children [and] approximately one third of victims had no symptoms. . . . The findings suggest the absence of any specific syndrome in sexually abused children."[21]

Moreover, children who have not been abused do not appreciably differ from abused children in how they play with anatomically detailed dolls; those prominent genitals are pretty interesting. Some children do bizarre things and it doesn't mean anything at all, except that the dolls are unreliable as diagnostic tests.[22] In one study headed by two eminent developmental psychologists, Maggie Bruck and Stephen Ceci, a child pounded a stick into the doll's vagina to show her parents what supposedly had happened to her during a doctor's exam that day.[23] The (videotaped) doctor had done no such thing, but you can imagine how you would feel if you watched your daughter playing so violently with the doll, and a psychiatrist told you solemnly it meant she had been molested. You would want that doctor's hide.

Many therapists who began to specialize in child abuse in the 1980s often feel extremely confident of their ability to determine whether a child has been molested; after all, they say, they have years of clinical experience to back up their judgments. Yet study after study shows that their confidence is mistaken. For example, clinical psychologist Thomas Horner and his colleagues examined the evaluations provided by a team of expert clinicians in a case in which a father was accused of molesting his three-year-old daughter. The experts reviewed transcripts, watched interviews of the child and videotapes of parent-child exchanges, and reviewed clinical findings. They had identical information, but some were convinced the abuse had occurred while others were just as convinced it had never happened. The researchers then recruited 129 other mental-health specialists and asked them to assess the evidence in this case, estimate the likelihood that the little girl had been molested by her father, and make a recommendation regarding custody. Again, the results ranged from certainty that the child had been molested to certainty that she had not. Some wanted to forbid the father to see his daughter ever again; others wanted to give him full custody. Those experts who were prone to believe that sexual abuse is rampant in families were quick to interpret ambiguous evidence in ways that supported that belief; those who were skeptical did not. For the unskeptical experts, the researchers said, "believing is seeing."[24]

Other studies of the unreliability of clinical predictions, and there are hundreds of them, are dissonance-creating news to the mental-health professionals whose self-confidence rests on the belief that their expert assessments are extremely accurate.[25] When we said that science is a form of arrogance control, that's what we mean.

o   o   o

"Believing is seeing" was the principle that created every one of the day-care scandals of the 1980s and 1990s. Just as in the McMartin case, each began with an accusation from a disturbed parent or the whimsical comments of a child, which provoked an investigation, which provoked panic. At the Wee Care Nursery School in New Jersey, for example, a four-year-old child was having his temperature taken rectally at his doctor's office when he said, "That's what my teacher [Kelly Michaels] does to me at school."[26] The child's mother notified the state's child protection agency. The agency brought the child to a prosecutor's office and gave him an anatomical doll to play with. The boy inserted his finger into the rectum of the doll and said that two other boys had had their temperature taken that way, too. Parents of children in the preschool were told to look for signs of abuse in their own children. Professionals were called in to interview the children. Before long, the children were claiming that Kelly Michaels had, among other things, licked peanut butter off their genitals, made them drink her urine and eat her feces, and raped them with knives, forks, and toys. These acts were said to have occurred during school hours over a period of seven months, although parents could come and go as they pleased, no child had complained, and none of the parents had noticed any problems in their children.

Kelly Michaels was convicted of 115 counts of sexual abuse and sentenced to forty-seven years in prison. She was released after five years, when an appeals court ruled that the children's testimony had been tainted by how they had been interviewed. And how was that? With the confirmation bias going at full speed and no reins of scientific caution to restrain it, a deadly combination that was the hallmark of the interviews of children conducted in all the day-care cases. For example, here is how Susan Kelley, a pediatric nurse who interviewed children in a number of these cases, used Bert and Ernie puppets to "aid" the children's recall:

Kelley: Would you tell Ernie?

Child: No.

Kelley: Ah, come on [pleading tone]. Please tell Ernie. Please tell me. Please tell me. So we could help you. Please . . . You whisper it to Ernie . . . Did anybody ever touch you right there? [*pointing to the vulva of a girl doll*]

Child: No.

Kelley: [*pointing to the doll's posterior*] Did anybody touch your bum?

Child: No.

Kelley: Would you tell Bert?

Child: They didn't touch me!

Kelley: Who didn't touch you?

Child: Not my teacher. Nobody.

Kelley: Did any big people, any adult, touch your bum there?

Child: No.[27]

"Who didn't touch you?" We are entering the realm of *Catch-22,* Joseph Heller's great novel, in which the colonel with the fat mustache says to Clevinger: "What did you mean when you said we couldn't punish you?" Clevinger replies: "I didn't say you couldn't punish me, sir." Colonel: "When didn't you say that we couldn't punish you?" Clevinger: "I always didn't say that you couldn't punish me, sir."

At the time, the psychotherapists and social workers who were called on to interview children believed that molested children won't tell you what happened to them until you press them by persistently asking leading questions, because they are scared or ashamed. In the absence of research, this was a reasonable assumption, and clearly it is sometimes true. [But when does pressing slide into coercion?] Psychological scientists have conducted experiments to investigate every aspect of children's memory and testimony: How do children understand what adults ask them? Do their responses depend on their age, verbal abilities, and the kinds of questions they are asked? Under what conditions are children likely to be telling the truth, and when are they likely to be suggestible, to say that something happened when it did not?[28]

For example, in an experiment with preschool children, Sena Garven and her colleagues used interview techniques that were based on the actual transcripts of interrogations of children in the Mc-Martin case. A young man visited children at their preschool, read them a story, and handed out treats. He did nothing aggressive, inappropriate, or surprising. A week later an experimenter questioned the children about the man's visit. She asked one group leading questions, such as "Did he shove the teacher? Did he throw a crayon at a kid who was talking?" She asked a second group the same questions along with influence techniques used by the McMartin interrogators: for example, telling the children what other kids had supposedly said, expressing disappointment if answers were negative, and praising children for making allegations. In the first group, children said "yes, it happened" to about 15 percent of the false allegations about the man's visit; not a high percentage, but not a trivial number, either. In the second group, however, the three-year-olds said "yes, it happened" to over 80 percent of the false allegations suggested to them, and the four- to six-year-olds said yes to about half the allegations. And those results occurred after interviews lasting only five to ten minutes; in actual criminal investigations, interviewers often question children repeatedly over weeks and months. In a similar study, this time with five- to seven-year-olds, the investigators found they could easily influence the children to agree with preposterous questions, such as "Did Paco take you flying in an airplane?" What was more troubling was that within a short time, many of the children's inaccurate statements had crystallized into stable, but false, memories.[29]

Research like this has enabled psychologists to improve their methods of interviewing children, so that they can help children who have been abused disclose what happened to them, but without increasing the suggestibility of children who have not been abused. The scientists have shown that very young children, under age five, often cannot tell the difference between something they were told and something that actually happened to them. If preschoolers overhear adults exchanging rumors about some event, for example, many of the children will later come to believe they actually experienced the event themselves.[30] In all these studies, the most powerful finding is that adults are highly likely to taint an interview when they go into it already convinced that a child has been molested. When that is so, there is only one "truth" they are prepared to accept when they ask the child to tell the truth. Like Susan Kelley, they never accept the child's "no"; "no" means the child is denying or repressing or afraid to tell. The child can do nothing to convince the adult she has not been molested.

We can understand why so many Susan Kelleys, prosecutors, and parents have been quick to assume the worst; no one wants to let a child molester go free. But no one should want to contribute to the conviction of an innocent adult, either. Today, informed by years of experimental research with children, the National Institute of Child Health and Human Development and some individual states, notably Michigan, have drafted new model protocols for social workers, police investigators, and others who conduct child interviews.[31] These protocols emphasize the hazards of the confirmation bias, instructing interviewers to test the hypothesis of possible abuse, and not assume they know what happened. The guidelines recognize that most children will readily disclose actual abuse, and some need prodding; the guidelines also caution against the use of techniques known to produce false reports.

This change, from the uncritical "believe the children" to "understand the children," reflects a recognition that mental-health professionals need to think more like scientists and less like advocates, weighing all the evidence fairly and considering the possibility that their suspicions are unfounded. If they do not, it will not be justice that is served, but self-justification.

Science, Skepticism, and Self-justification

When Judith Herman, an eminent psychiatrist, published *Father-Daughter Incest* in 1981, the patients she described remembered what had happened to them all too clearly. At the time, feminist clinicians like Herman were doing important work in raising public awareness of rape, child abuse, incest, and domestic violence. They were not claiming that their clients had repressed their memories; rather, these women said they had chosen to remain silent because they felt frightened and ashamed, and that no one would believe them. There is no entry for "repression" in the index of *Father-Daughter Incest.* Yet within ten years Herman had become a recovered-memory advocate: The very first sentence of her 1992 book *Trauma and Recovery* is "The ordinary response to atrocities is to banish them from consciousness." How did Herman and other highly experienced clinicians move from believing that traumatic experiences are rarely or never forgotten to believing that this response was "ordinary"? One step at a time.

Imagine that you are a therapist who cares deeply about the rights and safety of women and children. You see yourself as a skillful, compassionate practitioner. You know how hard it has been to get politicians and the public to pay serious attention to the problems of women and children. You know how difficult it has been for battered women to speak up. Now you start hearing about a new phenomenon: In therapy, women are suddenly recovering memories that had been repressed all their lives, memories of horrific events. These cases are turning up on talk shows, at the conferences you go to, and in a flurry of books, notably the hugely popular *The Courage to Heal.* It's true that the book's authors, Ellen Bass and Laura Davis, have had no training in any kind of psychotherapy, let alone science, which they freely admitted. "None of what is presented here is based on psychological theories," Bass explained in the preface, but this ignorance of psychology did not prevent them from defining themselves as healers and experts on sexual abuse, based on the workshops they had led.[32] They provided a list of symptoms, any of which, they said, suggest that a woman may be a victim of incest, including these: She feels powerless and unmotivated; she has an eating disorder or sexual problems; she feels there is something wrong with her deep down inside; she feels she has to be perfect; she feels bad, dirty, or ashamed. You are a therapist working with women who have some of these problems. Should you assume that years of incest, repressed from memory, are the primary cause?

There you are, at the top of the pyramid, with a decision to make: Leap onto the recovered-memory bandwagon or stay on the sidewalk. The majority of mental-health professionals were skeptical and did not go along. But a large number of therapists—between one-fourth and one-third, according to several surveys[33]—took that first step in the direction of belief, and, given the closed loop of clinical practice, we can see how easy it was for them to do so. Most had not been trained in the show-me-the-data spirit of skepticism. They did not know about the confirmation bias, so it did not occur to them that Bass and Davis were seeing evidence of incest in any symptom a woman has, and even in the fact that she has no symptoms. They lacked a deep appreciation of the importance of control groups, so they were unlikely to wonder how many women who were not molested nonetheless have eating disorders or feel powerless and unmotivated.[34] They did not pause to consider what reasons other than incest might cause their female clients to have sexual problems.

Even some skeptical practitioners were reluctant to slow the bandwagon by saying anything critical of their colleagues or of the women telling their stories. It's uncomfortable—dissonant—to realize that some of your colleagues are tainting your profession with silly or dangerous ideas. It's embarrassing—dissonant—to realize that not everything women and children say is true, especially after all your efforts to persuade victimized women to speak up and to get the world to recognize the problem of child abuse. Some therapists feared that to publicly question the likelihood of recovered memories was to undermine the credibility of the women who really had been molested or raped. Some feared that criticism of the recovered-memory movement would give ammunition and moral support to sexual predators and antifeminists. In the beginning, they could not have anticipated that a national panic about sexual abuse would erupt, and that innocent people would be swept up in the pursuit of the guilty. Yet by remaining silent as this happened, they furthered their own slide down the pyramid.

Today, some of the psychotherapists who joined the recovered-memory movement continue to do what they have been doing for years, helping clients uncover "repressed" memories. (Most have become cautious, however, fearing lawsuits.) Others have quietly dropped their focus on repressed memories of incest as the leading explanation of their clients' problems; it has gone out of fashion, just as penis envy, frigidity, and masturbatory insanity did decades ago. They drop one fad when it loses steam and sign on for the next, rarely pausing to question where all the repressed incest cases went. They might hear vaguely that there is controversy, but it's easier to stay with what they have always done, and maybe add a newer technique to go along with it.

But, undoubtedly, the practitioners who would have the greatest dissonance to resolve are the clinical psychologists and psychiatrists who spearheaded the recovered-memory movement to begin with. Many have impressive credentials. The movement gave them great fame and success. They were star lecturers at professional conferences. They were and still are called on to testify in court about whether a child has been abused or whether a plaintiff's recovered memory is reliable, and, as we saw, they usually made their judgments with a high degree of confidence. As the scientific evidence that they were wrong began to accumulate, how likely was it that they would have embraced it readily, being grateful for the studies of memory and children's testimony that would improve their practice? To do so would have been to realize that they had harmed the very women and children they were trying to help. It was much easier to preserve their commitments by rejecting the scientific research as being irrelevant to clinical practice. And as soon as they took that self-justifying step, they could not go back without enormous psychological difficulty.

Today, standing at the bottom of the pyramid, miles away professionally from their scientific colleagues, having devoted two decades to promoting a form of therapy that Richard McNally calls "the worst catastrophe to befall the mental-health field since the lobotomy era,"[35] most recovered-memory clinicians remain as committed as ever to their beliefs. How have they reduced their dissonance?

[One popular method is by minimizing the extent of the problem and the damage it caused.] Clinical psychologist John Briere, one of the earliest supporters of recovered-memory therapy, finally admitted at a conference that the numbers of memories recovered in the 1980s may have been caused, at least in part, by "over-enthusiastic" therapists who had inappropriately tried to "liposuction memories out of their [clients'] brains." Mistakes were made, by them. But only a few of them, he hastened to add. Recovered false memories are rare, he said; repressed true memories are far more common.[36]

[Others reduce dissonance by blaming the victim.] Colin Ross, a psychiatrist who rose to fame and fortune by claiming that repressed memories of abuse cause multiple personality disorder, eventually agreed that "suggestible individuals can have memories elaborated within their minds because of poor therapeutic technique." But because "normal human memory is highly error-prone," he concluded that "false memories are biologically normal and, therefore, not necessarily the therapist's fault." Therapists don't create false memories in their clients, because therapists are merely "consultants."[37] If a client comes up with a mistaken memory, therefore, it's the client's fault.

[The most ideologically committed clinicians reduce dissonance by killing the messenger.] In the late 1990s, when psychiatrists and psychotherapists were being convicted of malpractice for their use of coercive methods, and courts were ruling against them in cases of alleged recovered memories, D. Corydon Hammond advised his clinical colleagues at a convention thus: "I think it's time somebody called for an open season on academicians and researchers. In the United States and Canada in particular, things have become so extreme with academics supporting extreme false memory positions, so

I think it's time for clinicians to begin bringing ethics charges for scientific malpractice against researchers, and journal editors—most of whom, I would point out, don't have malpractice coverage."[38] Some psychiatrists and clinical psychologists took Hammond's advice, sending harassing letters to researchers and journal editors, making spurious claims of ethics violations against scientists studying memory and children's testimony, and filing nuisance lawsuits aimed at blocking publication of critical articles and books. None of these efforts have been successful at silencing the scientists.[39]

[There is one final way of reducing dissonance: Dismiss all the scientific research as being part of a backlash against child victims and incest survivors.]The concluding section of the third edition of *The Courage to Heal* is called "Honoring the Truth: A Response to the Backlash." There is no section called "Honoring the Truth: We Made Some Big Mistakes."[40]

o   o   o

There are almost no psychotherapists who practiced recovered-memory therapy who have admitted that they were wrong. Of course, they may fear lawsuits. But from the few who have publicly admitted their errors, we can see what it took to shake them out of their protective cocoons of self-justification. For Linda Ross, it was taking herself out of the closed loop of private therapy sessions and forcing herself to confront, in person, parents whose lives had been destroyed by their daughters' accusations. One of her clients brought her to a meeting of accused parents. Ross suddenly realized that a story that had seemed bizarre but possible when her client told it in therapy now seemed fantastical when multiplied by a roomful of similar tales. "I had been so supportive of women and their repressed memories," she said, "but I had never once considered what that experience was like for the parents. Now I heard how absolutely ludicrous it sounded. One elderly couple introduced themselves, and the wife told me that their daughter had accused her husband of murdering three people. . . . The pain in these parents' faces was so obvious. And the unique thread was that their daughters had gone to [recovered-memory] therapy. I didn't feel very proud of myself or my profession that day."

After that meeting, Ross said, she would frequently wake up in the middle of the night "in terror and anguish" as the cocoon began to crack open. She worried about being sued, but most of the time she "just thought about those mothers and fathers who wanted their children back." She called her former clients, trying to undo the damage she had caused, and she changed the way she practices therapy. In an interview on National Public Radio's *This American Life* with Alix Spiegel, Ross told of accompanying one of her clients to a meeting with the woman's parents, whose home had been dismantled by police trying to find evidence of a dead body that their daughter had claimed to remember in therapy.[41] There was no dead body, any more than there were underground torture chambers at the McMartin Preschool. "So I had a chance to tell them the part that I played," said Ross. "And to tell them that I completely understood that they would find it difficult for the rest of their lives to be able to find a place to forgive me, but that I was certainly aware that I was in need of their forgiveness."

At the end of the interview, Alix Spiegel said: "There are almost no people like Linda Ross, practicing therapists who have come forward to talk publicly about their experience, to admit culpability, or try to figure out how this happened. The experts, for once, are strangely silent."

CHAPTER 5

o   o   o

Law and Disorder

I guess it's really difficult for any prosecutor [to acknowledge errors and] to say, "Gee, we had 25 years of this guy's life. That's enough."
—Dale M. Rubin, lawyer for Thomas Lee Goldstein

THOMAS LEE GOLDSTEIN, a college student and ex-Marine, was convicted in 1980 of a murder he did not commit, and spent the next twenty-four years in prison. His only crime was being in the wrong place at the wrong time. Although he lived near the murder victim, the police found no physical evidence linking Goldstein to the crime: no gun, no fingerprints, no blood. He had no motive. He was convicted on the testimony of a jailhouse informant, improbably named Edward Fink, who had been arrested thirty-five times, had three felony convictions and a heroin habit, and had testified in ten different cases that the defendant had confessed to him while sharing a jail cell. (A prison counselor had described Fink as "a con man who tends to handle the facts as if they were elastic.") Fink lied under oath, denying that he had been given a reduced sentence in exchange for his testimony. The prosecution's only other support for its case was an eyewitness, Loran Campbell, who identified Goldstein as the killer after the police falsely assured him that Goldstein had failed a lie-detector test. None of the other five eyewitnesses identified Goldstein, and four of them said the killer was "black or Mexican." Campbell recanted his testimony later, saying he had been "a little overanxious" to help the police by telling them what they wanted to hear. It was too late. Goldstein was sentenced to twenty-seven years to life for the murder.

Over the years, five federal judges agreed that prosecutors had denied Goldstein his right to a fair trial by failing to tell the defense about their deal with Fink, but Goldstein remained in prison. Finally, in February 2004, a California Superior Court judge dismissed the case "in furtherance of justice," citing its lack of evidence and its "cancerous nature"—its reliance on a professional informer who perjured himself. Even then, the Los Angeles District Attorney's office refused to acknowledge that they might have made a mistake. Within hours, they filed new charges against Goldstein, set bail at $1 million, and announced they would retry him for the murder. "I am very confident we have the right guy," Deputy District Attorney Patrick Connolly said. Two months later, the DA's office conceded it had no case against Goldstein and released him.

o   o   o

On the night of April 19, 1989, the woman who came to be known as the Central Park Jogger was brutally raped and bludgeoned. The police quickly arrested five black and Hispanic teenagers from Harlem who had been in the park "wilding," randomly attacking and roughing up passersby. The police, not unreasonably, saw them as likely suspects for the attack on the jogger. They kept the teenagers in custody and interrogated them intensively for fourteen to thirty hours. The boys, ages fourteen to sixteen, finally confessed to the crime, but they did more than admit guilt: They reported lurid details of what they had done. One boy demonstrated how he had pulled off the jogger's pants. One told how her shirt was cut off with a knife, and how one of the gang repeatedly struck her head with a rock. Another expressed remorse for his "first rape," saying he had felt pressured by the other guys to do it, and promising he would never do it again. Although there was no physical evidence linking the teenagers to the crime—no matching semen, blood, or DNA—their confessions persuaded the police, the jury, forensic experts, and the public that the perpetrators had been caught. [Donald Trump spent $80,000 on newspaper ads calling for them to get the death penalty.]

And yet the teenagers were innocent. Thirteen years later, a felon named Matias Reyes, in prison for three rape-robberies and one rape-murder, admitted that he, and he alone, had committed the crime. He revealed details that no one else knew, and his DNA matched the DNA taken from semen found in the victim and on her sock. The Manhattan District Attorney's office, headed by Robert M. Morgenthau, investigated for nearly a year and could find no connection between Reyes and the boys who had been convicted. The DA's office supported the defense motion to vacate the boys' convictions, and in 2002 the motion was granted. But Morgenthau's decision was angrily denounced by former prosecutors in his office and by the police officers who had been involved in the original investigation, who refused to believe that the boys were innocent.[2] After all, they had confessed.

o   o   o

In 1932, Yale law professor Edwin Borchard published *Convicting the Innocent: Sixty-five Actual Errors of Criminal Justice.* Of those sixty-five cases that Borchard had investigated, eight involved defendants convicted of murder, even though the supposed victim turned up later, very much alive. You'd think that might be fairly convincing proof that police and prosecutors had made some serious mistakes, yet one prosecutor told Borchard, "Innocent men are never convicted. Don't worry about it, it never happens . . . It is a physical impossibility."

Then came DNA. Ever since 1989, the first year in which DNA testing resulted in the release of an innocent prisoner, the public has been repeatedly confronted with evidence that far from being an impossibility, convicting the innocent is much more common than we feared. The Innocence Project, founded by Barry Scheck and Peter J. Neufeld, keeps a running record on its Web site of the hundreds of people imprisoned for murder or rape who have been cleared, most often by DNA testing but also by other kinds of evidence, such as mistaken eyewitness identifications.[3] Death-row exonerations, of course, get the greatest public attention, but the number of wrongful convictions for lesser crimes is also alarming. After a comprehensive study of criminal cases in which the convicted person was indisputably exonerated, law professor Samuel R. Gross and his associates concluded that "if we reviewed prison sentences with the same level of care that we devote to death sentences, there would have been *over 28,500 non-death-row exonerations in the past 15 years* rather than the 255 that have in fact occurred."[4]

This is uncomfortably dissonant information for anyone who wants to believe that the system works. Resolving it is hard enough for the average citizen, but if you are a participant in the justice system, your motivation to justify its mistakes, let alone yours, will be immense. Social psychologist Richard Ofshe, an expert on the psychology of false confessions, once observed that convicting the wrong person is "one of the worst professional errors you can make—like a physician amputating the wrong arm."[5]

Suppose that you are presented with evidence that you did amputate the wrong arm: that you helped send the wrong person to prison. What do you do? Your first impulse will be to deny your mistake for the obvious reason of protecting your job, reputation, and colleagues. Besides, if you release someone who later commits a serious crime, or free someone who is innocent but who was erroneously imprisoned for a heinous crime such as child molesting, an outraged public may nail you for it; you have been "soft on crime."[6] You have plenty of such external incentives for denying that you made a mistake, but you have a greater internal one: You want to think of yourself as an honorable, competent person who would never convict the wrong guy. But how can you possibly think you got the right guy in the face of the new evidence to the contrary? Because, you convince yourself, the evidence is lousy, and look, he's a bad guy; even if he didn't commit this particular crime, he undoubtedly committed another one. The alternative, that you sent an innocent man to prison for fifteen years, is so antithetical to your view of your competence that you will go through mental hoops to convince yourself that you couldn't possibly have made such a blunder.

With every innocent person freed from years in prison through DNA testing, the public can almost hear the mental machinations of prosecutors, police, and judges who are busy resolving dissonance. One strategy is to claim that most of those cases don't reflect wrongful *convictions* but wrongful *pardons:* Just because a prisoner is exonerated doesn't mean he or she is innocent. And if the person really is innocent, well, that's a shame, but wrongful convictions are extremely rare, a reasonable price to pay for the superb system we already have in place. The real problem is that too many criminals get off on technicalities or escape justice because they are rich enough to buy a high-priced defense team. As Joshua Marquis, an Oregon district attorney and something of a professional defender of the criminal-justice system, put it, "Americans should be far more worried about the wrongfully freed than the wrongfully convicted."[7] When the nonpartisan Center for Public Integrity published its report of 2,012 cases of documented prosecutorial misconduct that had led to wrongful convictions, Marquis dismissed the numbers and report's implication that the problem might be "epidemic."

"The truth is that such misconduct is better described as episodic," he wrote, "those few cases being rare enough to merit considerable attention by both the courts and the media."

When mistakes or misconduct occur, Marquis added, the system has many self-correcting procedures in place to fix them immediately. In fact, he worries, if we start tinkering with the system to make corrections designed to reduce the rate of wrongful convictions, we will end up freeing too many guilty people. This claim reflects the perverted logic of self-justification. When an innocent person is falsely convicted, the *real* guilty party remains on the streets. "Alone among the legal profession," Marquis claims, "a prosecutor's sole allegiance is to the truth—even if that means torpedoing the prosecutor's own case."[8] That is an admirable, dissonance-reducing sentiment, one that reveals the underlying problem more than Marquis realizes. It is precisely because prosecutors believe they are pursuing the truth that they do not torpedo their own cases when they need to; because, thanks to self-justification, they rarely think they need to.

You do not have to be a scurrilous, corrupt DA to think this way. Rob Warden, executive director of the Center on Wrongful Convictions at Northwestern University's law school, has observed dissonance at work among prosecutors whom he considers "fundamentally good" and honorable people who want to do the right thing. When one exoneration took place, Jack O'Malley, the prosecutor on the case, kept saying to Warden, "How could this be? How could this happen?" Warden said, "He didn't get it. He didn't understand. He really didn't. And Jack O'Malley was a good man." Yet prosecutors cannot get beyond seeing themselves and the cops as good guys, and defendants as bad guys. "You get in the system," Warden says, "and you become very cynical. People are lying to you all over the place. Then you develop a theory of the crime, and it leads to what we call tunnel vision. Years later overwhelming evidence comes out that the guy was innocent. And you're sitting there thinking, 'Wait a minute. Either this overwhelming evidence is wrong or I was wrong—and I couldn't have been wrong because I'm a good guy.' That's a psychological phenomenon I have seen over and over."[9]

That phenomenon is self-justification. Over and over, as the two of us read the research on wrongful convictions in American history, we saw how self-justification can escalate the likelihood of injustice at every step of the process from capture to conviction. The police and prosecutors use methods gleaned from a lifetime of experience to identify a suspect and build a case for conviction. Usually, they are right. Unfortunately, those same methods increase their risks of pursuing the wrong suspect, ignoring evidence that might implicate another, increasing their commitment to a wrong decision, and, later, refusing to admit their error. As the process rolls along, those who are caught up in the effort to convict the original suspect often become more certain that they have the perpetrator and more committed to getting a conviction. Once that person goes to jail, *that fact alone justifies what we did to put him there.* Besides, the judge and jury agreed with us, didn't they? Self-justification not only puts innocent people in prison, but sees to it that they stay there.

The Investigators

On the morning of January 21, 1998, in Escondido, California, twelve-year-old Stephanie Crowe was found in her bedroom, stabbed to death. The night before, neighbors had called 911 to report their fears about a vagrant in the neighborhood who was behaving strangely—a man named Richard Tuite, who suffered from schizophrenia and had a history of stalking young women and breaking into their houses. But Escondido detectives and a team from the FBI's Behavioral Analysis Unit concluded almost immediately that the killing was an inside job. They knew that most murder victims are killed by someone related to them, not by crazy intruders.

Accordingly, the detectives, primarily Ralph Claytor and Chris McDonough, turned their attention to Stephanie's brother, Michael, then age fourteen. Michael, who was sick with a fever, was interrogated, without his parents' knowledge, for three hours at one sitting and then for another six hours, without a break. [The detectives lied to him:] They said they found Stephanie's blood in his room, that she had strands of his hair in her hand, that someone inside the house had to have killed her because all the doors and windows were locked, that Stephanie's blood was all over his clothes, and that he had failed the computerized Voice Stress Analyzer. (This is a pseudo-scientific technique that allegedly identifies liars by measuring "microtremors" in their voices. No one has scientifically demonstrated the existence of microtremors or the validity of this method.[10]) Although Michael repeatedly told them he had no memory of the crime and provided no details, such as where he put the murder weapon, [he finally confessed that he had killed her in a jealous rage.] Within days, the police also arrested Michael's friends Joshua Treadway and Aaron Houser, both fifteen. Joshua Treadway, after two interrogations that lasted twenty-two hours, produced an elaborate story of how the three of them had conspired to murder Stephanie.

On the eve of the trial, in a dramatic turn of events, Stephanie's blood was discovered on the sweatshirt that the vagrant, Richard Tuite, had been wearing the night of her murder. This evidence forced then–District Attorney Paul Pfingst to dismiss the charges against the teenagers, although, he said, he remained convinced of their guilt because of their confessions and would therefore not indict Tuite. The detectives who had pursued the boys, Claytor and McDonough, never gave up their certainty that they had nabbed the real killers. They self-published a book to justify their procedures and beliefs. In it, they claimed that Richard Tuite was just a fall guy, a scapegoat, a drifter who had been used as a pawn by politicians, the press, celebrities, and the criminal and civil lawyers hired by the boys' families to "shift blame from their clients and transfer it to him instead."[11]

The teenagers were released and the case was handed over to another detective in the department, Vic Caloca, to dispose of. Despite opposition by the police and the district attorneys, Caloca reopened the investigation on his own. Other cops stopped talking to him; a judge scolded him for making waves; the prosecutors ignored his requests for assistance. He had to get a court order to get evidence he sought from a crime lab. Caloca persisted, eventually compiling a 300-page report listing the "speculations, misjudgments and inconclusive evidence" used in the case against Michael Crowe and his friends. Because Caloca was not part of the original investigating team, and had not jumped to the wrong conclusion, the evidence implicating Tuite was not dissonant for him. It was simply evidence.

Caloca bypassed the local DA's office and took that evidence to the California State Attorney General's office in Sacramento. There, Assistant Attorney General David Druliner agreed to prosecute Tuite. In May 2004, six years after he had been ruled out by the investigating detectives as being nothing more than a bungling prowler, Richard Tuite was convicted of the murder of Stephanie Crowe. Druliner was highly critical of the initial investigation by the Escondido detectives. "They went off completely in the wrong direction to everyone's detriment," he said. "The lack of focus on Mr. Tuite—we could not understand that."[12]

Yet by now the rest of us can. It does seem ludicrous that the detectives did not change their minds, or at least entertain a moment of doubt, when Stephanie's blood turned up on Tuite's sweater. But once the detectives had convinced themselves that Michael and his friends were guilty, they started down the decision pyramid, self-justifying every bump to the bottom.

Let's begin at the top, with the initial process of identifying a suspect. Many detectives do just what the rest of us are inclined to do when we first hear about a crime: impulsively decide we know what happened and then fit the evidence to support our conclusion, ignoring or discounting evidence that contradicts it. Social psychologists have studied this phenomenon extensively by putting people in the role of jurors and seeing what factors influence their decisions. In one experiment, jurors listened to an audiotaped reenactment of an actual murder trial and then said how they would have voted and why. Instead of considering and weighing possible verdicts in light of the evidence, most people immediately constructed a story about what had happened and then, as evidence was presented during the mock trial, they accepted only the evidence that supported their pre-conceived version of what had happened. Those who jumped to a conclusion early on were also the most confident in their decision and were most likely to justify it by voting for an extreme verdict.[13] This is normal; it's also alarming.

In their first interview with a suspect, detectives tend to make a snap decision: Is this guy guilty or innocent? Over time and with ex-perience, the police learn to pursue certain leads and reject others, eventually becoming certain of their accuracy. Their confidence is partly a result of experience and partly a result of training techniques that reward speed and certainty over caution and doubt. Jack Kirsch, a former chief of the FBI's Behavioral Science Unit, told an inter-viewer that visiting police officers would come up to his team mem-bers with difficult cases and ask for advice. "As impromptu as it was, we weren't afraid to shoot from the hip and we usually hit our tar-gets," he said. "We did this thousands of times."[14]

This confidence is often well placed, because usually the police are dealing with confirming cases, the people who are guilty. Yet it also raises the risk of mislabeling the innocent as being guilty and of shutting the door on other possible suspects too soon. Once that door closes, so does the mind. Thus, the detectives didn't even try using their fancy voice analyzer on Tuite, as they had on Crowe. De-tective McDonough explained that "since Tuite had a history of mental illness and drug use, and might still be both mentally ill and using drugs currently, the voice stress testing might not be valid."[15] In other words, let's use our unreliable gizmo only on suspects we already believe are guilty, because whatever they do, it will confirm our belief; we won't use it on suspects we believe are innocent, because it won't work on them anyway.

The initial decision about a suspect's guilt or innocence appears obvious and rational at first: The suspect may fit a description given by the victim or an eyewitness, or the suspect fits a statistically likely category. Follow the trail of love and money, and the force is with you. Thus, in the case of most murders, the most probable killer is the victim's lover, spouse, ex-spouse, relative, or beneficiary. When a young woman is murdered, said Lieutenant Ralph M. Lacer, "the number one person you're going to look for is her significant other. You're not going to be looking for some dude out in a van." Lacer was justifying his certainty that a Chinese-American college student named Bibi Lee had been killed by her boyfriend, Bradley Page, which was why he did not follow up on testimony from eyewitnesses who had seen a man near the crime scene push a young "Oriental" woman into a van and drive away.[16] However, as attorney Steven Drizin observes, "Family members may be a legitimate starting point for an investigation but that's all they are. Instead of trying to prove the murder was intra-family, police need to explore all possible alternatives. All too often they do not."[17]

Once a detective decides that he or she has found the killer, the confirmation bias sees to it that the prime suspect becomes the only suspect. And once that happens, an innocent defendant is on the ropes. In the case of Patrick Dunn of Bakersfield, California, which we mentioned in the introduction, the police chose to believe the uncorroborated account of a career criminal, which supported their theory that Dunn was guilty, rather than corroborated statements by an impartial witness, which would have exonerated him. This decision was unbelievable to the defendant, who asked his lawyer, Stan Simrin, "But don't they want the truth?" "Yes," Simrin said, "and they are convinced they have found it. They believe the truth is you are guilty. And now they will do whatever it takes to convict you."[18]

Doing whatever it takes to convict leads to ignoring or discounting evidence that would require officers to change their minds about a suspect. In extreme cases, it can tempt individual officers and even entire departments to cross the line from legal to illegal actions. The Rampart Division of the Los Angeles Police Department set up an antigang unit in which dozens of officers were eventually charged with making false arrests, giving perjured testimony, and framing innocent people; nearly one hundred convictions that had been attained using these illegal methods were eventually overturned. And in New York, a state investigation in 1989 found that the Suffolk County Police Department had botched a number of major cases by brutalizing suspects, illegally tapping phones, and losing or faking crucial evidence.

Corrupt officers like these are made, not born. They are led down the slope of the pyramid by the culture of the police department and by their own loyalty to its goals. Law professor Andrew McClurg has traced the process that leads many officers to eventually behave in ways they never would have imagined when they started out as idealistic rookies. Being called on to lie in the course of their official duties at first creates dissonance: "I'm here to uphold the law" versus "And here I am, I'm breaking it myself." Over time, observes McClurg, they "learn to smother their dissonance under a protective mattress of self-justification." Once officers believe that lying is defensible and even an essential aspect of the job, he adds, "dissonant feelings of hypocrisy no longer arise. The officer learns to rationalize lying as a moral act or at least as not an immoral act. Thus, his self-concept as a decent, moral person is not substantially compromised."[19]

Let's say you're a cop serving a search warrant on a rock house, where crack cocaine is sold. You chase one guy to the bathroom, hoping to catch him before he flushes the dope, and your case, down the drain. You're too late. There you are, revved up, adrenaline flowing, you've put yourself in harm's way—and this bastard is going to get away? Here you are in a rock house, everyone knows what is going on, and these scumbags are going to walk? They are going to get a slick lawyer, and they will be out in a heartbeat. All that work, all that risk, all that danger, for nothing? Why not take a little cocaine out of your pocket and drop it on the floor of that bathroom, and nail the perp with it. All you'd have to say is, "Some of that crack fell out of his pocket before he could flush it all."[20]

It's easy to understand why you would do this, under the circumstances. It's because you want to do your job. You know it's illegal to plant evidence, but it seems so justifiable. The first time you do it, you tell yourself, "The guy is *guilty!*" This experience will make it easier for you to do the same thing again; in fact, you will be strongly motivated to repeat the behavior, because to do otherwise is to admit, if only to yourself, that it was wrong the first time you did it. Before long, you are breaking the rules in more ambiguous situations. Because police culture generally supports these justifications, it becomes even harder for an individual officer to resist breaking (or bending) the rules. Eventually, many cops will take the next steps, proselytizing other officers, persuading them to behave as they have, and shunning or sabotaging officers who do not go along. They are a reminder of the moral road not taken.

And, in fact, the 1992 Mollen Commission, reporting on patterns of corruption in the New York Police Department, concluded that the practice of police falsification of evidence is "so common in certain precincts that it has spawned its own word: 'testilying.'"[21] In such police cultures, police routinely lie to justify searching anyone they suspect of having drugs or guns, swearing in court that they stopped a suspect because his car ran a red light, because they saw drugs changing hands, or because the suspect dropped the drugs as the officer approached, giving him probable cause to arrest and search the guy. Norm Stamper, a police officer for thirty-four years and former chief of the Seattle Police Department, has written that there isn't a major police force in the country that has escaped the problem of officers who convert drugs to their own use, planting them on suspects or robbing and extorting pushers.[22] The most common justification for lying and planting evidence is that the end justifies the means. One officer told the Mollen Commission investigators that he was "doing God's work." Another said, "If we're going to catch these guys, fuck the Constitution." When one officer was arrested on charges of perjury, he asked in disbelief, "What's wrong with that? They're guilty."[23]

What's "wrong with that" is that there is nothing to prevent the police from planting evidence and committing perjury to convict someone they believe is guilty—someone who is innocent. Corrupt cops are certainly a danger to the public, but so are many of the well-intentioned ones who would never dream of railroading an innocent person into prison. In a sense, honest cops are even more dangerous than corrupt cops, because they are far more numerous and harder to detect. The problem is that once they have decided on a likely suspect, they don't think it's possible that he or she is innocent. And then they behave in ways to confirm that initial judgment, justifying the techniques they use in the belief that only guilty people will be vulnerable to them.

The Interrogators

The most powerful piece of evidence a detective can produce in an investigation is a confession, because it is the one thing most likely to convince a prosecutor, jury, and judge of a person's guilt. Accordingly, police interrogators are trained to get it, even if that means lying to the suspect and using, as one detective proudly admitted to a reporter, "trickery and deceit."[24] Most people are surprised to learn that this is entirely legal. Detectives are proud of their ability to trick a suspect into confessing; it's a mark of how well they have learned their trade. The greater their confidence, the greater the dissonance they will feel if confronted with evidence that they were wrong, and the greater the need to reject that evidence.

Inducing an innocent person to confess is obviously one of the most dangerous mistakes that can occur in police interrogation, but most detectives, prosecutors, and judges don't think it is possible. "The idea that somebody can be induced to falsely confess is ludicrous," says Joshua Marquis. "It's the Twinkie defense of [our time]. It's junk science at its worst."[25] Most people agree, because we can't imagine ourselves admitting to a crime if we were innocent. We'd protest. We'd stand firm. We'd call for our lawyer . . . wouldn't we? Yet studies of unequivocally exonerated prisoners have found that between 15 to 25 percent of them had confessed to a crime they had not committed. Social scientists and criminologists have analyzed these cases and conducted experimental research to demonstrate how this can happen.

The bible of interrogation methods is *Criminal Interrogation and Confessions,* written by Fred E. Inbau, John E. Reid, Joseph P. Buckley, and Brian C. Jayne. John E. Reid and Associates offers training programs, seminars, and videotapes on the 9-Step Reid Technique, and on their Web site they claim that they have trained more than 300,000 law-enforcement workers in the most effective ways of eliciting confessions. The manual starts right off reassuring readers that "none of the steps is apt to make an innocent person confess, and that all the steps are legally as well as morally justifiable"[26]:

> It is our clear position that merely introducing fictitious evidence during an interrogation would not cause an innocent person to confess. It is absurd to believe that a suspect who knows he did not commit a crime would place greater weight and credibility on alleged evidence than his own knowledge of his innocence. Under this circumstance, the *natural human reaction* would be one of anger and mistrust toward the investigator. The net effect would be the suspect's further resolution to maintain his innocence.[27]

Wrong. The "natural human reaction" is usually not anger and mistrust but confusion and hopelessness—dissonance—because most innocent suspects trust the investigator not to lie to them. The interrogator, however, is biased from the start. Whereas an interview is a conversation designed to get general information from a person, an interrogation is designed to get a suspect to admit guilt. (The suspect is often unaware of the difference.) The manual states this explicitly: "An interrogation is conducted only when the investigator is reasonably certain of the suspect's guilt." The danger of that attitude is that once the investigator is "reasonably certain," the suspect cannot dislodge that certainty. On the contrary, anything the suspect does will be interpreted as evidence of lying, denial, and evading the truth, including repeated claims of innocence. Interrogators are explicitly instructed to think this way. They are taught to adopt the attitude "Don't lie; we know you are guilty," and to reject the suspect's denials. We've seen this self-justifying loop before, in the way some therapists and social workers interview children they believe have been molested. Once an interrogation like this has begun, there is no such thing as disconfirming evidence.[28]

Promulgators of the Reid Technique have an intuitive understanding of how dissonance works (at least in other people). They realize that if a suspect is given the chance to protest his innocence, he will have made a public commitment and it will be harder for him to back down and later admit guilt. "The more the suspect denies his involvement," writes Louis Senese, vice president of Reid and Associates, "the more difficult it becomes for him to admit that he committed the crime"—precisely, because of dissonance. Therefore, Senese advises interrogators to be prepared for the suspect's denials and head them off at the pass. Interrogators, he says, should watch for nonverbal signs that the suspect is about to deny culpability ("holding his hand up or shaking his head no or making eye contact"), and if the suspect says, straight out, "Could I say something?," interrogators should respond with a command, using the suspect's first name ("Jim, hold on for just a minute") and then return to their questioning.[29]

The interrogator's presumption of guilt creates a self-fulfilling prophecy. It makes the interrogator more aggressive, which in turn makes innocent suspects behave more suspiciously. In one experiment, social psychologist Saul Kassin and his colleagues paired individuals who were either guilty or innocent of theft with interrogators who were told they were guilty or innocent. There were therefore four possible combinations of suspect and interrogator: You're innocent and he thinks you're innocent; you're innocent and he thinks you're guilty; you're guilty and he thinks you're innocent; or you're guilty and he thinks you're guilty. The deadliest combination, the one that produced the greatest degree of pressure and coercion by the interviewer, was the one that paired an interrogator convinced of a suspect's guilt with a suspect who was actually innocent. In such circumstances, the more the suspect denied guilt, the more certain the interrogator became that the suspect was lying, and he upped the pressure accordingly.

Kassin lectures widely to detectives and police officers to show them how their techniques of interrogation can backfire. They always nod knowingly, he says, and agree with him that false confessions are to be avoided; but then they immediately add that they themselves have never coerced anyone into a false confession. "How do you know?" Kassin asked one cop. "Because I never interrogate innocent people," he said. Kassin found that this certainty of infallibility starts at the top. "I was at an International Police Interviewing conference in Quebec, on a debate panel with Joe Buckley, president of the Reid School," he told us. "After his presentation, someone from the audience asked whether he was concerned that innocent people might confess in response to his techniques. Son of a gun if he didn't say it, word for word; I was so surprised at his overt display of such arrogance that I wrote down the quote and the date on which he said it: 'No, because we don't interrogate innocent people.'"[30]

In the next phase of training, detectives learn to become confident of their ability to read the suspect's nonverbal cues: eye contact, body language, posture, hand gestures, and vehemence of denials. If the person won't look you in the eye, the manual explains, that's a sign of lying. If the person slouches (or sits rigidly), those are signs of lying. If the person denies guilt, that's a sign of lying. Yet the Reid Technique advises interrogators to "deny suspect eye contact." Deny a suspect the direct eye contact that they themselves regard as evidence of innocence?

The Reid Technique is thus a closed loop: How do I know a suspect is guilty? Because he's nervous and sweating (or too controlled) and because he won't look me in the eye (and I wouldn't let him if he wanted to). So my partners and I interrogate him for twelve hours using the Reid Technique, and he confesses. Therefore, because innocent people never confess, his confession confirms my belief that his being nervous and sweating (or too controlled), or looking me in the eye (or not) is a sign of guilt. By the logic of this system, the only error the detective can make is failing to get a confession.

The manual is written in an authoritative tone as if it were the voice of God revealing indisputable truths, but in fact it fails to teach its readers a core principle of scientific thinking: the importance of examining and ruling out other possible explanations for a person's behavior before deciding which one is the most likely. Saul Kassin, for example, was involved in a military case in which investigators had relentlessly interrogated a defendant against whom there was no hard evidence. (Kassin believed the man to be innocent, and indeed he was acquitted.) When one of the investigators was asked why he pursued the defendant so aggressively, he said: "We gathered that he was not telling us the whole truth. Some examples of body language is that he tried to remain calm, but you could tell that he was nervous and every time we tried to ask him a question his eyes would roam and he would not make direct contact, and at times he would act pretty sporadic and he started to cry at one time."

"What he described," says Kassin, "is a person under stress." Students of the Reid Technique generally do not learn that being nervous, fidgeting, avoiding eye contact, and slouching uncomfortably might be signs of something other than guilt. They might be signs of nervousness, adolescence, cultural norms, deference to authority—or anxiety about being falsely accused.

Promoters of the manual claim that their method trains investigators to determine whether someone is telling the truth or lying with an 80 to 85 percent level of accuracy. There is simply no scientific support for this claim. As with the psychotherapists we discussed in chapter 4, training does not increase accuracy; it increases people's confidence in their accuracy. In one of numerous studies that have documented the false-confidence phenomenon, Kassin and his colleague Christina Fong trained a group of students in the Reid Technique. They watched the Reid training videos, read the manual, and were tested on what they had learned to make sure they got it. Then they were asked to watch videotapes of people being interviewed by an experienced police officer. The taped suspects were either guilty of a crime but denying it, or were denying it because they were innocent. The training did not improve the students' accuracy by an iota. They did no better than chance, but it did make them feel more confident of their abilities. Still, they were only college students, not professionals. So Kassin and Fong asked forty-four professional detectives in Florida and Ontario, Canada, to watch the tapes. These professionals averaged nearly fourteen years of experience each, and two-thirds had had special training, many in the Reid Technique. Like the students, they did no better than chance, yet they were convinced that their accuracy rate was close to 100 percent. Their experience and training did not improve their performance. Their experience and training simply increased their belief that it did.[31]

Nonetheless, why doesn't an innocent suspect just keep denying guilt? Why doesn't the target get angry at the interrogator, as the manual says any innocent person would do? Let's say you are an innocent person who is called in for questioning, perhaps to "help the police in their investigation." You have no idea that you are a prime suspect. You trust the police and want to be helpful. Yet here is a detective telling you that your fingerprints are on the murder weapon. That you failed a lie detection test. That your blood was found on the victim, or the victim's blood was on your clothes. These claims will create considerable cognitive dissonance:

Cognition 1: I was not there. I didn't commit the crime. I have no memory of it.

Cognition 2: Reliable and trustworthy people in authority tell me that my fingerprints are on the murder weapon, the victim's blood was on my shirt, and an eyewitness saw me in a place where I am sure I've never been.

How will you resolve this dissonance? If you are strong enough, wealthy enough, or have had enough experience with the police to know that you are being set up, you will say the four magic words: "I want a lawyer." But many people believe they don't need a lawyer if they are innocent.[32] Believing as they do that the police are not allowed to lie to them, they are astonished to hear that there is evidence against them that they cannot explain. And what damning evidence at that—their fingerprints! The manual claims that the "self-preservation instincts of an innocent person during an interrogation" will override anything an interrogator does, but for vulnerable people, the need to make sense of what is happening to them even trumps the need for self-preservation.

Bradley Page: Is it possible that I could have done this terrible thing and blanked it out?

Lieutenant Lacer: Oh, yes. It happens all the time.

And now the police offer you an explanation that makes sense, a way to resolve your dissonance: You don't remember because you blanked it out; you were drunk and lost consciousness; you repressed the memory; you didn't know that you have multiple personality disorder, and one of your other personalities did it. This is what the detectives did in their interrogations of Michael Crowe. They told him that there might have been "two Michaels," a good one and a bad one, and the bad Michael committed the crime without the good Michael even being aware of it.

Sure, you might say, Michael was fourteen; no wonder the police could scare him into confessing. It is true that juveniles and the mentally ill are particularly vulnerable to these tactics, but so are healthy adults. In a close examination of 125 cases in which prisoners were later exonerated despite having given false confessions, Steven Drizin and Richard Leo found that forty were minors, twenty-eight were mentally retarded, and fifty-seven were competent adults. Of the cases in which length of interrogation could be determined, more than 80 percent of the false confessors had been grilled for more than six hours straight, half for more than twelve hours, and some almost nonstop for two days.[33]

That was what happened to the teenagers arrested on the night the Central Park Jogger was attacked. When social scientists and legal scholars were able to examine the videotapes of four of the five teenagers (the fifth was not taped), and when District Attorney Robert Morgenthau's office reexamined this evidence starting from the assumption that the boys might be innocent rather than guilty, the dramatic persuasiveness of their confessions melted in the light. Their statements turned out to be full of contradictions, factual errors, guesses, and information planted by the interrogator's biased questions.[34] And contrary to the public impression that all of them confessed, in fact none of the defendants ever admitted that he personally raped the jogger. One said he "grabbed at" her. Another stated that he "felt her tits." One said he "held and fondled her leg." The district attorney's motion to vacate their convictions observed that "the accounts given by the five defendants differed from one another on the specific details of virtually every major aspect of the crime—who initiated the attack, who knocked the victim down, who undressed her, who struck her, who held her, who raped her, what weapons were used in the course of the assault, and when in the sequence of events the attack took place."[35]

After long hours of interrogation, wanting nothing more than to be allowed to go home, the exhausted suspect accepts the explanation the interrogators offer as the only one possible, the only one that makes sense. And confesses. Usually, the moment the pressure is over and the target gets a night's sleep, he or she immediately retracts the confession. It will be too late.

The Prosecutors

In that splendid film *The Bridge on the River Kwai,* Alec Guinness and his soldiers, prisoners of the Japanese in World War II, build a railway bridge that will aid the enemy's war effort. Guinness agrees to this demand by his captors as a way of building unity and restoring morale among his men, but once he builds it, it becomes *his*—a source of pride and satisfaction. When, at the end of the film, Guinness finds the wires revealing that the bridge has been mined and realizes that Allied commandoes are planning to blow it up, his first reaction is, in effect: "You can't! It's *my* bridge. How dare you destroy it!" To the horror of the watching commandoes, he tries to cut the wires to protect the bridge. Only at the very last moment does Guinness cry, "What have I done?," realizing that he was about to sabotage his own side's goal of victory to preserve his magnificent creation.

In the same way, many prosecutors end up being prepared to sabotage their own side's goal of justice to preserve their convictions, in both meanings of the word. By the time prosecutors go to trial, they often find themselves in the real-world equivalent of a justification-of-effort experiment. They have selected this case out of many because they are convinced the suspect is guilty and that they have the evidence to convict. They often have invested many months on a case. They have worked intensely with police, witnesses, and the victim's shattered, often vengeful family. In the case of crimes that have roused public emotions, they are under enormous pressure to get a conviction quickly. Any doubts they might have are drowned in the satisfaction of feeling that they are representing the forces of good against a vile criminal. And so, with a clear conscience, prosecutors end up saying to a jury: "This defendant is subhuman, a monster. Do the right thing. Convict." Occasionally they have so thoroughly convinced themselves that they have a monster that they, like the police, go too far: coaching witnesses, offering deals to jailhouse informants, or failing to give the defense all the information they are legally obliged to hand over.

How, then, will most prosecutors react when, years later, the convicted rapist or murderer, still maintaining innocence (as, let's keep in mind, plenty of guilty felons do), demands a DNA test? Or claims that his or her confession was coerced? Or produces evidence suggesting that the eyewitness testimony that led to conviction was wrong? What if the defendant might not be a monster, after all that hard work to convince themselves and everyone else that he is? The response of prosecutors in Florida is typical. After more than 130 prisoners had been freed by DNA testing in the space of fifteen years, prosecutors decided they would respond by mounting a vigorous challenge to similar new cases. Wilton Dedge had to sue the state to have the evidence in his case retested, over the fierce objections of prosecutors who said that the state's interest in finality and the victim's feelings should supersede concerns about Dedge's possible innocence.[36] Dedge was finally exonerated and released.

That finality and the victim's feelings should preclude justice seems an appalling argument by those we entrust to provide justice, but that's the power of self-justification. (Besides, wouldn't the victims feel better if the real murderer of their loved one had been caught and punished?) Across the country, as DNA testing has freed hundreds of prisoners, news accounts often include a quote or two from the prosecutors who originally tried them. For example, in Philadelphia, District Attorney Bruce L. Castor Jr. was asked by reporters what scientific basis he had for rejecting a DNA test that exonerated a man who had been in prison for 20 years. He replied, "I have no scientific basis. I know because I trust my detective and my tape-recorded confession."[37]

How do we know that this casual dismissal of DNA testing, which is persuasive to just about everyone else on the planet, is a sign of self-justification and not simply an honest assessment of the evidence? It's like the horse-race study we described in chapter 1: Once we have placed our bets, we don't want to entertain any information that casts doubt on that decision. That is why prosecutors will interpret the same evidence in two ways, depending on when it is discovered. Early in an investigation, the police use DNA to confirm a suspect's guilt or rule the person out. But when DNA tests are conducted after a defendant has been indicted and convicted, the prosecutors typically dismiss it as being irrelevant, not important enough to reopen the case. Texas prosecutor Michael McDougal said that the fact that the DNA found in a young rape-murder victim did not match that of Roy Criner, the man convicted of the crime, did not mean Criner was innocent. "It means that the sperm found in her was not his," he said. "It doesn't mean he didn't rape her, doesn't mean he didn't kill her."[38]

Technically, of course, McDougal is right; Criner could have raped the woman in Texas and ejaculated somewhere else—Arkansas, perhaps. But DNA evidence should be used the same way whenever it turns up; it is the need for self-justification that prevents most prosecutors from being able to do that. Defense attorney Peter J. Neufeld says that in his experience, reinterpreting the evidence to justify the original verdict is extremely common among prosecutors and judges. During the trial, the prosecutor's theory is that one person alone, the defendant, seized and raped the victim. If, after the defendant is convicted, DNA testing excludes him as the perpetrator, prosecutors miraculously come up with other theories. Our own favorite is what Neufeld calls the "unindicted co-ejaculator" theory: The convicted defendant held the woman down while a mysterious second man actually committed the rape. Or the victim was lying there helpless, and a male predator "comes along and sees an opportunity and takes it," as one prosecutor claimed.[39] Or the defendant wore a condom, and the victim had consensual sex with someone else shortly before she was raped. (When Roy Criner's case was sent to the Texas Court of Criminal Appeals, Chief Judge Sharon Keller ruled that DNA "showing the sperm was not that of a man convicted of rape was not determinative because he might have worn a condom.") If the victim protests that she has not had intercourse in the previous three days, prosecutors advance the theory—again, after the trial—that she is lying: She doesn't want to admit that she had illicit sex because her husband or boyfriend will be angry.

Self-justifications like these create a double tragedy: They keep innocent people in prison and allow the guilty to remain free. The same DNA that exonerates an innocent person can be used to identify the guilty one, but this does not happen nearly as often as it should.[40] Of all the cases of wrongful conviction the Innocence Project has succeeded in overturning so far, in the great majority the real perpetrator of the crime has never been found. The police and prosecutors just close the books on the case completely, as if to obliterate its silent accusation of the mistake they made.

Jumping to Convictions

> If the system can't function fairly, if the system can't correct its own mistakes and admit that it makes mistakes and give people an opportunity to [correct] them, then the system is broken.
>
> —appellate lawyer Michael Charlton, who represented Roy Criner

All citizens have a right to expect that our criminal-justice system will have procedures in place not only to convict the guilty, but also to protect the innocent, and when mistakes are made, to remedy them with alacrity. Legal scholars and social scientists have suggested various constitutional remedies and important piecemeal improvements to reduce the risk of false confessions, unreliable eyewitness testimony, police "testilying," and so forth.[41] But from our vantage point, the greatest impediment to admitting and correcting mistakes in the criminal-justice system is that most of its members reduce dissonance by denying that there is a problem. "Our system has to create this aura of close to perfection, of certainty that we don't convict innocent people," says former prosecutor Bennett Gershman.[42] The benefit of this certainty to police officers, detectives, and prosecutors is that they do not have sleepless nights, worrying that they might have put an innocent person in prison. But a few sleepless nights are called for. Doubt is not the enemy of justice; overconfidence is.

Currently, the professional training of most police officers, detectives, judges, and attorneys includes almost no information about their own cognitive biases; how to correct for them, as much as possible; and how to manage the dissonance they will feel when their beliefs meet disconfirming evidence. On the contrary, much of what they learn about psychology comes from self-proclaimed experts with no training in psychological science and who, as we saw, do not teach them to be more accurate in their judgments, merely more confident that they are accurate: "An innocent person would never confess." "I saw it with my own eyes; therefore I'm right." "I can tell when someone is lying; I've been doing this for years." Yet that kind of certainty is the hallmark of pseudoscience. True scientists speak in the careful language of probability—"Innocent people most certainly can be induced to confess, under particular conditions; let me explain why I think this individual's confession is likely to have been coerced"—which is why scientists' testimony is often exasperating. Many judges, jurors, and police officers prefer certainties to science. Law professor D. Michael Risinger and attorney Jeffrey L. Loop have lamented "the general failure of the law to reflect virtually any of the insights of modern research on the characteristics of human perception, cognition, memory, inference or decision under uncertainty, either in the structure of the rules of evidence themselves, or the ways in which judges are trained or instructed to administer them."[43]

Yet training that promotes the certainties of pseudoscience, rather than a humbling appreciation of our cognitive biases and blind spots, increases the chances of wrongful convictions in two ways. First, it encourages law-enforcement officials to jump to conclusions too quickly. A police officer decides that a suspect is the guilty party, and then closes the door to other possibilities. A district attorney decides impulsively to prosecute a case, especially a sensational one, without having all the evidence; she announces her decision to the media; and then finds it difficult to back down when subsequent evidence proves shaky. Second, once a case is prosecuted and a conviction won, officials will be motivated to reject any subsequent evidence of the defendant's innocence.

The antidote to these all-too-human mistakes is to ensure that in police academies and law schools, students learn about their own vulnerability to self-justification. They must learn to look for the statistically likely suspect (a jealous boyfriend) without closing their minds to the statistically less likely suspect, if that is where some evidence leads. They need to learn that even if they are confident that they can tell if a suspect is lying, they could be wrong. They need to learn how and why innocent people can be induced to confess to a crime they did not commit, and how to distinguish confessions that are likely to be true from those that have been coerced.[44] They need to learn that the popular method of profiling, that beloved staple of the FBI and TV shows, carries significant risks of error because of the confirmation bias: When investigators start looking for elements of a crime that match a suspect's profile, they also start overlooking elements that do not match. In short, investigators need to learn to change trees once they realize they are barking up the wrong one.

Law professor Andrew McClurg would go further in the training of police. He has long advocated the application of cognitive-dissonance principles to keep highly motivated rookies from taking that first step down the pyramid in a dishonest direction, by calling on their own self-concept as good guys fighting crime and violence. He proposes a program of integrity training in dealing with ethical dilemmas, in which cadets would be instilled with the values of telling the truth and doing the right thing as a central part of their emerging professional identity. (Currently, in most jurisdictions, police trainees get one evening or a couple of hours on dealing with ethical problems.) Because such values are quickly trumped on the job by competing moral codes—"You don't rat on a fellow officer"; "In the real world, the only sure way to get a conviction is to fudge the truth"—McClurg proposes that rookies be partnered with experienced, ethical mentors who, in the manner of Alcoholics Anonymous sponsors, would help rookies maintain their honesty commitment. "The only hope of substantially reducing police lying is a preventative approach aimed at keeping good cops from turning bad," he argues. Cognitive dissonance theory offers "a potent, inexpensive, and inexhaustible tool for accomplishing this goal: the officer's own self-concept."[45]

Because no one, no matter how well trained or well intentioned, is completely immune to the confirmation bias and to his or her own cognitive blind spots, the leading social scientists who have studied wrongful conviction are unanimous in recommending safeguards, such as the videotaping of all interviews. Currently, only a handful of states require the police to electronically record their interrogations.[46] Police and prosecutors have long resisted this requirement, fearing, we suspect, the embarrassing, dissonance-generating revelations it might create. Ralph Lacer, one of the interrogators of Bradley Page, justified this position on the grounds that "a tape is inhibiting" and makes it "hard to get at the truth."[47] Suppose, he complained, the interview goes on for ten hours. The defense attorney will make the jury listen to all ten hours, instead of just the fifteen-minute confession, and the jury will be confused and overwhelmed. Yet in the Page case, the prosecution's argument rested heavily on a segment of the audiotaped interview that was missing. Lacer admitted that he had turned off the cassette player just before he said the words that convinced Page to confess. According to Page, during that missing segment, Lacer had asked him to imagine how he *might* have killed his girlfriend. (This is another maneuver recommended by the creators of the Reid Technique.) Page thought he was being asked to construct an imaginary scenario to help the police; he was stunned when Lacer used it as a legitimate confession. The jury did not hear the full context—the question that elicited the alleged confession.

In fact, in jurisdictions that do videotape interrogations, law enforcement has come to favor it. The Center on Wrongful Convictions surveyed 238 law enforcement agencies that currently record all interrogations of felony suspects, and found that virtually every officer with whom they spoke was enthusiastic about the practice. Videotaping, with a camera angle that includes both interviewer and interviewee, eliminates the problem of suspects changing their stories, and it satisfies jurors that the confession was obtained honestly.

And of course it permits independent experts and jurors to assess the techniques that were used and determine whether any of them were deceptive or coercive.[48]

Reforms like these are slowly being implemented in Canada and Great Britain, which are instituting procedures to minimize the chances of wrongful convictions. In the United States, the many exonerations due to DNA are also slowly bringing legal changes: improved oversight of crime labs, tougher standards for eyewitness identification, giving inmates (varying) degrees of access to DNA evidence, and, in a few states, the creation of commissions to expedite cases of wrongful conviction and find remedies. These reforms are essential and long overdue. But according to legal scholars and social scientists Deborah Davis and Richard Leo, American law enforcement remains steeped in its traditions, including adherence to the Reid Technique and similar procedures, maintaining "near absolute denial" that these techniques can and do produce false confessions and wrongful convictions.[49] The American criminal-justice system's unwillingness to admit fallibility compounds the injustices it creates. Many states do absolutely nothing for people who have been exonerated. They provide no compensation for the many years of life and earnings lost. They do not even offer an official apology. Cruelly, they often do not expunge the exonerated person's record, making it difficult for the person to get an apartment or a job.

From the viewpoint of dissonance theory, we can see why the victims of wrongful convictions are treated so harshly. That harshness is in direct proportion to the system's inflexibility. If you know that errors are inevitable, you will not be surprised when they happen and you will have contingencies in place to remedy them. But if you refuse to admit to yourself or the world that mistakes do happen, then every wrongfully imprisoned person is stark, humiliating evidence of how wrong you are. Apologize to them? Give them money? Don't be absurd. They got off on a technicality. Oh, the technicality was DNA? Well, they were guilty of something else.

And yet, every so often, a man or woman of integrity rises above the common impulse to sacrifice truth in the service of self-justification: A police officer blows the whistle on corruption; a detective reopens a case that was apparently solved; a district attorney owns up to a miscarriage of justice. Thomas Vanes, now an attorney in Merrillville, Indiana, was a prosecutor for thirteen years. "I was not bashful then in seeking the death penalty," he wrote.[50] "When criminals are guilty, they deserve to be punished." But Vanes learned that mistakes are made, and he had made them, too.

> I learned that a man named Larry Mayes, whom I had prosecuted and convicted, had served more than 20 years for a rape he did not commit. How do we know? DNA testing. . . . Two decades later, when he requested a DNA retest on that rape kit, I assisted in tracking down the old evidence, convinced that the current tests would put to rest his long-standing claim of innocence. But he was right, and I was wrong.
>
> Hard facts trumped opinion and belief, as they should. It was a sobering lesson, and none of the easy-to-reach rationalizations (just doing my job, it was the jurors who convicted him, the appellate courts had upheld the conviction) completely lessen the sense of responsibility—moral, if not legal—that comes with the conviction of an innocent man.

CHAPTER 6

o   o   o

Love's Assassin:
Self-justification in Marriage

Love ... is the extremely difficult realization that something other
than oneself is real.

—novelist Iris Murdoch

WHEN WILLIAM BUTLER YEATS got married in 1917, his father wrote him a warm letter of congratulations. "I think it will help
you in your poetic development," he said. "No one really knows
human nature, men as well as women," who has not lived in marriage—"the enforced study of a fellow creature."[1] Married partners
are forced to learn more about each other than they ever expected
(or perhaps wanted) to know. With no one else, not even with our
children or parents, do we learn so much about another human
being's adorable and irritating habits, ways of handling frustrations
and crises, and private, passionate desires. Yet, as John Butler Yeats
knew, marriage also forces couples to face themselves, to learn more
about themselves and how they behave with an intimate partner

than they ever expected (or perhaps wanted) to know. No other relationship so profoundly tests the extent of our own willingness to be flexible and forgiving, to learn and change—if we can resist the allure of self-justification.

Benjamin Franklin, who advised, "Keep your eyes wide open before marriage, and half shut afterward," understood the power of dissonance in relationships. Couples first justify their decision to be together, and then to stay together. When you buy a house, you will start reducing dissonance immediately. You will tell your friends the wonderful things you love about it—the view of the trees, the space, the original old windows—and minimize the things that are wrong with it—the view of the parking lot, the cramped guest room, the drafty old windows. In this case, self-justification will keep you feeling happy about your beautiful new home. If before you fell in love with it, a geologist had told you that the cliff above you was unstable and might give way at any moment, you would welcome the information and walk away, sad but not heartbroken. But once you have fallen in love with your house, spent more than you could afford to buy it, and moved in with your unwilling cat, you have too much invested, emotionally and financially, to walk away easily. If after you are in the house, someone tells you that the cliff above you is precarious, that same impulse to justify your decision may keep you there far too long. The people who live in houses along the beach in La Conchita, California, in the shadow of cliffs that have a habit of crashing down on them during heavy winter rains, live with constant dissonance, which they resolve by saying: "It won't happen again." This allows them to remain until it does happen again.

A relationship with a house is simpler than a relationship with another human being. For one thing, it's only one-way. The house can't blame you for being a bad owner or for not keeping it clean, though it also can't give you a nice back rub after a hard day. Marriage, though, is the greatest two-way decision of most people's lives, and couples are enormously invested in making it work. A moderate amount of postwedding, eyes-half-shut dissonance reduction, in which partners emphasize the positive and overlook the negative, allows things to hum along in harmony. But the identical mechanism allows some people to remain in marriages that are the psychological equivalent of La Conchita, on the brink of constant disaster. What do deliriously happy newlyweds have in common with unhappy couples who have remained together, in bitterness or weariness, for many years? An unwillingness to take heed of dissonant information. Many newlyweds, seeking confirming signs that they have married the perfect person, overlook or dismiss any discrepant evidence that might be a warning sign of trouble or conflict ahead: ["He goes into a sulk if I even chat with another man; how cute, it means he loves me." "She's so casual and relaxed about household matters; how charming, it means she'll make me less compulsive."] Unhappy spouses who have long tolerated one another's cruelty, jealousy, or humiliation are also busy reducing dissonance. To avoid facing the devastating possibility that they invested so many years, so much energy, so many arguments, in a failed effort to achieve even peaceful coexistence, they say something like "All marriages are like this. Nothing can be done about it, anyway. There are enough good things about it. Better to stay in a difficult marriage than to be alone."

Self-justification doesn't care whether it reaps benefits or wreaks havoc. It keeps many marriages together (for better or worse) and it tears others asunder (for better or worse). Couples start off blissfully optimistic, and over the years some will move in the direction of greater closeness and affection, others in the direction of greater distance and hostility. Some couples find in marriage a source of solace and joy, a place to replenish the soul, a relationship that allows them to flourish as individuals and as a couple. For others, marriage becomes a source of bickering and discord, a place of stagnation, a relationship that squashes their individuality and dissipates their bond. Our goal in this chapter is not to imply that all relationships can and should be saved, but rather to show how self-justification contributes to these two different outcomes.

Of course, some couples separate because of a cataclysmic revelation, an act of betrayal, or violence that one partner can no longer tolerate or ignore. But the vast majority of couples who drift apart do so slowly, over time, in a snowballing pattern of blame and self-justification. Each partner focuses on what the other one is doing wrong, while justifying his or her own preferences, attitudes, and ways of doing things. Each side's intransigence, in turn, makes the other side even more determined not to budge. Before the couple realizes it, they have taken up polarized positions, each feeling right and righteous. Self-justification will then cause their hearts to harden against the entreaties of empathy.

∘   ∘   ∘

To show how this process works, let's consider the marriage of Debra and Frank, taken from Andrew Christensen and Neil Jacobson's insightful book *Reconcilable Differences*.[2] Most people enjoy her-version/his-version accounts of a marriage (except when it's their own), shrugging their shoulders and concluding that there are two sides to every story. We think there's more to it than that. Let's start with Debra's version of their marital problems:

> [Frank] just plods through life, always taking care of business, pre-occupied with getting his work done but never showing much excitement or pain. He says his style shows how emotionally stable he is. I say it just shows he's passive and bored. In many ways I'm just the opposite: I have a lot of ups and downs. But most of the time I'm energetic, optimistic, spontaneous. Of course I get upset, angry, and frustrated sometimes. He says this range of feeling shows I'm emotionally immature, that "I have a lot of growing up to do." I think it just shows I'm human.

I remember one incident that kind of sums up the way I see Frank. We went out to dinner with a charming couple who had just moved to town. As the evening wore on, I became more and more aware of how wonderful their life was. They seemed genuinely in love with one another, even though they had been married longer than we have. No matter how much the man talked to us, he always kept in contact with his wife: touching her, or making eye contact with her, or including her in the conversation. And he used "we" a lot to refer to them. Watching them made me realize how little Frank and I touch, how rarely we look at each other, and how separately we participate in conversation. Anyway, I admit it, I was envious of this other couple. They seemed to have it all: loving family, beautiful home, leisure, luxury. What a contrast to Frank and me: struggling along, both working full-time jobs, trying to save money. I wouldn't mind that so much, if only we worked at it *together*. But we're so distant.

When we got home, I started expressing those feelings. I wanted to reevaluate our life—as a way of getting closer. Maybe we couldn't be as wealthy as these people, but there was no reason we couldn't have the closeness and warmth they had. As usual, Frank didn't want to talk about it. When he said he was tired and wanted to go to bed, I got angry. It was Friday night, and neither of us had to get up early the next day; the only thing keeping us from being together was his stubbornness. It made me mad. I was fed up with giving in to his need to sleep whenever I brought up an issue to discuss. I thought, Why can't he stay awake just for me sometimes?

I wouldn't let him sleep. When he turned off the lights, I turned them back on. When he rolled over to go to sleep, I kept talking. When he put a pillow over his head, I talked louder. He told me I was a baby. I told him he was insensitive. It escalated from there and got ugly. No violence but lots of words. He finally went to the guest bedroom, locked the door, and went to sleep. The next morning we were both worn out and distant. He criticized me for being so irrational. Which was probably true. I do get irrational when I get desperate. But I think he uses that accusation as a way of justifying himself. It's sort of like "If you're irrational, then I can dismiss all your complaints and I am blameless."

This is Frank's version:

Debra never seems to be satisfied. I'm never doing enough, never giving enough, never loving enough, never sharing enough. You name it, I don't do enough of it. Sometimes she gets me believing I really am a bad husband. I start feeling as though I've let her down, disappointed her, not met my obligations as a loving, supportive husband. But then I give myself a dose of reality. What have I done that's wrong? I'm an okay human being. People usually like me, respect me. I hold down a responsible job. I don't cheat on her or lie to her. I'm not a drunk or a gambler. I'm moderately attractive, and I'm a sensitive lover. I even make her laugh a lot. Yet I don't get an ounce of appreciation from her—just complaints that I'm not doing enough.

I'm not thrown by events the way Debra is. Her feelings are like a roller coaster: sometimes up, sometimes down. I can't live that way. A nice steady cruising speed is more my style. But I don't put Debra down for being the way she is. I'm basically a tolerant person. People, including spouses, come in all shapes and sizes. They aren't tailored to fit your particular needs. So I don't take offense at little annoyances; I don't feel compelled to talk about every difference or dislike; I don't feel every potential area of disagreement has to be explored in detail. I just let things ride. When I show that kind of tolerance, I expect my partner to do the same for me. When she doesn't, I get furious. When Debra picks at me about every detail that doesn't fit with her idea of what's right, I do react strongly. My cool disappears, and I explode.

I remember driving home with Debra after a night out with an attractive, impressive couple we had just met. On the way home I was wondering what kind of impression I'd made on them. I was tired that evening and not at my best. Sometimes I can be clever and funny in a small group, but not that night. Maybe I was trying too hard. Sometimes I have high standards for myself and get down on myself when I can't come up to them.

Debra interrupted my ruminations with a seemingly innocent question: "Did you notice how much in tune those two were with each other?" Now I know what's behind that kind of question—or at least where that kind of question will lead. It always leads right back to us, specifically to me. Eventually the point becomes "We aren't in tune with each other," which is code for "You're not in tune with me." I dread these conversations that chew over what's wrong with us as a couple, because the real question, which goes unstated in the civil conversations, but gets stated bluntly in the uncivil ones, is "What's wrong with Frank?" So I sidestepped the issue on this occasion by answering that they were a nice couple.

But Debra pushed it. She insisted on evaluating them in comparison to us. They had money and intimacy. We had neither. Maybe we couldn't be wealthy, but we could at least be intimate. Why couldn't we be intimate? Meaning: Why couldn't *I* be intimate? When we got home, I tried to defuse the tension by saying I was tired and suggesting that we go to bed. I *was* tired, and the last thing I wanted was one of these conversations. But Debra was relentless. She argued that there was no reason we couldn't stay up and discuss this. I proceeded with my bedtime routine, giving her the most minimal of responses. If she won't respect my feelings, why should I respect hers? She talked at me while I put on my pajamas and brushed my teeth; she wouldn't even let me alone in the bathroom. When I finally got into bed and turned off the light, she turned it back on. I rolled over to go to sleep, but she kept talking. You'd think she'd have gotten the message when I put the pillow over my head—but no, she pulled it off. At that point I lost it. I told her she was a baby, a crazy person—I don't remember everything I said. Finally, in desperation, I went to the guest bedroom and locked the door. I was too upset to go to sleep right away, and I didn't sleep at all. In the morning, I was still angry at her. I told her she was irrational. For once, she didn't have much to say.

Have you taken sides yet? Do you think this couple would be fine if she only stopped trying to get him to talk or if he would only stop hiding under the pillow, literally and figuratively? And what is their major problem—that they are temperamentally incompatible, that they don't understand each other, that they are angry?

Every couple has differences. Even identical twins have differences. For Frank and Debra, like most couples, the differences are precisely why they fell in love: He thought she was terrific because she was sociable and outgoing, a perfect antidote to his reserve; she was drawn to his calmness and unflappability in a storm. All couples have conflicts, too: small irritants that are amusing to everyone but the participants—she wants dirty dishes washed immediately, and he lets them pile up for only one cleanup a day (or week)—or larger disagreements about money, sex, in-laws, or any of countless other issues. Differences need not cause rifts. But once there is a rift, the couple explains it as being an inevitable result of their differences.

Moreover, Frank and Debra actually understand their situation very well. They agree on everything that happened the night of their great blowup: on what set it off, on how they both behaved, on what each wanted from the other. They both agree that comparing themselves to the new couple made them feel unhappy and self-critical. They agree that she is more roller-coastery and he more placid, a gender complaint as common as ragweed in summer. They are clear about what they want from the relationship and what they feel they aren't getting. They even are very good, perhaps better than most, at understanding the other person's point of view.

Nor is this marriage deteriorating because Frank and Debra get angry at one another. Successful couples have conflicts and get angry, just as unhappy couples do. But happy couples know how to manage their conflicts. If a problem is annoying them, they either talk and fix the problem, let it go, or learn to live with it.[3] Unhappy couples are pulled further apart by angry confrontations. When Frank and Debra get into a quarrel, they retreat to their familiar positions, brood, and stop listening to each other. If they do listen, they don't hear. Their attitude is: "Yeah, yeah, I know how you feel about this, but I'm not going to change because I'm right."

To show what we think Frank and Debra's underlying problem is, let's rewrite the story of their trip home. Suppose that Frank had anticipated Debra's fears and concerns, which he knows very well by now, and expressed his genuine admiration for her sociability and ease with new people. Suppose he anticipated that she would compare their marriage unfavorably with this appealing couple's relationship and said something like "You know, tonight I realized that even though we don't live in the luxury they do, I am awfully lucky to have you." Suppose that Frank had admitted candidly to Debra that being with this new couple made him feel "down on himself" about his participation that evening, a revelation that would have evoked her concern and sympathy. For her part, suppose that Debra had short-circuited her own self-pitying ruminations and paid attention to her husband's low mood, saying something like "Honey, you didn't seem to be up to par tonight. Are you feeling okay? Was it something about that couple you didn't like? Or were you just tired?" Suppose she, too, had been honest in expressing what she dislikes about herself, such as her envy of the other couple's affluence, instead of expressing what she dislikes about Frank. Suppose she had turned her attention to the qualities she does love about Frank. Hmmm, come to think of it, he's right about being a "sensitive lover."

From our standpoint, therefore, misunderstandings, conflicts, personality differences, and even angry quarrels are not the assassins of love; self-justification is. Frank and Debra's evening with the new couple might have ended very differently if each of them had not been so busy spinning their own self-justifications and blaming the other, and had thought about the other's feelings first. Each of them understands the other's point of view perfectly, but their need for self-justification is preventing them from accepting their partner's position as being as legitimate as their own. It is motivating them to see their own way as the better way, indeed the only reasonable way.

We are not referring here to the garden-variety kind of self-justification that we are all inclined to use when we make a mistake or disagree about relatively trivial matters, like who left the top off the salad dressing or who forgot to pay the water bill or whose memory of a favorite scene in an old movie is correct. In those circumstances, self-justification momentarily protects us from feeling clumsy, incompetent, or forgetful. The kind that can erode a marriage, however, reflects a more serious effort to protect not *what we did* but *who we are,* and it comes in two versions: "I'm right and you're wrong" and "Even if I'm wrong, too bad; that's the way I am." Frank and Debra are in trouble because they have begun to justify their fundamental self-concepts, the qualities about themselves that they value and do not wish to alter or that they believe are inherent in their nature. They are not saying to each other, "I'm right and you're wrong about that memory." They are saying, "I am the right kind of person and you are the wrong kind of person. And because you are the wrong kind of person, you cannot appreciate my virtues; foolishly, you even think some of my virtues are flaws."

Thus, Frank justifies himself by seeing his actions as those of a good, loyal, steady husband—that's who he is—and so he thinks everything would be fine if Debra quit pestering him to talk, if she would forgive his imperfections as he forgives hers. Notice his language: "What have I done that's wrong?" asks Frank. "I'm an okay human being." Frank justifies his unwillingness to discuss difficult or painful topics in the name of his "tolerance" and ability to "just let things ride." For her part, Debra thinks her emotional expressiveness "just shows I'm human"—that's who she is—and that everything would be fine if Frank weren't so "passive and bored." Debra got it right when she observed that Frank justifies ignoring her demands to communicate by attributing them to her irrational nature. But she doesn't see that she is doing the same thing, that she justifies ignoring his wishes not to talk by attributing them to his stubborn nature.

Every marriage is a story, and like all stories, it is subject to its participants' distorted perceptions and memories that preserve the narrative as each side sees it. Frank and Debra are at a crucial decision point on the pyramid of their marriage, and the steps they take to resolve the dissonance between "I love this person" and "This person is doing some things that are driving me crazy" will enhance their love story or destroy it. They are going to have to decide how to answer some key questions about those crazy things their partner does: Are they due to an unchangeable personality flaw? Can I live with them? Are they grounds for divorce? Can we find a compromise? Could I—horror of horrors—learn something from my partner, maybe improve my own way of doing things? And they are going to have to decide how to think about their own way of doing things. Seeing as how they have lived with themselves their whole lives, "their own way" feels natural, inevitable. Self-justification is blocking each partner from asking: Could I be wrong? Could I be making a mistake? Could I change?

[As Debra and Frank's problems accumulated, each developed an implicit theory of how the other person was wrecking the marriage. (These theories are called "implicit" because people are often unaware that they hold them.)]Debra's implicit theory is that Frank is socially awkward and passive; his theory is that Debra is insecure and cannot accept herself, or him, as they are. The trouble is that once people develop an implicit theory, the confirmation bias kicks in and they stop seeing evidence that doesn't fit it. As Frank and Debra's therapist observed, Debra now ignores or plays down all the times that Frank isn't awkward and passive with her or others—the times he's been funny and charming, the many times he has gone out of his way to be helpful. For his part, Frank now ignores or plays down evidence of Debra's psychological security, such as her persistence and optimism in the face of disappointment. "They each think the other is at fault," their therapists observed, "and thus they selectively remember parts of their life, focusing on those parts that support their own points of view."[4]

Our implicit theories of why we and other people behave as we do come in one of two versions. We can say it's because of something in the situation or environment: "The bank teller snapped at me because she is overworked today; there aren't enough tellers to handle these lines." Or we can say it's because something is wrong with the person: "That teller snapped at me because she is plain rude." When we explain our own behavior, self-justification allows us to flatter ourselves: We give ourselves credit for our good actions but let the situation excuse the bad ones. When we do something that hurts another, for example, we rarely say, "I behaved this way because I am a cruel and heartless human being." We say, "I was provoked; anyone would do what I did"; or "I had no choice"; or "Yes, I said some awful things, but that wasn't *me*—it's because I was drunk." Yet when we do something generous, helpful, or brave, we don't say we did it because we were provoked or drunk or had no choice, or because the guy on the phone guilt-induced us into donating to charity. We did it because we are generous and open-hearted.

Successful partners extend to each other the same self-forgiving ways of thinking we extend to ourselves: They forgive each other's missteps as being due to the situation, but give each other credit for the thoughtful and loving things they do. If one partner does something thoughtless or is in a crabby mood, the other tends to write it off as a result of events that aren't the partner's fault: "Poor guy, he is under a lot of stress"; "I can understand why she snapped at me; she's been living with back pain for days." But if one does something especially nice, the other credits the partner's inherent good nature and sweet personality: "My honey brought me flowers for no reason at all," a wife might say; "he is the dearest guy."

[While happy partners are giving each other the benefit of the doubt, unhappy partners are doing just the opposite.[5] If the partner does something nice, it's because of a temporary fluke or situational demands: "Yeah, he brought me flowers, but only because all the other guys in his office were buying flowers for their wives."] If the partner does something thoughtless or annoying, though, it's because of the partner's personality flaws: "She snapped at me because she's a bitch." Frank doesn't say that Debra did a crazy *thing*, following him around the house demanding that he talk to her, and he doesn't say she acted that way because she was feeling frustrated that he would not talk to her; he calls her a crazy *person*. Debra doesn't say that Frank avoided talking after the dinner party because he was weary and didn't want to have a confrontation last thing at night; she says he is a passive *person*.

Implicit theories have powerful consequences because they affect, among other things, how couples argue, and even the very purpose of an argument. If a couple is arguing from the premise that each is a good person who did something wrong but fixable, or who did something blunderheaded because of momentary situational pressures, there is hope of correction and compromise. But, once again, unhappy couples invert this premise. Because each partner is expert at self-justification, they each blame the other's unwillingness to change on personality flaws, but excuse their own unwillingness to change on the basis of their personality virtues. If they don't want to admit they were wrong or modify a habit that annoys or distresses their partner, they say, "I can't help it. It's natural to raise your voice when you're angry. That's the way I am." You can hear the self-justification in these words because, of course, they *can* help it. They help it every time they don't raise their voice with a police officer, their employer, or a 300-pound irritating stranger on the street.

The shouter who protests, "That's the way I am!" is, however, rarely inclined to extend the same self-forgiving justification to the partner. On the contrary, he or she is likely to turn it into an infuriating insult: "That's the way you are—you're just like your mother!" Generally, the remark does not refer to your mother's sublime baking skills or her talent at dancing the tango. It means that you are like your mother genetically and irredeemably; there's nothing you can do about it. And when people feel they can't do anything about it, they feel unjustly accused, as if they were being criticized for being too short or too freckled. Social psychologist June Tangney has found that being criticized for who you are rather than for what you did evokes a deep sense of shame and helplessness; it makes a person want to hide, disappear.[6] Because the shamed person has nowhere to go to escape the desolate feeling of humiliation, Tangney found, shamed spouses tend to strike back in anger: "You make me feel that I did an awful thing because I'm reprehensible and incompetent. Since I don't think I am reprehensible and incompetent, you must be reprehensible to humiliate me this way."

By the time a couple's style of argument has escalated into shaming and blaming each other, the very purpose of their quarrels has shifted. It is no longer an effort to solve a problem or even to get the other person to modify his or her behavior; it's just to wound, to insult, to score. That is why shaming leads to fierce, renewed efforts at self-justification, a refusal to compromise, and the most destructive emotion a relationship can evoke: contempt. In his groundbreaking study of more than 700 couples, whom he followed over a period of years, psychologist John Gottman found that contempt—criticism laced with sarcasm, name calling, and mockery—is one of the strongest signs that a relationship is in free fall.[7] Gottman offered this example:

> *Fred:* Did you pick up my dry cleaning?
> *Ingrid (mocking):* "Did you pick up my dry cleaning?" Pick up your own damn dry cleaning. What am I, your maid?
> *Fred:* Hardly. If you were a maid, at least you'd know how to clean.

Contemptuous exchanges like this one are devastating because they destroy the one thing that self-justification is designed to protect: our feelings of self-worth, of being loved, of being a good and respected person. Contempt is the final revelation to the partner that "I don't value the 'who' that you are." We believe that contempt is a predictor of divorce not because it causes the wish to separate, but because it reflects the couple's feelings of psychological separation. Contempt emerges only after years of squabbles and quarrels that keep resulting, as for Frank and Debra, in yet another unsuccessful effort to get the other person to behave differently. It is an indication that the partner is throwing in the towel, thinking, "There's no point hoping that you will ever change; you are just like your mother after all." Anger reflects the hope that a problem can be corrected. When it burns out, it leaves the ashes of resentment and contempt. And contempt is the handmaiden of hopelessness.

o   o   o

Which comes first, a couple's unhappiness with each other, or their negative ways of thinking about each other? Am I unhappy with you because of your personality flaws, or does my belief that you have personality flaws (rather than forgivable quirks or external pressures) eventually make me unhappy with you? Obviously it works in both directions. But because most new partners do not start out in a mood of complaining and blaming, psychologists have been able to follow couples over time to see what sets some of them, but not others, on a downward spiral. They have learned that negative ways of thinking and blaming usually come first and are unrelated to the couple's frequency of anger, either party's feelings of depression, or other negative emotional states.[8] Happy and unhappy partners simply think differently about each other's behavior, even when they are responding to identical situations and actions.

That is why we think that self-justification is the prime suspect in the murder of a marriage. Each partner resolves the dissonance caused by conflicts and irritations by explaining the spouse's behavior in a particular way. That explanation, in turn, sets them on a path down the pyramid. Those who travel the route of shame and blame will eventually begin rewriting the story of their marriage. As they do, they seek further evidence to justify their growing pessimistic or contemptuous views of each other. They shift from minimizing negative aspects of the marriage to overemphasizing them, seeking every bit of supporting evidence to fit their new story. As the new story takes shape, with husband and wife rehearsing it privately or with sympathetic friends, the partners become blind to each other's good qualities, the very ones that initially caused them to fall in love.

The tipping point at which a couple starts rewriting their love story, Gottman finds, is when the "magic ratio" dips below five-to-one: Successful couples have a ratio of five times as many positive interactions (such as expressions of love, affection, and humor) to negative ones (such as expressions of annoyance and complaints). It doesn't matter if the couple is emotionally volatile, quarreling eleven times a day, or emotionally placid, quarreling once a decade; it is the ratio that matters. "Volatile couples may yell and scream a lot, but they spend five times as much of their marriage being loving and making up," Gottman found. "Quieter, avoidant couples may not display as much passion as the other types, but they display far less criticism and contempt as well—the ratio is still 5 to 1."[9] When the ratio is five to one or better, any dissonance that arises is generally reduced in a positive direction. For example, social psychologist Ayala Pines, in a study of burnout in marriage, reported how a happily married woman she called Ellen reduced the dissonance caused by her husband's failure to give her a birthday present. "I wish he would have given me something—anything—I told him that, like I am telling him all of my thoughts and feelings," Ellen said to Pines. "And as I was doing that I was thinking to myself how wonderful it is that I can express openly all of my feelings, even the negative ones . . . The left over negative feelings I just sent down with the water under the bridge."[10]

When the positive-negative ratio has shifted in favor of those negative feelings, however, couples resolve dissonance *caused by the same events* in a way that increases their alienation from one another. Pines reported how an unhappily married woman, Donna, reacted to the same problem that upset Ellen: no birthday present from her husband. But whereas Ellen decided to accept that her husband was never going to become the Bill Gates of domestic giving, Donna interpreted her husband's behavior quite differently:

> One of the things that actually cemented my decision to divorce was my birthday, which is a symbolic day for me. I got a phone call at six o'clock in the morning from Europe, from a cousin, to wish me a happy birthday. Here is someone miles away who's taken the trouble. And he was sitting there listening, and didn't wish me a happy birthday. . . . And I suddenly realized, you know, that here are all these people who do love me, and here's a person who doesn't appreciate me. He doesn't value me, he doesn't love me. If he did he wouldn't treat me the way he did. He would want to do something special for me.

It is entirely possible, of course, that Donna's husband doesn't love and appreciate her. And of course we don't have his side of the story about the birthday gift; perhaps he had tried giving her gifts for years but she never liked any of them. Presumably, though, most people don't decide to divorce because of a missing birthday present. Because Donna has decided that her husband's behavior is not only unmodifiable but intolerable, she now interprets everything he does as unmistakable evidence that "he doesn't value me, he doesn't love me." Donna actually took the confirmation bias further than most spouses do: She told Pines that whenever her husband made her feel depressed and upset, she wrote it down in a "hate book." Her hate book gave her all the evidence she needed to justify her decision to divorce.

When the couple has hit this low point, they start revising their memories, too. Now the incentive for both sides is not to send down the negative things "with the water under the bridge," but to encourage every negative thing to bubble up to the surface. Distortions of past events—or complete amnesia—kick in to confirm the couple's suspicion that they married a complete stranger, and not a particularly appealing one, either. Clinical psychologist Julie Gottman worked with an angry couple in therapy. When she asked, "How did the two of you meet?" the wife said, contemptuously, "At school, where I mistakenly thought he was smart."[11] In this twist of memory, she announces that she didn't make a mistake in choosing him; he made the mistake, by deceiving her about his intelligence.

"I have found that nothing foretells a marriage's future as accurately as how a couple retells their past," John Gottman observes.[12] Rewriting history begins even before a couple is aware their marriage is in danger. Gottman and his team conducted in-depth interviews of fifty-six couples, and were able to follow up on forty-seven of them three years later. At the time of the first interview, none of the couples had planned to separate, but the researchers were able to predict with 100 percent accuracy the seven couples who divorced. (Of the remaining forty couples, the researchers predicted that thirty-seven would still be together, still an astonishing accuracy rate.) During the first interview, those seven couples had already begun recasting their history, telling a despondent story with confirming details to fit. For example, they told Gottman they had married not because they were in love and couldn't bear to be apart, but because marriage seemed "natural, the next step." The first year, the divorced couples now recalled, was full of letdowns and disappointments. "A lot of things went wrong but I don't remember what they were," said one soon-to-be-ex-husband. Happy couples, however, called the same difficulties "rough spots" and saw them as challenges that they proudly had survived, with humor and affection.

Thanks to the revisionist power of memory to justify our decisions, by the time many couples divorce, they can't remember why they married. It's as if they have had a nonsurgical lobotomy that excised the happy memories of how each partner once felt toward the other. Over and over we have heard people say, "I knew the week after the wedding I'd made a terrible mistake." "But why did you have three children and stay together for the next twenty-seven years?" "Oh, I don't know; I just felt obligated, I guess."

Of course, some people do make the decision to separate as a result of a clear-eyed weighing of current benefits and problems; but for most, it's a decision fraught with historical revisionism and dissonance reduction. How do we know? Because even when the problems remain the same, the justifications change as soon as one or both parties decides to leave. As long as couples have decided to stay in a relationship that is far from their ideal, they reduce dissonance in ways that support their decision: "It's not really that bad." "Most marriages are worse than mine—or certainly no better." "He forgot my birthday, but he does many other things that show me he loves me." "We have problems, but overall I love her." When one or both partners starts thinking of divorce, however, their efforts to reduce dissonance will now justify the decision to leave: "This marriage really *is* that bad." "Most marriages are better than mine." "He forgot my birthday, and it means he doesn't love me." And the pitiless remark said by many a departing spouse after twenty or thirty years, "I never loved you."

The cruelty of that last particular lie is commensurate with the teller's need to justify his or her behavior. Couples who part because of clear external reasons—say, because one spouse is physically or emotionally abusive—will feel no need for additional self-justification. Nor will those rare couples who part in complete amicability, or who eventually restore warm feelings of friendship after the initial pain of separation. They feel no urgency to vilify their former partner or forget happier times, because they are able to say, "It didn't work out," "We just grew apart," or "We were so young when we married and didn't know better." But when the divorce is wrenching, momentous, and costly, and especially when one partner wants the separation and the other does not, both sides will feel an amalgam of painful emotions. In addition to the anger, anguish, hurt, and grief that almost invariably accompany divorce, these couples will also feel the pain of dissonance. That dissonance, and the way many people choose to resolve it, is one of the major reasons for postdivorce vindictiveness.

If you are the one being left, you may suffer the ego-crushing dissonance of "I'm a good person and I've been a terrific partner" and "My partner is leaving me. How could this be?" You could conclude that you're not as good a person as you thought, or that you are a good person but you were a pretty bad partner, but few of us choose to reduce dissonance by plunging darts into our self-esteem. It's far easier to reduce dissonance by plunging darts into the partner, so to speak—say, by concluding that your partner is a difficult, selfish person, only you hadn't realized it fully until now.

If you are the one who is leaving, you also have dissonance to reduce, to justify the pain you are inflicting on someone you once loved. Because you are a good person, and a good person doesn't hurt another, your partner must have deserved your rejection, perhaps even more than you realized. Observers of divorcing couples are often baffled by what seems like unreasonable vindictiveness on the part of the person who initiated the separation; what they are observing is dissonance reduction in action. A friend of ours, lamenting her son's divorce, said: "I don't understand my daughter-in-law. She left my son for another man who adores her, but she won't marry him or work full-time just so that my son has to keep paying her alimony. My son has had to take a job he doesn't like to afford her demands. Given that she's the one who left, and that she has another relationship, the way she treats my son seems inexplicably cruel and venge-ful." From the daughter-in-law's standpoint, however, her behavior toward her ex is perfectly justifiable. If he were such a good guy, she'd still be with him, wouldn't she?

Divorce mediators, and anyone else who has tried to be helpful to warring friends in the throes of divorce, have seen this process up close. Mediators Donald Saposnek and Chip Rose describe the "ten-dency of one spouse to cast the other in a vilified image, for example, 'He's a weak, violent drunk,' or, 'She's a two-faced, selfish, patholog-ical liar who can't ever be trusted.' These intensely negative, polarized characterizations that high conflict divorcing couples make of each other become reified and immutable over time."[13] The reason they do is that once a couple starts reducing dissonance by taking the ego-preserving route of vilifying the former partner, they need to keep justifying their position. Thus they fight over every nickel and dime that one party is "entitled to" and the other "doesn't deserve," furi-ously denying or controlling custody matters and the ex's visitation rights because, look, the ex is a terrible person. Neither party pauses in mid-rant to consider that the terribleness might be a result of the terrible situation, let alone a response to their own behavior. Each ac-tion that one partner takes evokes a self-justified retaliation from the other, and voilà, they are on a course of reciprocal, escalating ani-mosity. Each partner, having induced the other to behave badly, uses that bad behavior both to justify his or her own retaliation and to marshal support for the ex's inherently "evil" qualities.

By the time these couples seek mediation, they have slid pretty far down the pyramid. Don Saposnek told us that in the more than 4,000 custody mediations he has done, "I have *never* had one in which a parent has said, 'You know, I really think that she should get custody, since she really is the better parent and the kids are closer to her.' It is virtually always a bilateral stand-off of 'why I am the better and more deserving parent.' Not a single point of acknowledgment is ever given to the other parent, and even when they freely admit their own acts of retaliation, they always justify it: 'He deserved it, after what he's done—breaking up our family!' The agreements they reach are invariably some kind of compromise which each experiences as 'giving up my position because I felt coerced, I'm exhausted fighting, or I ran out of money for mediation . . . even though I know that I'm the better parent.'"

Dissonance theory would lead us to predict that it is the very people with the greatest initial ambivalence about their decision to divorce, or who feel the greatest guilt over their unilateral decision, who have the greatest urgency to justify their decision to leave. In turn, the bereft partner feels a desperate urgency to justify any retaliation as payback for having been treated so cruelly and unfairly. As both parties come up with confirming memories and all those horrible recent examples of the ex's bad behavior to support their new accounts, the ex turns completely villainous. Self-justification is the route by which ambivalence morphs into certainty, guilt into rage. The love story has become a hate book.

o   o   o

Our colleague Leonore Tiefer, a clinical psychologist, told us about a couple in their late thirties, married ten years, whom she saw in therapy. They could not make a decision about having children because each wanted to be sure before even raising the issue with the other. They could not make a decision about how to balance her demanding business career with their activities together, because she felt justified in working as much as she wanted. They could not resolve their quarrels over his drinking, because he felt justified in drinking as much as he wanted. Each had had an affair, which they justified as being a response to the other's.

Yet their normal, if difficult, problems were not what doomed this marriage; their obstinate self-justifications were. "They do not know what to give up in order to be a couple," says Tiefer. "They each want to do what they feel entitled to do, and they can't discuss the important issues that affect them as a pair. And as long as they stay mad at each other, they don't have to discuss those matters, because discussion might actually require them to compromise or consider the partner's point of view. They have a very difficult time with empathy, each one feeling completely confident that the other's behavior is less reasonable than their own. So they bring up old resentments to justify their current position and their unwillingness to change, or forgive."

In contrast, the couples who grow together over the years have figured out a way to live with a minimum of self-justification, which is another way of saying that they are able to put empathy for the partner ahead of defending their own territory. Successful, stable couples are able to listen to the partner's criticisms, concerns, and suggestions undefensively. In our terms, they are able to yield, just enough, on the self-justifying excuse "That's the kind of person I am." They reduce the dissonance caused by small irritations by overlooking them, and they reduce the dissonance caused by their mistakes and major problems by solving them.

We interviewed several couples who have been together for many years, the kind of couples Frank and Debra admired, who by their own accounts have an unusually tight and affectionate marriage. We didn't ask them, "What is the secret of your long marriage?" because people rarely know the answer; they will say something banal or unhelpful, such as "We never went to bed angry" or "We share a love of golf." (Plenty of happy couples do go to bed angry because they would rather not have an argument when they are dead tired, and plenty of happy couples do not share hobbies and interests.) Instead, we asked these couples, in effect, how, over the years, they reduced the dissonance between "I love this person" and "This person is doing something that is driving me crazy."

One especially illuminating answer came from a couple we will call Charlie and Maxine, who have been married more than forty years. Like all couples, they have many small differences that could easily flare into irritation, but they have come to accept most of them as facts of life, not worth sulking about. Charlie says, "I like to eat dinner at five; my wife likes to eat at eight; we compromise—we eat at five to eight." The important thing about this couple is how they handle the big problems. When they first fell in love, in their early twenties, Charlie was attracted to a quality of serenity in Maxine's soul that he found irresistible; she was, he said, an oasis in a tumultuous world. She was attracted to his passionate energy, which he brought to everything from finding the perfect peach to writing the perfect sentence. But the passionate quality she enjoyed in him when it was attached to love, sex, travel, music, and movies was alarming to her when it was attached to anger. When he was angry, he would yell and pound the table, something no one in her family had ever done. Within a few months of their marriage, she told him, tearfully, that his anger was frightening her.

Charlie's first impulse was to justify himself. He didn't think that raising his voice was a desirable trait, exactly, but he saw it as one that was part of who he was, an aspect of his authenticity. "My father yelled and pounded tables," he said to her. "My grandfather yelled and pounded tables! It's my right! I can't do anything about it. It's what a man does. You want me to be like those wimpy guys who are always talking about their 'feelings'?" Once he stopped yelling and considered how his behavior was affecting Maxine, he realized that of course he could modify his behavior, and, slowly and steadily, he reduced the frequency and intensity of his flare-ups. But Maxine, too, had to change; she had to stop justifying her belief that all forms of anger are dangerous and bad. ("In my family no one ever expressed anger. Therefore, that's the only right way to be.") When she did, she was able to learn to distinguish legitimate feelings of anger from unacceptable ways of expressing them, such as pounding tables, and for that matter from unconstructive ways of *not* expressing them, such as crying and retreating—her own "unchangeable" habit.

Over the years, a different problem emerged, one that had developed slowly, as it does for many couples who divide up tasks on the initial basis of who's better at them. The down side of Maxine's serenity was unassertiveness and a fear of confrontation; she would never dream of complaining about a bad meal or flawed merchandise. And so it always fell to Charlie to return the coffeepot that didn't work, call customer service with complaints, or deal face-to-face with the landlord who wouldn't fix the plumbing. "You're so much better at this than I am," she would say, and because he was, he would do it. Over time, however, Charlie grew tired of shouldering this responsibility and was becoming irritated by what he was now seeing as Maxine's passivity. "Why am I always the one handling these unpleasant confrontations?" he said to himself.

He was at a choice point. He could have let it slide, saying that's just the way she is, and continued to do all the dirty work. Instead, Charlie suggested that perhaps it was time for Maxine to learn how to be more assertive, a skill that would be useful to her in many contexts, not only in their marriage. Initially, Maxine responded by saying, "That's the way I am, and you knew it when you married me. Besides, no fair changing the rules after all these years." As they talked more, she was able to hear his concern without letting the jangle of self-justification get in the way. As soon as that happened, she could empathize with his feelings and understand why he thought the division of labor had become unfair. She realized that her options were not as limited as she had always assumed. She took an assertiveness-training course, diligently practiced what she learned there, got better at standing up for her rights, and before long was enjoying the satisfaction of speaking her mind in a way that usually got results. Charlie and Maxine made it clear that he did not turn into a lamb nor did she turn into a tiger; personality, history, genetics, and temperament do put limitations on how much anyone can change.[14] But each of them moved. In this marriage, assertiveness and the constructive expression of anger are no longer polarized skills, his and hers.

In good marriages, a confrontation, difference of opinion, clashing habits, and even angry quarrels can bring the couple closer, by helping each partner learn something new and by forcing them to examine their assumptions about their abilities or limitations. It isn't always easy to do this. Letting go of the self-justifications that cover up our mistakes, that protect our desires to do things just the way we want to, and that minimize the hurts we inflict on those we love can be embarrassing and painful. Without self-justification, we might be left standing emotionally naked, unprotected, in a pool of regrets and losses.

Yet, in the final analysis, we believe it is worth it, because no matter how painful it can be to let go of self-justification, the result teaches us something deeply important about ourselves and can bring the peace of insight and self-acceptance. At the age of sixty-five, the feminist writer and activist Vivian Gornick wrote a dazzlingly honest essay about her lifelong efforts to balance work and love, and to lead a life based on exemplary egalitarian principles in both arenas. "I'd written often about living alone because I couldn't figure out why I *was* living alone," she wrote. For years her answer, the answer of so many in her generation, was sexism: Patriarchal men were forcing strong, independent women to choose between their careers and their relationships. That answer isn't wrong; sexism has sunk many marriages and shot holes through countless others that are barely afloat. But today Gornick realizes that it was not the full answer. Looking back, without the comfort of her familiar self-justifications, she was able to see her own role in determining the course of her relationships, realizing "that much of my loneliness was self-inflicted, having more to do with my angry, self-divided personality than with sexism."[15]

"The reality was," she wrote, "that I was alone not because of my politics but because I did not know how to live in a decent way with another human being. In the name of equality I tormented every man who'd ever loved me until he left me: I called them on everything, never let anything go, held them up to accountability in ways that wearied us both. There was, of course, more than a grain of truth in everything I said, but those grains, no matter how numerous, need not have become the sandpile that crushed the life out of love."

CHAPTER 7

○   ○   ○

Wounds, Rifts, and Wars

High-stomached are they both, and full of ire,
In rage deaf as the sea, hasty as fire.
—William Shakespeare, *Richard II*

ONE YEAR AFTER HE had confessed his affair, Jim felt there was no letup in Diane's anger. Every conversation eventually turned to the affair. She watched him like a hawk, and when he caught her gaze her expression was full of suspicion and pain. Couldn't she realize that it had just been a small mistake on his part? He was hardly the first person on the planet to make such a mistake. He had been honest enough to admit the affair, after all, and strong enough to end it. He had apologized, and told her a thousand times that he loved her and wanted the marriage to continue. Couldn't she understand that? Couldn't she just focus on the good parts of their marriage and get over this setback?

Diane found Jim's attitude incredible. He seemed to want compliments for confessing the affair and ending it, rather than criticism for having had the affair to begin with. Couldn't he understand that? Couldn't he just focus on her pain and distress and quit trying to justify himself? He never even apologized, either. Well, he said he was sorry, but that was pathetic. Why couldn't he give her a genuine, heartfelt apology? She didn't need him to prostrate himself; she just wanted him to know how she felt and make amends.

But Jim was finding it difficult to make the amends Diane wanted because of her intense anger, which made him feel like retaliating. The message he heard in her anger was "You have committed a horrible crime" and "You are less than human for doing what you did to me." He was deeply sorry that he had hurt her, of course, and he would give the world if he could only make her feel better, but he didn't think that he had committed a horrible crime or that he was inhuman, and the kind of groveling apology she seemed to want was not the kind he was prepared to give. So instead, he tried to convince her that the affair was not serious and that the other woman meant little to him. Diane, however, interpreted Jim's attempts to explain the affair as an effort to invalidate her feelings. The message she heard in his reaction was "You shouldn't be so upset; I didn't do anything bad." His efforts to explain himself made her angrier, and her anger made it more difficult for him to empathize with her suffering and respond to it.[1]

o   o   o

In 2005 the country was mesmerized by the last battle in the terrible family war over the life and death of Terri Schiavo, in which her parents, Robert and Mary Schindler, fought her husband, Michael Schiavo, over control of her life, or what remained of it. "It is almost beyond belief, given the sea of distance between them now, that Terri Schiavo's husband and parents once shared a home, a life, a goal," wrote one reporter. Of course, it is not at all beyond belief to students of self-justification. At the start of Terri and Michael's marriage, the couple and her parents stood close together at the top of the pyramid. Michael called his in-laws Mom and Dad. The Schindlers paid the couple's rent in their early struggling years. When Terri Schiavo suffered massive brain damage in 1990, the Schindlers moved in with their daughter and son-in-law to jointly take care of her, and that is what they did for nearly three years. And then, the root of many rifts—money—was planted. In 1993, Michael Schiavo won a malpractice case against one of Terri's physicians, and was awarded $750,000 for her care and $300,000 for the loss of his wife's companionship. A month later, husband and parents quarreled over the award. Michael Schiavo said it began when his father-in-law asked how much money he, Robert, would receive from the malpractice settlement. The Schindlers said the fight was about what kind of treatment the money should be spent on; the parents wanted intensive, experimental therapy and the husband wanted to give her only basic care.

The settlement was the first straw, forcing parents and husband to make a decision about how it should be spent and who deserved the money, because each side legitimately felt entitled to make the ultimate decisions about Terri's life and death. Accordingly, Michael Schiavo briefly blocked the Schindlers' access to his wife's medical records; they tried for a time to have him removed as her guardian. [He was offended by what he saw as a crass effort by his father-in-law to claim some of the settlement money; they were offended by what they saw as his selfish motives to get rid of his wife.] By the time the country witnessed this family's final, furious confrontation, one inflamed by the media and opportunistic politicians, their reciprocally intransigent positions seemed utterly irrational and insoluble.

o   o   o

In January 1979, the shah of Iran, Mohammad Reza Pahlavi, faced with a growing public insurrection against him, fled Iran for safety in Egypt, and two weeks later the country welcomed the return of its new Islamic fundamentalist leader, Ayatollah Ruhollah Khomeini, whom the shah had sent into exile more than a decade earlier. In October, the Carter administration reluctantly permitted the shah to make a brief stopover in the United States on humanitarian grounds, for medical treatment for his cancer. Khomeini denounced the American government as the "Great Satan," urging Iranians to demonstrate against the United States and Israel, the "enemies of Islam." Thousands of them heeded his call and gathered outside the American embassy in Tehran. On November 4, several hundred Iranian students seized the main embassy building and took most of its occupants captive, of whom fifty-two remained as hostages for the next 444 days. The captors demanded that the shah be returned to Iran for trial, along with the billions of dollars they claimed the shah had stolen from the Iranian people. The Iran hostage crisis was the 9/11 of its day; according to one historian, it received more coverage on television and in the press than any other event since World War II. Ted Koppel informed the nation of each day's (non)events in a new late-night show, *America Held Hostage,* which was so popular that when the crisis was over it continued as *Nightline.* Americans were riveted to the story, furious at the Iranians' actions and demands. So they were mad at the shah; what the hell were they angry at us about?

o   o   o

Thus far in this book we have been talking about situations in which mistakes were definitely made—memory distortions, wrongful convictions, misguided therapeutic practices. We move now to the far more brambly territory of betrayals, rifts, and violent hostilities. Our examples will range from family quarrels to the Crusades, from routine meanness to systematic torture, from misdemeanors in marriage to the escalations of war. These conflicts between friends, cousins, and countries may differ profoundly in cause and form, but they are woven together with the single, tenacious thread of self-justification. In pulling out that common thread, we do not mean to overlook the complexity of the fabric or to imply that all garments are the same.

Sometimes both sides agree on who is to blame, as Jim and Diane did; Jim did not try to shift the blame, as he might have done, by claiming, for example, that Diane drove him to have an affair by being a bad wife. And sometimes it is all too certain who the guilty party is even when the guilty party is busy denying it with a litany of excuses and self-justifications. Enslaved people are not partly to blame for slavery, children do not provoke pedophiles, women do not ask to be raped, the Jews did not bring the Holocaust on themselves.

We want to start, though, with a more common problem: the many situations in which it isn't clear who is to blame, "who started this," or even when this started. Every family has tales to tell of insults, unforgivable slights and wounds, and never-ending feuds: "She didn't come to my wedding, and she didn't even send a gift." "He stole my inheritance." "When my father was sick, my brother totally disappeared and I had to take care of him myself." In a rift, no one is going to admit that they lied or stole or cheated without provocation; only a bad person would do that, just as only a heartless child would abandon a parent in need. Therefore, each side justifies its own position by claiming that the other side is to blame; each is simply responding to the offense or provocation as any reasonable, moral person would do. "Yeah, you bet I didn't come to your wedding, and where were you seven years ago when I was going through that bad breakup and you vanished?" "Sure, I took some money and possessions from our parents' estate, but it wasn't stealing—you started this forty years ago when you got to go to college and I didn't." "Dad likes you better than me anyway, he was always so hypercritical of me, so it's right that you take care of him now."

In most rifts each side accuses the other of being inherently selfish, stubborn, mean, and aggressive, but the need for self-justification trumps personality traits. In all likelihood, the Schindlers and Michael Schiavo are not characteristically obstinate or irrational. Rather, their obstinate and irrational behavior in relation to each other was the result of twelve years of decisions (fight or yield on this one? resist or compromise?), subsequent self-justifications, and further actions designed to reduce dissonance and ambivalence. Once they became more and more entrapped by their choices, they could not find a way back. To justify their initial, understandable decision to keep their daughter alive, Terri's parents found themselves needing to justify their next decisions to keep her alive at all costs. Unable to accept the evidence that she was brain dead, Terri's parents justified their actions by accusing Michael of being a controlling husband, an adulterer, possibly a murderer, who wanted Terri to die because she had become a burden. To justify his equally understandable decision to let his wife die naturally, Michael, too, found himself on a course of action from which he could not turn back. To justify those actions, he accused Terri's parents of being opportunistic media manipulators who were denying him the right to keep his promise to Terri that he would not let her live this way. The Schindlers were angry that Michael Schiavo would not listen to them or respect their religious beliefs. Michael Schiavo was angry that the Schindlers took the case to the courts and the public. Each side felt the other was behaving offensively; each felt profoundly betrayed by the other. Who started the final confrontation over control of Terri's death? Each says the other. What made it intractable? Self-justification.

When the Iranian students took those Americans hostage in 1979, the event seemed a meaningless act of aggression, a bolt that came out of the blue as far as the Americans were concerned; Americans saw themselves as having been attacked without provocation by a bunch of crazy Iranians. But to the Iranians, it was the Americans who started it, because American intelligence forces had aided in a coup in 1953 that unseated their charismatic, democratically elected leader, Mohammed Mossadegh, and installed the shah. Within a

decade, many Iranians were growing resentful of the shah's accumu-
lation of wealth and the westernizing influence of the United States.
In 1963, the shah put down an Islamic fundamentalist uprising led
by Khomeini and sent the cleric into exile. As opposition to the
shah's government mounted, he allowed his secret police, SAVAK, to
crack down on dissenters, fueling even greater anger.

When did the hostage crisis begin? When the United States supported the coup against Mossadegh? When it kept supplying the
shah with arms? When it turned a blind eye to the cruelties committed by SAVAK? When it admitted the shah for medical treatment?
Did it begin when the shah exiled Khomeini, or when the ayatollah,
after his triumphant return, saw a chance to consolidate his power
by focusing the nation's frustrations on America? Did it begin during the protests at the embassy, when Iranian students allowed themselves to be Khomeini's political pawns? Most Iranians chose answers
that justified their anger at the United States, and most Americans
chose answers that justified their anger at Iran. Each side convinced
itself that it was the injured party, and consequently was entitled to
retaliate. Who started the hostage crisis? Each says the other. What
made it intractable? Self-justification.

Of all the stories that people construct to justify their lives, loves,
and losses, the ones they weave to account for being the instigator or
recipient of injustice or harm are the most compelling and have the
most far-reaching consequences. In such cases, the hallmarks of self-
justification transcend the specific antagonists (lovers, parents and
children, friends, neighbors, or nations) and their specific quarrels (a
sexual infidelity, a family inheritance, a property line, a betrayal of a
confidence, or a military invasion). We have all done something that
made others angry at us, and we have all been spurred to anger by
what others have done to us. We all have, intentionally or unintentionally, hurt another person who will forever regard us as the villain,
the betrayer, the scoundrel. And we have all felt the sting of being on
the receiving end of an act of injustice, nursing a wound that never

seems to fully heal. The remarkable thing about self-justification is that it allows us to shift from one role to the other and back again in the blink of an eye, without applying what we have learned from one role to the other. Feeling like a victim of injustice in one situation does not make us less likely to commit an injustice against someone else, nor does it make us more sympathetic to victims. It's as if there is a brick wall between those two sets of experiences, blocking our ability to see the other side.

One of the reasons for that brick wall is that pain felt is always more intense than pain inflicted, even when the actual amount of pain is identical. The old joke—the other guy's broken leg is trivial; our broken fingernail is serious—turns out to be an accurate description of our neurological wiring. English neurologists paired people in a tit-for-tat experiment. Each pair was hooked up to a mechanism that exerted pressure on their index fingers, and each participant was instructed to apply the same force on their partner's finger that they had just felt. They could not do it fairly, although they tried hard to do so. Every time one partner felt the pressure, he retaliated with considerably greater force, thinking he was giving what he had gotten. The researchers concluded that the escalation of pain is "a natural by-product of neural processing."[3] It helps explain why two boys who start out exchanging punches on the arm as a game soon find themselves in a furious fistfight, and why two nations find themselves in a spiral of retaliation: "They didn't take an eye for an eye, they took an eye for a tooth. We must get even—let's take a leg." Each side justifies what it does as merely evening the score.

Social psychologist Roy Baumeister and his colleagues showed how smoothly self-justification works to minimize any bad feelings we might have as doers of harm, and to maximize any righteous feelings we might have as victims.[4] They asked sixty-three people to provide autobiographical accounts of a "victim story," when they had been angered or hurt by someone else, and a "perpetrator story," a time when they had made someone else angry. They did not use the term *perpetrator* in its common criminal sense, to describe someone actually guilty of a crime or other wrongdoing, and in this section neither will we; we will use the word, as they do, to mean anyone who perpetrated an action that harmed or offended another.

From both perspectives, accounts involved the familiar litany of broken promises and commitments; violated rules, obligations, or expectations; sexual infidelity; betrayal of secrets; unfair treatment; lies; and conflicts over money and possessions. Notice that this was not a he-said/she-said study, the kind that marriage counselors and mediators present when they describe their cases; rather, it was a he-said-this-*and*-he-said-that study, in which everyone reported an experience of being on each side. The benefit of this method, the researchers explained, is that "it rules out explanations that treat victims and perpetrators as different kinds of people. Our procedures indicate how ordinary people define themselves as victims or as perpetrators—that is, how they construct narratives to make sense of their experiences in each of those roles." Again, personality differences have nothing to do with it. Sweet, kind people are as likely as crabby ones to be victims or perpetrators, and to justify themselves accordingly.

When we construct narratives that "make sense," however, we do so in a self-serving way. Perpetrators are motivated to reduce their moral culpability; victims are motivated to maximize their moral blamelessness. Depending on which side of the wall we are on, we systematically distort our memories and account of the event to produce the maximum consonance between what happened and how we see ourselves. By identifying these systematic distortions, the researchers showed how the two antagonists misperceive and misunderstand each other's actions.

In their narratives, perpetrators drew on different ways to reduce the dissonance caused by realizing they did something wrong. The first, naturally, was to say they did nothing wrong at all: "I lied to him, but it was only to protect his feelings." "Yeah, I took that bracelet from my sister, but it was originally mine, anyway." Only a few perpetrators admitted that their behavior was immoral or deliberately hurtful or malicious. Most said their offending behavior was justifiable, and some of them, the researchers added mildly, "were quite insistent about this." Most of the perpetrators reported, at least in retrospect, that what they did was reasonable; their actions might have been regrettable, but they were understandable, given the circumstances.

The second strategy was to admit wrongdoing but excuse or minimize it. "I know I shouldn't have had that one-night stand, but in the great cosmos of things, what harm did it do?" "It might have been wrong to take Mom's diamond bracelet when she was ill, but she would have wanted me to have it. And besides, my sisters got so much more than I did." More than two-thirds of the perpetrators claimed external or mitigating circumstances for what they did—"I was abused as a child myself"; "I've been under a lot of stress lately"—but victims were disinclined to grant their perpetrators these forgiving explanations. Nearly half the perpetrators said they "couldn't help" what happened; they had simply acted impulsively, mindlessly. Others passed the buck, maintaining that the victim had provoked them or was otherwise partly responsible.

The third strategy, when the perpetrators' backs were to the wall and they could not deny or minimize responsibility, was to admit they had done something wrong and hurtful, and then try to get rid of the episode as fast as possible. Whether they accepted the blame or not, most perpetrators, eager to exorcise their dissonant feelings of guilt, bracketed the event off in time. They were far more likely than victims to describe the episode as an isolated incident that was now over and done with, that was not typical of them, that had no lasting negative consequences, and that certainly had no implications for the present. Many even told stories with happy endings that provided a reassuring sense of closure, along the lines of "everything is fine now, there was no damage to the relationship; in fact, today we are good friends."

For their part, the victims had a rather different take on the perpetrators' justifications, which might be summarized as "Oh, yeah? No damage? Good friends? Tell it to the marines." Perpetrators may be motivated to get over the episode quickly and give it closure, but victims have long memories; an event that is trivial and forgettable to the former may be a source of lifelong rage to the latter. Only one of the sixty-three victim stories described the perpetrator as having been justified in behaving as he did, and none thought the perpetrators' actions "could not be helped." Accordingly, most victims reported lasting negative consequences of the rift or quarrel. More than half said it had seriously damaged the relationship. They reported continuing hostility, loss of trust, unresolved negative feelings, or even the end of the former friendship, which they apparently neglected to tell the perpetrator.

Moreover, whereas the perpetrators thought their behavior made sense at the time, many victims said they were unable to make sense of the perpetrators' intentions, even long after the event. "Why did he *do* that?" "What was she *thinking*?" The incomprehensibility of the perpetrator's motives is a central aspect of the victim identity and the victim story. "Not only did he do that terrible thing; he doesn't even understand that it *is* a terrible thing!" "Why can't she admit how cruelly she treated me?"

One reason he doesn't understand and she can't admit it is that perpetrators are preoccupied with justifying what they did, but another reason is that they really do not know how the victim feels. Many victims initially stifle their anger, nursing their wounds and brooding about what to do. They ruminate about their pain or grievances for months, sometimes for years, and sometimes for decades. One man we know told us that after eighteen years of marriage, his wife announced "out of the blue, at breakfast," that she wanted a divorce. "I tried to find out what I'd done wrong," he said, "and I told her I wanted to make amends, but there were eighteen years of dustballs under the bed." That wife brooded for eighteen years; the Iranians brooded for twenty-six years. By the time many victims get around to expressing their pain and anger, especially over events that the perpetrators have wrapped up and forgotten, perpetrators are baffled. No wonder most thought their victims' anger was an over-reaction, though few victims felt that way. The victims are thinking, "Overreacted? But I thought about it for months before I spoke. I consider that an underreaction!"

Some victims justify their continued feelings of anger and their unwillingness to let it go because rage itself is retribution, a way to punish the offender, even when the offender wants to make peace, is long gone from the scene, or has died. In *Great Expectations,* Charles Dickens gave us the haunting figure of Miss Havisham, who, having been jilted on her wedding day, sacrifices the rest of her life to be-come a professional victim, clothed in self-righteous wrath and her yellowing bridal gown, raising her ward Estella to exact her revenge on men. Many victims are unable to resolve their feelings because they keep picking at the scab on their wound, asking themselves re-peatedly, "How could such a bad thing have happened to me, a good person?" This is perhaps the most painful dissonance-arousing ques-tion that we confront in our lives. It is the reason for the countless books offering spiritual or psychological advice to help victims find closure—and consonance.

Whether it is Jim and Diane, the Schiavo and Schindler families, or the Iran hostage crisis, the gulf between perpetrators and victims, and the habits of self-justification that create it, can be seen in the way each side tells the same story. Perpetrators, whether individuals or nations, write versions of history in which their behavior was jus-tified and provoked by the other side; their behavior was sensible and meaningful; if they made mistakes or went too far, at least everything turned out for the best in the long run; and it's all in the past now anyway. Victims tend to write accounts of the same history in which they describe the perpetrator's actions as arbitrary and meaningless, or else intentionally malicious and brutal; in which their own retaliation was impeccably appropriate and morally justified; and in which nothing turned out for the best. In fact, everything turned out for the worst, and we are still irritated about it.

Thus, Americans who live in the North and West learn about the Civil War as a matter of ancient history, in which our brave Union troops forced the South to abandon the ugly institution of slavery, we defeated the traitor Jefferson Davis, and the country remained united. (We'll just draw a veil over our own complicity as perpetrators and abetters of slavery; that was then.) But most white Southerners tell a different story, one in which the Civil War is alive and kicking; then is *now*. Our brave Confederate troops were victims of greedy, crude Northerners who defeated our noble leader, Jefferson Davis, destroyed our cities and traditions, and are still trying to destroy our states' rights. There is nothing united about us Southerners and you damned Yankees; we'll keep flying our Confederate flag, thank you, that's *our* history. Slavery may be gone with the wind, but grudges aren't. That is why history is written by the victors, but it's victims who write the memoirs.

Perpetrators of Evil

The first shot I saw [from Abu Ghraib], of Specialist Charles A. Graner and Pfc. Lynndie R. England flashing thumbs up behind a pile of their naked victims, was so jarring that for a few seconds I took it for a montage. . . . There was something familiar about that jaunty insouciance, that unabashed triumph at having inflicted misery upon other humans. And then I remembered: the last time I had seen that conjunction of elements was in photographs of lynchings.[5]

—writer Luc Sante

It may sometimes be hard to define good, but evil has its unmistakable odor: Every child knows what pain is. Therefore, each time we deliberately inflict pain on another, we know what we are doing. We are doing evil.[6]

—Israeli novelist and social critic Amos Oz

Did Charles Graner and Lynndie England know what they were doing, let alone believe they were "doing evil" while they were deliberately inflicting pain and humiliation on their Iraqi prisoners and then laughing at them? No, they didn't, and that is why Amos Oz is wrong. Oz didn't reckon with the power of self-justification: We are good people. Therefore, if we deliberately inflict pain on another, the other must have deserved it. Therefore, we are not doing evil, quite the contrary. We are doing good. The relatively small percentage of people who cannot or will not reduce dissonance this way pay a large psychological price in guilt, anguish, anxiety, nightmares, and sleepless nights. The pain of living with horrors they have committed, but cannot morally accept, would be searing, which is why most people will reach for any justification available to assuage the dissonance. In the previous chapter, we saw on a smaller scale why many divorcing couples justify the hurt they inflict on each other. In the horrifying calculus of self-deception, the greater the pain we inflict on others, the greater the need to justify it to maintain our feelings of decency and self-worth. Because our victims deserved what they got, we hate them even more than we did before we harmed them, which in turn makes us inflict even more pain on them.

Experiments have confirmed this mechanism many times. In one experiment by Keith Davis and Edward Jones, students watched another student being interviewed and then, on instruction by the experimenters, had to report to the target student that they found him to be shallow, untrustworthy, and dull. As a result of making this rather nasty assessment, the participants succeeded in convincing themselves that the victim actually deserved their criticism, and they found him less appealing than they had before they hurt his feelings. Their change of heart occurred even though they knew that the other student had done nothing to merit their criticism, and that they were simply following the experimenter's instructions.[7]

Are all perpetrators alike? No; not everyone feels the need to reduce dissonance by denigrating the victim. Who do you imagine would be most likely to blame the victim: perpetrators who think highly of themselves and have strong feelings of self-worth, or those who are insecure and have low self-worth? Dissonance theory makes the nonobvious prediction that it will be the former. For people who have low self-esteem, treating others badly or going along mindlessly with what others tell them to do is not terribly dissonant with their self-concept. Moreover, they are more likely to be self-deprecating and modest, because they don't think they are especially wonderful. It is the people who think the most of themselves who, if they cause someone pain, must convince themselves the other guy is a rat. Because terrific guys like me don't hurt innocent people, that guy must deserve every nasty thing I did to him. An experiment by David Glass confirmed this prediction: The higher the perpetrators' self-esteem, the greater their denigration of their victims.[8]

Are all victims alike in the eyes of the perpetrator? No; they differ in their degree of helplessness. Suppose you are a marine in a hand-to-hand struggle with an armed enemy soldier. You kill him. Do you feel much dissonance? Probably not. The experience may be unpleasant, but it does not generate dissonance and needs no additional justification: "It was him or me . . . I killed an enemy . . . We are in this to win . . . I have no choice here." But now suppose that you are on a mission to firebomb a house that you were told contains enemy troops. You and your team destroy the place, and then discover you have blown up a household of old men, children, and women. Under these circumstances, most soldiers will try to find additional self-justifications to reduce the dissonance they feel about killing innocent civilians, and the leading one will be to denigrate and dehumanize their victims: "Stupid jerks, they shouldn't have been there . . . they were probably aiding the enemy . . . All those people are vermin, gooks, subhuman." Or, as General William West-moreland famously said of the high number of civilian casualties during the Vietnam War, "The Oriental doesn't put the same high price on life as does a Westerner. Life is plentiful. Life is cheap in the Orient."[9]

Dissonance theory would therefore predict that when victims are armed and able to strike back, perpetrators will feel less need to reduce dissonance by belittling them than when their victims are helpless. In an experiment by Ellen Berscheid and her associates, par-ticipants were led to believe that they would be delivering a painful electric shock to another person as part of a test of learning. Half were told that later they would be reversing roles, so the victim would be in position to retaliate. As predicted, the only participants who denigrated their victims were those who believed the victims were helpless and would not be able to respond in kind.[10] This was precisely the situation of the people who took part in Stanley Mil-gram's 1963 obedience experiment. Many of those who obeyed the experimenter's orders to deliver what they thought were dangerous amounts of shock to a "learner" justified their actions by blaming the victim. As Milgram himself put it, "Many subjects harshly devalue the victim *as a consequence* of acting against him. Such comments as, 'He was so stupid and stubborn he deserved to get shocked,' were common. Once having acted against the victim, these subjects found it necessary to view him as an unworthy individual, whose punish-ment was made inevitable by his own deficiencies of intellect and character."[11]

The implications of these studies are ominous: Combine perpe-trators who have high self-esteem and victims who are helpless, and you have a recipe for the escalation of brutality. This brutality is not confined to brutes—sadists or psychopaths. It can be, and usually is, committed by ordinary individuals, people who have children and lovers, "civilized" people who enjoy music and food and making love and gossiping as much as anyone else. This is one of the most thoroughly documented findings in social psychology, but it is also the most difficult for many people to accept because of the enormous dissonance it produces: "What can I possibly have in common with perpetrators of murder and torture?" It is much more reassuring to believe that they are evil and be done with them.[12] We dare not let a glimmer of their humanity in the door, because it might force us to face the haunting truth of Pogo's great line, "We have met the enemy and he is us."

On the other hand, if the perpetrators are one of us, many people will reduce dissonance by coming to their defense or minimizing the seriousness or illegality of their actions, anything that makes their actions seem fundamentally different from what the enemy does. For example, torture is something that only villains like Idi Amin or Saddam Hussein do. But as John Conroy showed in *Unspeakable Acts, Ordinary People,* it is not only interrogators in undemocratic countries who have violated the Geneva Convention's prohibitions against "violence to life and person, in particular murder of all kinds, mutilation, cruel treatment and torture . . . [and] outrages upon personal dignity, in particular, humiliating and degrading treatment." In his investigation of documented cases of abuse of prisoners, Conroy found that almost every military or police official he interviewed, whether British, South African, Israeli, or American, justified their practices by saying, in effect, our torture is never as severe and deadly as their torture:

> Bruce Moore-King [of South Africa] told me that when he administered electrical torture he never attacked the genitals, as torturers elsewhere are wont to do . . . Hugo Garcia told me the Argentine torturers were far worse than the Uruguayan. Omri Kochva assured

me that the men of the Natal battalion had not descended to the level of the Americans in Vietnam. . . . The British comforted themselves with the rationalization that their methods were nothing compared to the suffering created by the IRA. The Israelis regularly argue that their methods pale in comparison to the torture employed by Arab states.[13]

In the aftermath of Abu Ghraib, impartial investigations revealed that American interrogators and their allies have been using sleep deprivation, prolonged isolation, waterboarding, sexual humiliation, induced hypothermia, beatings, and other harsh methods on terrorist suspects, not only at Abu Ghraib but also at Guantánamo Bay and "black sites" in other countries. How to reduce the dissonance caused by the information that America, too, has been systematically violating the Geneva Convention? One way is to say that if we do it, it isn't torture. "We do not torture," said George Bush, when he was confronted with evidence that we do. "We use an alternative set of procedures." A second way to reduce dissonance is to say that if we do torture anyone, it's justified. The prisoners at Abu Ghraib deserved everything they got, said Senator James Inhofe (R-OK), because "they're murderers, they're terrorists, they're insurgents. Many of them probably have American blood on their hands." He seemed unaware that most of the prisoners had been picked up for arbitrary reasons or minor crimes, and were never formally accused. Indeed, several military intelligence officers told the International Committee of the Red Cross that between 70 and 90 percent of the Iraqi detainees had been arrested by mistake.[14]

The universal justification for torture is the ticking-time-bomb excuse. As the columnist Charles Krauthammer put it, "A terrorist has planted a nuclear bomb in New York City. It will go off in one hour. A million people will die. You capture the terrorist. He knows where it is. He's not talking. Question: If you have the slightest belief that hanging this man by his thumbs will get you the information to save a million people, are you permitted to do it?" Yes, says Krauthammer, and not only are you permitted to, it's your moral duty.[15] You don't have time to call the Geneva Convention people and ask them if it's okay; you will do whatever you can to get the terrorist to tell you the bomb's location.

Few deny that the ticking-time-bomb justification for torture would be reasonable under those circumstances. The trouble is that those circumstances are very rare, so the "saving lives" excuse starts being used even when there is no ticking and there is no bomb. Secretary of State Condoleezza Rice, on a visit to Germany where she was bombarded by protests from European leaders about the American use of torture on terrorist suspects held in secret jails, denied that any torture was being used. Then she added that her critics should realize that interrogations of these suspects have produced information that "stopped terrorist attacks and saved innocent lives— in Europe as well as in the United States."[16] She seemed unconcerned that these interrogations have also ruined innocent lives. Rice admitted that "mistakes were made" when the United States abducted an innocent German citizen on suspicions of terrorism and subjected him to harsh and demeaning treatment for five months.

Once torture is justified in rare cases, it is easier to justify it in others: Let's torture not only this bastard we are sure knows where the bomb is, but this other bastard who *might* know where the bomb is, and also this bastard who might have some general information that could be useful in five years, and also this other guy who might be a bastard only we aren't sure. William Schulz, director of Amnesty International, observed that according to credible Israeli, international, and Palestinian human-rights organizations, Israelis used methods of interrogation from 1987 to 1993 that constituted torture. "While originally justified on the grounds of finding 'ticking bombs,'" he said, "the use of such methods of torture became routine."[17] A sergeant in the U.S. Army's 82nd Airborne Division described how this process happens in treating Iraqi detainees:

The "Murderous Maniacs" was what they called us at our camp. . . . When [the detainees] came in, it was like a game. You know, how far could you make this guy go before he passes out or just collapses on you. From stress positions to keeping them up two days straight, depriving them of food, water, whatever. . . . We were told by intel that these guys were bad, but sometimes they were wrong.[18]

"Sometimes they were wrong," the sergeant says, but nonetheless we treated them all the same way.

The debate about torture has properly focused on its legality, its morality, and its utility. As social psychologists, we want to add one additional concern: what torture does to the individual perpetrator and to the ordinary citizens who go along with it. Most people want to believe that their government is working in their behalf, that it knows what it's doing, and that it's doing the right thing. Therefore, if our government decides that torture is necessary in the war against terrorism, most citizens, to avoid dissonance, will agree. Yet, over time, that is how the moral conscience of a nation deteriorates. Once people take that first small step off the pyramid in the direction of justifying abuse and torture, they are on their way to hardening their hearts and minds in ways that might never be undone. Uncritical patriotism, the kind that reduces the dissonance caused by information that their government has done something immoral and illegal, greases the slide down the pyramid.

Once a perpetrator has decided on a course of action, he or she will justify that decision in ways that avoid any conflict between "We are the good guys" and "We are doing some awful things." Even the most awful guys think they are good guys. During his four-year trial for war crimes, crimes against humanity, and genocide, Slobodan Milosevic, the "Butcher of the Balkans," justified his policy of ethnic cleansing that caused the deaths of more than 200,000 Croats, Bosnian Muslims, and Albanians. He was not responsible for those deaths, he kept repeating at his trial; Serbs had been victims of Muslim propaganda. War is war; he was only responding to the aggression *they* perpetrated against the innocent Serbians. Riccardo Orizio interviewed seven other dictators, including Idi Amin, Jean-Claude "Baby Doc" Duvalier, Mira Markovic (the "Red Witch," Milosevic's wife), and Jean-Bédel Bokassa of the Central African Republic (known to his people as the Ogre of Berengo). Every one of them claimed that everything they did—torturing or murdering their opponents, blocking free elections, starving their citizens, looting their nation's wealth, launching genocidal wars—was done for the good of their country. The alternative, they said, was chaos, anarchy, and bloodshed. Far from seeing themselves as despots, they saw themselves as self-sacrificing patriots.[19] "The degree of cognitive dissonance involved in being a person who oppresses people out of love for them," wrote Louis Menand, "is summed up in a poster that Baby Doc Duvalier had put up in Haiti. It read, 'I should like to stand before the tribunal of history as the person who irreversibly founded democracy in Haiti.' And it was signed, 'Jean-Claude Duvalier, president-for-life.' "[20]

If the good-of-the-country justification isn't enough, there is always that eternally popular dissonance reducer: "They started it." Even Hitler said they started it, "they" being the victorious nations of World War I who humiliated Germany with the Treaty of Versailles, and Jewish "vermin" who were undermining Germany from within. The problem is, how far back do you want to go to show that the other guy started it? As our opening example of the Iran hostage crisis suggests, victims have long memories, and they can call on real or imagined episodes from the recent or distant past to justify their desire to retaliate now. For example, in the centuries of war between Muslims and Christians, sometimes simmering and sometimes erupting, who are the perpetrators and who the victims? There is no simple answer, but let's examine how each side has justified its actions.

When, after 9/11, George Bush announced that he was launching a crusade against terrorism, most Americans welcomed the metaphor.

In the West, *crusade* has positive connotations, associated with the good guys—think of the Billy Graham Crusades; Holy Cross's football team, the Crusaders; and, of course, Batman and Robin, the Caped Crusaders. The actual historical Crusades in the Middle East began more than a thousand years ago and ended in the late thirteenth century; could anything be more "over" than that? Not to most Muslims, who were angered and alarmed by Bush's use of the term. For them, the Crusades created feelings of persecution and victimization that persist to the present. The First Crusade of 1095, during which Christians captured Muslim-controlled Jerusalem and mercilessly slaughtered almost all its inhabitants, might just as well have occurred last month, it's that vivid in the collective memory.

The Crusades indeed gave European Christians license to massacre hundreds of thousands of Muslim "infidels." (Thousands of Jews were also slaughtered as the pilgrims marched through Europe to Jerusalem, which is why some Jewish historians call the Crusades "the first Holocaust.") From the West's current standpoint, the Crusades were unfortunate, but, like all wars, they produced benefits all around; for instance, the Crusades opened the door to cultural and trade agreements between the Christian West and the Muslim East. Some books have gone so far as to argue that Christians were merely defending themselves and their interests from the holy wars that had motivated the Muslim invasion of formerly Christian countries. For example, the cover of Robert Spencer's book, *The Politically Incorrect Guide to Islam (and the Crusades),* states boldly: "The Crusades were defensive conflicts." So we actually were not the perpetrators that so many Muslims think we were. We were the victims.

Who were the victims? It depends on how many years, decades, and centuries you take into account. By the middle of the tenth century, more than a century before the Crusades began, half the Christian world had been conquered by Muslim Arab armies: the city of Jerusalem and countries in which Christianity had been established for centuries, including Egypt, Sicily, Spain, and Turkey. In 1095, Pope Urban II called on the French aristocracy to wage holy war against all Muslims. A pilgrimage to regain Jerusalem would give European towns an opportunity to extend their trade routes; it would organize the newly affluent warrior aristocracy and mobilize the peasants into a unified force; and it would unite the Christian world, which had been split into Eastern and Roman factions. The Pope assured his forces that killing a Muslim was an act of Christian penance. Anyone killed in battle, the Pope promised, would bypass thousands of years of torture in purgatory and go directly to heaven. Does this incentive to generate martyrs who will die for your cause sound familiar? It has everything but the virgins.

The First Crusade was enormously successful in economic terms for European Christians; inevitably, it provoked the Muslims to organize a response. By the end of the twelfth century, the Muslim general Saladin had recaptured Jerusalem and retaken almost every state the Crusaders had won. (Saladin signed a peace treaty with King Richard I of England in 1192.) So the Crusades, brutal and bloody as they were, were preceded and followed by Muslim conquests. Who started it?

Likewise, the intractable battles between Israelis and Arabs have their own litany of original causes. On July 12, 2006, Hezbollah militants kidnapped two Israeli reservists, Ehud Goldwasser and Eldad Regev. Israel retaliated, sending rockets into Hezbollah-controlled areas of Lebanon, killing many civilians. Historian Timothy Garton Ash, observing the subsequent retaliations of both sides, wrote, "When and where did this war begin?" On July 12, or a month earlier, when Israeli shells killed seven Palestinian civilians? The preceding January, when Hamas won the Palestinian elections? In 1982, when Israel invaded Lebanon? In 1979, with the fundamentalist revolution in Iran? In 1948, with the creation of the state of Israel? Ash's own answer to "What started this?" is the virulent

European anti-Semitism of the nineteenth and twentieth centuries, which included Russian pogroms, French mobs screaming "Down with Jews!" at the trial of Captain Alfred Dreyfus, and the Holocaust. The "radical European rejection" of the Jews, he writes, produced the driving forces of Zionism, Jewish emigration to Palestine, and creation of the state of Israel:

> Even as we criticize the way the Israeli military is killing Lebanese civilians and U.N. monitors in the name of recovering Gold-wasser . . . , we must remember that all of this almost certainly would not be happening if some Europeans had not attempted, a few decades back, to remove everyone named Goldwasser from the face of Europe—if not the Earth.[21]

And Ash is only moving the start date back a couple of centuries. Others would move it back a couple of millennia.

Once people commit themselves to an opinion about "Who started this?," whatever the "this" may be—a family quarrel or an international conflict—they become less able to accept information that is dissonant with their position. Once they have decided who the perpetrator is and who the victim is, their ability to empathize with the other side is weakened, even destroyed. How many arguments have you been in that sputtered out with unanswerable "but what about?"s? As soon as you describe the atrocities that one side has committed, someone will protest: "But what about the other side's atrocities?"

We can all understand why victims would want to retaliate. But retaliation often makes the original perpetrator minimize the severity and harm of its side's actions and also claim the mantle of victim, thereby setting in motion a cycle of oppression and revenge. "Every successful revolution," observed the historian Barbara Tuchman, "puts on in time the robes of the tyrant it has deposed." Why not? The victors, former victims, feel justified.

Truth and Reconciliation

In our favorite version of an ancient Buddhist parable, a group of monks is returning to their monastery from a long pilgrimage. Over high mountains and across low valleys they trek, until one day they come to a raging river, where a beautiful young woman stands. She approaches the eldest monk and says, "Forgive me, Roshi, but would you be so kind as to carry me across the river? I cannot swim, and if I remain here or attempt to cross on my own I shall surely perish." The monk smiles at her warmly and says, "Of course I will help you." With that he picks her up and carries her across the river. On the other side, he gently sets her down. She thanks him, departs, and the monks continue their journey.

After five more days of arduous travel, the monks arrive at their monastery, and the moment they do, they turn on the elder in a fury. "How could you do that?" they admonish him. "You broke your vow—you touched that woman!"

The elder replies, "I only carried her across the river. You have been carrying her for five days."

The monks carried the woman in their hearts for days; some perpetrators and victims carry their burdens of guilt, grief, anger, and revenge for years. What does it take to set those burdens down? Anyone who has tried to intervene between warring couples or nations knows how painfully difficult it is for both sides to let go of self-justification, especially after years of fighting, defending their position, and moving farther down the pyramid away from compromise and common ground. Mediators and negotiators therefore have two challenging tasks: to require perpetrators to acknowledge and atone for the harm they caused; and to require victims to relinquish the impulse for revenge while helping them feel validated in the harm they have suffered.

For example, in their work with married couples in which one partner had deeply hurt or betrayed the other, clinical psychologists Andrew Christensen and Neil Jacobson described three possible ways out of the emotional impasse. In the first, the perpetrator unilaterally puts aside his or her own feelings and, realizing that the victim's anger masks enormous suffering, responds to that suffering with genuine remorse and apology. In the second, the victim unilaterally lets go of his or her repeated, angry accusations—after all, the point has been made—and expresses pain rather than anger, a response that may make the perpetrator more empathic and caring rather than defensive. "Either one of these actions, if taken unilaterally, is difficult and for many people impossible," Christensen and Jacobson say.[22] The third way, they suggest, is the hardest but most hopeful for a long-term resolution of the conflict: Both sides drop their self-justifications and agree on steps they can take together to move forward. If it is only the perpetrator who apologizes and tries to atone, it may not be done honestly or in a way that assuages and gives closure to the victim's suffering. But if it is only the victim who lets go and forgives, the perpetrator may have no incentive to change, and therefore may continue behaving unfairly or callously.[23]

Christensen and Jacobson were speaking of two individuals in conflict. But their analysis, in our view, applies to group conflicts as well, where the third way is not merely the best way; it is the only way. In South Africa, the end of apartheid could easily have left a legacy of self-justifying rage on the part of the whites who supported the status quo and the privileges it conferred on them, and of self-justified fury on the part of the blacks who had been its victims. It took the courage of a white man, Frederik de Klerk, and a black man, Nelson Mandela, to avert the bloodbath that has followed in the wake of most revolutions, and to create the conditions that made it possible for their country to move forward as a democracy.

De Klerk, who had been elected president in 1989, knew that a violent revolution was all but inevitable. The fight against apartheid was escalating; sanctions imposed by other countries were having a significant impact on the nation's economy; supporters of the banned African National Congress were becoming increasingly violent, killing and torturing people whom they believed were collaborating with the white regime. De Klerk could have tightened the noose by instituting even more repressive policies in the desperate hope of preserving white power. Instead, he revoked the ban on the ANC and freed Mandela from the prison in which he had spent twenty-seven years. For his part, Mandela could have allowed his anger to consume him; he could have emerged from that prison with a determination to take revenge that many would have found entirely legitimate. Instead, he relinquished anger for the sake of the goal to which he had devoted his life. "If you want to make peace with your enemy, you have to work with your enemy," said Mandela. "Then he becomes your partner." In 1993, both men shared the Nobel Peace Prize, and the following year Mandela was elected president of South Africa.

Virtually the first act of the new democracy was the establishment of the Truth and Reconciliation Commission, chaired by Archbishop Desmond Tutu. (Three other commissions, on human rights violations, amnesty, and reparation and rehabilitation, were also created.) The goal of the TRC was to give victims of brutality a forum where their accounts would be heard and vindicated, where their dignity and sense of justice would be restored, and where they could express their grievances in front of the perpetrators themselves. In exchange for amnesty, the perpetrators had to drop their denials, evasions, and self-justifications and admit the harm they had done, including torture and murder. The commission emphasized the "need for understanding but not for vengeance, a need for reparation but not for retaliation, a need for *ubuntu* [humanity toward others] but not for victimization."

The goals of the TRC were inspiring, if not entirely honored in practice. The commission produced grumbling, mockery, protests, and anger. Many black victims of apartheid, such as the family of activist Stephen Biko, who had been murdered in prison, were furious at the provisions of amnesty to the perpetrators. Many white perpetrators did not apologize with anything remotely like true feelings of remorse, and many white supporters of apartheid were not interested in listening to the broadcast confessions of their peers. South Africa has hardly become a paradise; it is still suffering from poverty and high crime rates. Yet it averted a bloodbath. When psychologist Solomon Schimmel traveled there, interviewing people across the political and cultural spectrum for his book on victims of injustice and atrocities, he expected to hear them describe their rage and desire for revenge. "What most impressed me overall," he reported, "was the remarkable lack of overt rancor and hatred between blacks and whites, and the concerted effort to create a society in which racial harmony and economic justice will prevail."[24]

Understanding without vengeance, reparation without retaliation, are possible only if we are willing to stop justifying our own position. Many years after the Vietnam War, veteran William Broyles Jr. traveled back to Vietnam to try to resolve his feelings about the horrors he had seen there and those he had committed. He went because, he said, he wanted to meet his former enemies "as people, not abstractions." In a small village that had been a Marine base camp, he met a woman who had been with the Viet Cong. As they talked, Broyles realized that her husband had been killed at exactly the time that he and his men had been patrolling. "My men and I might have killed your husband," he said. She looked at him steadily and said, "But that was during the war. The war is over now. Life goes on."[25] Later, Broyles reflected on his healing visit to Vietnam:

I used to have nightmares. Since I've been back from that trip, I haven't had any. Maybe that sounds too personal to support any larger conclusions, but it tells me that to end a war you have to return to the same personal relationships you would have had with people before it. You do make peace. Nothing is constant in history.

CHAPTER 8

o   o   o

Letting Go and Owning Up

A man travels many miles to consult the wisest guru in the land. When he arrives, he asks the wise man: "Oh, wise guru, what is the secret of a happy life?"

"Good judgment," says the guru.

"But oh, wise guru," says the man, "how do I achieve good judgment?"

"Bad judgment," says the guru.

ON JANUARY 26, 2006, an astonishing cultural event occurred: Oprah Winfrey devoted an entire show to apologizing for making a mistake. Oprah had endorsed James Frey and his self-proclaimed memoir of drug addiction and recovery, *A Million Little Pieces,* an endorsement that had boosted Frey's sales into the millions. On January 8, The Smoking Gun, an investigative Web site, had shown that Frey had fabricated many parts of his story and greatly embellished others. Oprah's first reaction, faced with this dissonant information—"I supported and praised this guy, and now it turns out he lied and deceived me"—was to do what most of us would be inclined to do: Keep supporting the guy, to smother the feeling that you have been duped. Accordingly, when Larry King interviewed Frey after The Smoking Gun report had appeared, Oprah called in to the show and justified her support of Frey: "The underlying message of redemption in James Frey's memoir still resonates with me," she said, "and I know that it resonates with millions of other people." Besides, she added, if mistakes were made, they were the publisher's; she and her producers had relied on the publisher's claim that this was a work of nonfiction.

There Oprah was, at the top of the moral pyramid, having taken a first step in the direction of maintaining her original commitment to Frey. Yet instead of continuing to justify that decision, sliding further down the pyramid claiming "the publisher did it" or "my producers were to blame" or "the emotional truth of this book is truer than the true truth," and other buck-passing maneuvers so common in our culture these days, Oprah stopped in her tracks. Perhaps she personally had a change of heart; perhaps her producers yanked her back from the ledge, advising her that her defense of Frey was not helping her reputation. But regardless of whether Oprah was heeding her conscience or her producers, the next decision was surely hers. And that decision made her the poster girl for taking responsibility for a mistake and correcting it in a straight-talking, nonmealymouthed way. She brought Frey onto her show and started right off with an apology for her call to Larry King: "I regret that phone call," she said to her audience. "I made a mistake and I left the impression that the truth does not matter. And I am deeply sorry about that, because that is not what I believe. I called in because I love the message of this book and—at the time, and every day I was reading e-mail after e-mail from so many people who have been inspired by it. And I have to say that I allowed that to cloud my judgment. And so to everyone who has challenged me on this issue of truth, you are absolutely right."[1]

She turned to Frey and continued: "It is difficult for me to talk to you, because I really feel duped. . . . I have been really embarrassed, but now I feel that you conned us all." Later in the show, she told Richard Cohen, a *Washington Post* columnist who had called Frey a liar and said of Oprah that she was "not only wrong, but deluded," that she was impressed with what he said, because "sometimes criticism can be very helpful, so thank you very much. You were right, I was wrong." [*You were right, I was wrong?*] How often have Americans heard that euphonious sentence from their spouses and parents, let alone from television personalities, pundits, and politicians? Cohen practically had to go lie down to recover. "The year is very new," he told Oprah, "but I still name you Mensch of the Year, for standing up and saying you were wrong. [That] takes a lot of courage, all right? I've never done that."

Throughout the show, Oprah did not let James Frey off the hook. Frey kept trying to justify his actions, saying, "I think I made a lot of mistakes in writing the book and, you know, promoting the book." Oprah went ballistic. She was the one who made mistakes, she reminded him, by calling Larry King and "leaving the impression that the truth doesn't matter"; but he lied. "Do you think you lied, or do you think you made a mistake?" she asked. Frey said, hesitantly, "I—I think probably both."

> *Frey:* I mean, I feel like I came here and I have been honest with you. I have, you know, essentially admitted to . . .
> *Winfrey:* Lying.

Toward the end of the hour, the *New York Times* columnist Frank Rich appeared on the show to echo Richard Cohen, giving kudos to Oprah for speaking up, for taking a stand for books that do not distort the truth in order to sell. "The hardest thing to do is admit a mistake," he said. Oprah told him she didn't want praise. "It really wasn't that hard," she said.

o   o   o

Sometimes, as we have seen throughout this book, it really is that hard. It was for Linda Ross, the psychotherapist who had practiced recovered-memory therapy until she realized how misguided she had been; for Grace, whose false recovered memories tore her family apart for years; for Thomas Vanes, the district attorney who learned that a man he had convicted of rape, who had spent twenty years in prison, was innocent; for the couples and political leaders who manage to break free from the spirals of rage and retaliation. And it is hardest of all for those whose mistakes cost lives, especially the lives of friends and coworkers they know and care about.

Certainly, N. Wayne Hale Jr. knows what we mean. Hale had been launch integration manager at NASA in 2003, when seven astronauts died in the explosion of the space shuttle *Columbia.* In a public e-mail to the space shuttle team, Hale took full responsibility for the disaster:

> I had the opportunity and the information and I failed to make use of it. I don't know what an inquest or a court of law would say, but I stand condemned in the court of my own conscience to be guilty of not preventing the Columbia disaster. We could discuss the particulars: inattention, incompetence, distraction, lack of conviction, lack of understanding, a lack of backbone, laziness. The bottom line is that I failed to understand what I was being told; I failed to stand up and be counted. Therefore look no further; I am guilty of allowing Columbia to crash.[2]

These courageous individuals take us straight into the heart of dissonance and its innermost irony: The mind wants to protect itself from the pain of dissonance with the balm of self-justification; but the soul wants to confess. To reduce dissonance, most of us put an enormous amount of mental and physical energy into protecting ourselves and propping up our self-esteem when it sags under the realization that we have been foolish, gullible, mistaken, corrupted, or otherwise human. And yet, much of the time, all this investment of energy is surprisingly unnecessary. Linda Ross is still a psychotherapist; a better one. Thomas Vanes is still a successful prosecutor. Grace got her parents back. Wayne Hale was promoted to manager of the Space Shuttle program for NASA at the Johnson Space Center.

Imagine with us, for a moment, how you would feel if your partner, your grown child, or your parent said: "I want to take responsibility for that mistake I made; we have been quarreling about it all this time, and now I realize that you were right, and I was wrong." Or if your employer started a meeting by saying, "I want to hear every possible objection to this proposal before we go ahead with it—every mistake we might be making." Or if a district attorney held a press conference and said, "I made a horrendous mistake. I failed to reopen a case in which new evidence showed that I and my office sent an innocent man to prison. I will apologize, but being sorry is not enough. I will also reassess our procedures to reduce the likelihood of ever convicting an innocent person again."

How would you feel about these people? Would you lose respect for them? Chances are that if they are friends or relatives, you will feel relieved and delighted. "My God, Harry actually admitted he made a mistake! What a generous guy!" And if they are professionals or political leaders, you will probably feel reassured that you are in the capable hands of someone big enough to do the right thing, which is to learn from the wrong thing. The last American president to tell the country he had made a terrible mistake was John F. Kennedy in 1961. He had believed the claims and faulty intelligence reports of his top military advisers, who assured him that once

Americans invaded Cuba at the Bay of Pigs, the people would rise up in relief and joy and overthrow Castro. The invasion was a disaster, but Kennedy learned from it. He reorganized his intelligence system and determined that he would no longer accept uncritically the claims of his military advisers, a change that helped him steer the country successfully through the subsequent Cuban missile crisis. After the Bay of Pigs fiasco, Kennedy spoke to newspaper publishers and said: "This administration intends to be candid about its errors. For as a wise man once said, 'An error does not become a mistake until you refuse to correct it.' . . . Without debate, without criticism, no administration and no country can succeed—and no republic can survive." The final responsibility for the failure of the Bay of Pigs invasion was, he said, "mine, and mine alone." Kennedy's popularity soared.

We want to hear, we *long* to hear, "I screwed up. I will do my best to ensure that it will not happen again." Most of us are not impressed when a leader offers the form of Kennedy's admission without its essence, as in Ronald Reagan's response to the Iran-Contra scandal, which may be summarized as "I didn't do anything wrong myself, but it happened on my watch, so, well, I guess I'll take responsibility."[3] That doesn't cut it. Daniel Yankelovich, the highly regarded survey researcher, reports that although polls find that the public has an abiding mistrust of our major institutions, right below that cynicism is a "genuine hunger" for honesty and integrity. "People want organizations to operate transparently," he says, "to show a human face to the outside world, to live up to their own professed standards of behavior, and to demonstrate a commitment to the larger society."[4]

That longing to hear authorities own up, without weaseling or blowing smoke, underlies the recent movement in the health-care system to encourage doctors and hospitals to admit and correct their mistakes. (We are talking about honest mistakes, human error, not about repeated acts of incompetent malpractice.) Traditionally, of course, most doctors have been adamant in their refusal to admit mistakes in diagnosis, procedure, or treatment on the self-justifying grounds that doing so would encourage malpractice suits. They are wrong. Studies of hospitals across the country have found that patients are actually less likely to sue when doctors admit and apologize for mistakes, and when changes are implemented so that future patients will not be harmed in the same way. "Being assured that it won't happen again is very important to patients, more so than many caregivers seem to appreciate," says Lucian Leape, a physician and professor of health policy at the Harvard School of Public Health. "It gives meaning to patients' suffering."[5]

Doctors' second self-justification for not disclosing mistakes is that doing so would puncture their aura of infallibility and omniscience, which, they maintain, is essential to their patients' confidence in them and compliance. They are wrong about this, too. The image of infallibility that many physicians try to cultivate often backfires, coming across as arrogance and even heartlessness. "Why can't they just tell me the truth, and apologize?" patients and their families lament. In fact, when competent physicians come clean about their mistakes, they are still seen as competent, but also as human beings capable of error. In one of his essays on medicine for the *New York Times,* physician Richard A. Friedman beautifully summarized the difficulties and benefits of owning up. "Like every doctor," he began, "I've made plenty of mistakes along the way." In one case, he failed to anticipate a potentially dangerous drug interaction, and his patient ended up in the intensive care unit. (She survived.) "Needless to say, I was distraught about what had happened," he says. "I wasn't sure what went wrong, but I felt that it was my fault, so I apologized to the patient and her family. They were shaken and angry, and they quite naturally blamed me and the hospital . . . but in the end they decided this was an unfortunate but 'honest' medical error and took no legal action." The disclosure of fallibility humanizes doctors and builds trust, Friedman concluded. "In the end, most patients will forgive their doctor for an error of the head, but rarely for one of the heart."[6]

Recipients of an honest admission of error are not the only beneficiaries. When we ourselves are forced to face our own mistakes and take responsibility for them, the result can be an exhilarating, liberating experience. Management consultant Bob Kardon told us about the time he led a seminar at the National Council of Nonprofit Associations' conference. The seminar was entitled, simply, "Mistakes," and twenty leaders of the statewide associations attended. Kardon told them that the only ground rules for the session were that participants had to tell about a mistake they had made as a leader, and not to try to clean it up by telling how they had corrected it—or dodged responsibility for it. He did not allow them to justify what they did. "In other words," he told them, "stay with the mistake":

> As we went around the circle the magnitude of the mistakes burgeoned. By the time we reached the halfway point these executives were copping to major errors, like failing to get a grant request in on time and costing their organization hundreds of thousands of dollars in lost revenue. Participants would often get uncomfortable hanging out there with the mistake, and try to tell a redeeming anecdote about a success or recovery from the mistake. I enforced the ground rules and cut off the face-saving attempt. A half hour into the session laughter filled the room, that nearly hysterical laughter of release of a great burden. It got so raucous that attendees at other seminars came to our session to see what the commotion was all about.

Kardon's exercise illuminates just how difficult it is to say, "Boy, did I mess up," without the protective postscript of self-justification—to say "I dropped a routine fly ball with the bases loaded" rather than "I dropped the ball because the sun was in my eyes" or "because a bird flew by" or "because it was windy" or "because a fan called me a jerk." A friend returning from a day in traffic school told us that as participants went around the room, reporting the violations that had brought them there, a miraculous coincidence occurred: Not one of them was responsible for breaking the law. They all had justifications for why they were speeding, had ignored a stop sign, ran a red light, or made an illegal U-turn. He became so dismayed by the litany of flimsy excuses that, when his turn came, he was embarrassed to give in to the same impulse. He said, "I didn't stop at a stop sign. I was entirely wrong and I got caught." There was a moment's silence, and then the room erupted in cheers for his candor.

There are plenty of good reasons for admitting mistakes, starting with the simple likelihood that you will probably be found out anyway—by your family, your company, your colleagues, your enemies, your biographer. Psychology professor Bob Abelson once had a graduate student who was persisting with an idea he was testing experimentally, hoping against hope it would come out the way he wanted it to. Finally Abelson said to him gently, "Would you rather admit you're wrong now or wait until someone else proves it?" But there are more positive reasons for owning up. Other people will like you more. Someone else may be able to pick up your fumble and run with it; your error might inspire someone else's solution. Children will realize that everyone screws up on occasion and that even adults have to say "I'm sorry." And if you can admit a mistake when it is the size of an acorn, it is easier to repair than when it has become the size of a tree, with deep, wide-ranging roots.

If letting go of self-justification and admitting mistakes is so beneficial to the mind and relationships, why aren't more of us doing it? If we are so grateful to others when they do it, why don't we do it more often? First, we don't do it because, as we have seen, most of the time we aren't even aware that we need to. Self-justification purrs along automatically, just beneath consciousness, protecting us from the dissonant realization that we did anything wrong. "Mistake? What mistake? I didn't make a mistake . . . The tree jumped in front of my car . . . And what do I have to be sorry about, anyway? She started it . . . He stole it . . . Not my fault." Second, America is a mistake-phobic culture, one that links mistakes with incompetence and stupidity. So even when people are aware of having made a mistake, they are often reluctant to admit it, even to themselves, because they take it as evidence that they are a blithering idiot. If we really want more people to take responsibility for their mistakes and then strive to correct them, we need to overcome these two impediments.

As we have tracked the trail of self-justification through the territories of family, memory, therapy, law, prejudice, conflict, and war, two lessons from dissonance theory emerge: First, the ability to reduce dissonance helps us in countless ways, preserving our beliefs, confidence, decisions, self-esteem, and well-being. Second, this ability can get us into big trouble. People will pursue self-destructive courses of action to protect the wisdom of their initial decisions. They will treat people they have hurt even more harshly, because they convince themselves that their victims deserve it. They will cling to outdated and sometimes harmful procedures in their work. They will support torturers and tyrants who are on the right side—that is, theirs. People who are insecure in their religious beliefs may feel the impulse to silence and harass those who disagree with them, because their mere existence arouses the painful dissonance of doubt.

The need to reduce dissonance is a universal mental mechanism, but that doesn't mean we are doomed to be controlled by it. Human beings may not be eager to change, but we have the ability to change, and the fact that many of our self-protective delusions and blind spots are built into the way the brain works is no justification for not trying. Is the brain designed to defend our beliefs and convictions? Fine—the brain wants us to stock up on sugar, too, but most of us learn to enjoy vegetables. Is the brain designed to make us flare in anger when we think we are being attacked? Fine—but most of us learn to count to ten and find alternatives to beating the other guy with a cudgel. An appreciation of how dissonance works, in ourselves and others, gives us some ways to override our wiring. And protect us from those who can't.

Living with Dissonance

Perhaps the greatest lesson of dissonance theory is that we can't wait around for people to have moral conversions, personality transplants, sudden changes of heart, or new insights that will cause them to sit up straight, admit error, and do the right thing. Most human beings and institutions are going to do everything in their power to reduce dissonance in ways that are favorable to them, that allow them to justify their mistakes and maintain business as usual. They will not be grateful for the evidence that their methods of interrogation have put innocent people in prison for life. They are not going to thank us for pointing out to them why their study of some new drug, into whose development they have poured millions, is fatally flawed. And no matter how deftly or gently we do it, even the people who love us dearly are not going to be amused when we correct their fondest self-serving memory . . . with the facts.

The ultimate correction for the tunnel vision that afflicts all of us mortals is more light. Because most of us are not self-correcting and because our blind spots keep us from knowing that we need to be, external procedures must be in place to correct the errors that human beings will inevitably make and to reduce the chances of future ones. In the legal domain, we have seen that mandatory videotaping of all

forensic interviews is one obvious and relatively inexpensive correc-
tive to the confirmation bias; any bias or coercion that creeps in can
be assessed later by independent observers. But it is not only potential police bias we need to worry about; it is also prosecutorial bias.
Unlike physicians, who can be sued for malpractice if they amputate
the wrong arm, prosecutors generally have immunity from civil suits
and are subject to almost no judicial review. Most of their decisions
occur outside of public scrutiny, because fully 95 percent of the cases
that the police hand over to a prosecutor's office never reach a jury.
But power without accountability is a recipe for disaster in any
arena, and in the criminal justice system that combination permits
individuals and even entire departments to do anything for a win,
with self-justification to smooth the way.[7] When district attorneys do
actively seek to release an inmate found to be innocent (as opposed
to grudgingly accepting a court order to do so), it is usually because,
like Robert Morgenthau, who reopened the Central Park Jogger
case, and the Sacramento district attorneys who prosecuted Richard
Tuite, they were not the original prosecutors and have the power
to withstand the heat that such a decision often produces. That is
why independent commissions must often be empowered to investigate charges of corruption in a department or determine whether
to reopen a case. Their members must have no conflicts of interest,
no decisions to justify, no cronies to protect, and no dissonance to
reduce.[8]

Few organizations, however, welcome outside supervision and
correction. If those in power prefer to maintain their blind spots at
all costs, then impartial review boards must improve their vision,
against their will, if it comes to that. The scientific model of independent, external peer review is an excellent paradigm, although
even it has required tinkering of late. Scientific and medical journals,
aware of the taint on research when conflicts of interest are involved
and having been deceived by a few investigators who faked their

data, are instituting stronger measures to reduce the chances of publishing biased, corrupt, or fraudulent research. Many scientists are calling for greater transparency in the review process, the same solution that reformers of the criminal-justice system are seeking. If we human beings are inevitably afflicted with tunnel vision, at least our errors are more likely to be reduced, or corrected, if the tunnel is made of glass.

Organizational consultants Warren Bennis and Burt Nanus suggest that institutions can be designed to reward admissions of mistakes as part of the organizational culture, rather than, as now, making it uncomfortable for people to own up. This is a change, naturally, that must come from the top. Bennis and Nanus offer a story about the legendary Tom Watson Sr., IBM's founder and its guiding inspiration for over forty years. "A promising junior executive of IBM was involved in a risky venture for the company and managed to lose over $10 million in the gamble," they wrote. "It was a disaster. When Watson called the nervous executive into his office, the young man blurted out, 'I guess you want my resignation?' Watson said, 'You can't be serious. We've just spent $10 million educating you!'"[9]

But what are we supposed to do in our everyday lives? Call an external review board of cousins and in-laws to adjudicate every family quarrel? Videotape all parental interrogations of their teenagers? In our private relationships, we are on our own, and that calls for some self-awareness. Once we understand how and when we need to reduce dissonance, we can become more vigilant about the process and often nip it in the bud; like Oprah, we can catch ourselves before we slide too far down the pyramid. By looking at our actions critically and dispassionately, as if we were observing someone else, we stand a chance of breaking out of the cycle of action followed by self-justification, followed by more committed action. We can learn to put a little space between what we feel and how we respond, insert a moment of reflection, and think about whether we really want to buy that canoe in January, really want to send good money after bad, really want to hold on to a belief that is unfettered by facts. We might even change our minds before our brains freeze our thoughts into consistent patterns.

Becoming aware that we are in a state of dissonance can help us make sharper, smarter, conscious choices instead of letting automatic, self-protective mechanisms resolve our discomfort in our favor. Suppose your unpleasant, aggressive coworker has just made an innovative suggestion at a group meeting. You could say to yourself, "An ignorant jerk like her could not possibly have a good idea about anything," and shoot her suggestion down in flames because you dislike the woman so much (and, you admit it, you feel competitive with her for your manager's approval). Or you could give yourself some breathing room and ask: "Could the idea be a smart one? How would I feel about it if it came from my ally on this project?" If it is a good idea, you might support your coworker's proposal even if you continue to dislike her as a person. You keep the message separate from the messenger.

The goal is to become aware of the two dissonant cognitions that are causing distress and find a way to resolve them constructively, or, when we can't, learn to live with them. In 1985, Israeli prime minister Shimon Peres was thrown into dissonance by an action taken by his ally and friend Ronald Reagan. Peres was angry because Reagan had accepted an invitation to pay a state visit to the Kolmeshohe Cemetery at Bitburg, Germany, to symbolize the two nations' postwar reconciliation. The announcement of the proposed visit enraged Holocaust survivors and many others, because forty-nine Nazi Waffen-SS officers were buried there. Reagan, however, did not back down from his decision to visit the cemetery. When reporters asked Peres what he thought of Reagan's action, Peres neither condemned Reagan personally nor minimized the seriousness of the visit to Bitburg. Instead, Peres took a third course. "When a friend makes a mistake," he said, "the friend remains a friend, and the mistake remains a mistake."[10]

Consider for a moment the benefits of being able to separate dissonant thoughts as clearly as Peres did: Friendships that might otherwise be terminated in a huff are preserved; mistakes that might otherwise be dismissed as unimportant are properly criticized and their perpetrator held accountable. People could remain passionately committed to their nation, religion, political party, spouse, and family, yet understand that it is not disloyal to disagree with actions or policies they find inappropriate, misguided, or immoral.

In an online discussion for psychologists working in the field of trauma research and treatment, one young psychotherapist posted a note expressing his enthusiasm for a recent hot fad in psychotherapy. He was unprepared for the reaction from psychological scientists, who deluged him with the systematic research showing that the therapy's gimmick was ineffective and the theory behind it was spurious. Their response put him in big-time dissonance: "I've spent time, money, and effort on this new method and I'm getting excited about it" bumped into "but eminent scientists I admire tell me it's nonsense." The usual, knee-jerk dissonance-reducing strategy would be to dismiss the scientists as ivory-tower know-nothings. Instead, the young man replied with the open-mindedness of the scientist and the self-insight of the clinician, a model that might serve us all.

"Thanks for your thoughts and comments on this topic, even though they were hard to accept at first," he wrote. He read the research they recommended, and concluded that he had become so enamored of the new approach that he did not devote enough attention to studies that had evaluated it and found it wanting. "I used my own practice as validation," he admitted, "and allowed my thrill to overtake my critical thinking. It is part of the scientific attitude to change one's beliefs once they are discredited. Well, it's not an easy thing to do. Combine invested time, invested money, high hopes, high expectations, and a relative amount of pride, and you're up for quite a challenge when confronted with contradicting evidence. Very humbling this experience has been."[11]

Humbling, yes, but ultimately that's the point. Understanding how the mind yearns for consonance, and rejects information that questions our beliefs, decisions, or preferences, teaches us to be open to the possibility of error. It also helps us let go of the need to be right. Confidence is a fine and useful quality; none of us would want a physician who was forever wallowing in uncertainty and couldn't decide how to treat our illness, but we do want one who is open-minded and willing to learn. Nor would most of us wish to live without passions or convictions, which give our lives meaning and color, energy and hope. But the unbending need to be right inevitably produces self-righteousness. When confidence and convictions are un-leavened by humility, by an acceptance of fallibility, people can easily cross the line from healthy self-assurance to arrogance. In this book, we have met many who crossed that line: the psychiatrists who are certain that they can tell if a recovered memory is valid; the physicians and judges who are certain that they are above conflicts of interest; the police officers who are certain that they can tell if a suspect is lying; the prosecutors who are certain that they convicted the guilty party; the husbands and wives who are certain that their interpretation of events is the right one; the nations who are certain that their version of history is the only one.

All of us have hard decisions to make at times in our lives; not all of them will be right, and not all of them will be wise. Some are complicated, with consequences we could never have foreseen. If we can resist the temptation to justify our actions in a rigid, overconfident way, we can leave the door open to empathy and an appreciation of life's complexity, including the possibility that what was right for us might not have been right for others. "I know what hard decisions look like," says a woman we will call Betty.

When I decided to leave my husband of twenty years, that decision was right for one of my daughters—who said, "What took you so long?"—but a disaster for the other; she was angry at me for years. I worked hard in my mind and brain to resolve that conflict and to justify what I did. I blamed my daughter for not accepting it and understanding my reasons. By the end of my mental gymnastics I had turned myself into Mother Teresa and my daughter into a selfish, ungrateful brat. But over time, I couldn't keep it up. I missed her. I remembered her sweetness and understanding, and realized she wasn't a brat but a child who had been devastated by the divorce. And so finally I sat down with her. I told her that although I am still convinced that the divorce was the right decision for me, I understood now how much it had hurt her. I told her I was ready to listen. "Mom," she said, "let's go to Central Park for a picnic and talk, the way we did when I was a kid." And we did, and that was the beginning of our reconciliation. Nowadays, when I feel passionate that I am 100 percent right about a decision that others question, I look at it again; that's all.

Betty did not have to admit that she made a mistake; she didn't make a mistake. But she did have to let go of her need to be right.

Mistakes Were Made—by Me

> It is considered unhealthy in America to remember mistakes, neurotic to think about them, psychotic to dwell upon them.
>
> —playwright Lillian Hellman

Dissonance may be hardwired, but how we think about mistakes is not. After the disastrous bloodbath of Pickett's Charge at the Battle of Gettysburg, in which more than half of his 12,500 men were slaughtered by Union soldiers, Robert E. Lee said: "All this has been my fault. I asked more of my men than should have been asked of them."[12] Robert E. Lee was a great general who made a tragic miscalculation, but that mistake did not make him an incompetent military leader. If Robert E. Lee could take responsibility for an action that cost thousands of lives, why can't all those people in traffic school even admit they ran a red light?

Most Americans know they are supposed to say "we learn from our mistakes," but deep down, they don't believe it for a minute. They think that mistakes mean you are stupid. Combined with the culture's famous amnesia for anything that happened more than a month ago, this attitude means that people treat mistakes like hot potatoes, eager to get rid of them as fast as possible, even if they have to toss them in someone else's lap.

One lamentable consequence of the belief that mistakes equal stupidity is that when people do make a mistake, they don't learn from it. They throw good money after bad, and the con artists are right there to catch it. Do you know anyone who has been victimized by a scam? About a fourth of the entire American adult population has been taken in by one scam or another, some silly, some serious: sweepstakes offers of having won a million dollars, if only you send us the tax on that amount first; gold coins you can buy at a tenth of their market value; a miracle bed that will cure all your ailments, from headaches to arthritis. Every year, Americans lose more than $40 billion to telemarketing frauds alone, and older people are especially susceptible to them.

Con artists know all about dissonance and self-justification. They know that when people are caught between "I am a smart and capable person" and "I have spent thousands of dollars on magazine subscriptions I don't need and on bogus sweepstakes entries," few will reduce dissonance by deciding they aren't smart and capable. Instead, many will justify their spending that money by spending even more money to recoup their losses. This way of resolving dissonance protects their self-esteem but virtually guarantees their further victimization: "If only I subscribe to *more* magazines, I'll win the big prize," they say; or "That nice, thoughtful person who made me the investment offer would never cheat me, and besides, they advertise on Christian radio." Older people are especially vulnerable to reducing dissonance in this direction because many of them are already worried that they are "losing it"—their competence as well as their money. And they don't want to give their grown children grounds for taking control of their lives.

Understanding how dissonance operates helps us rethink our own muddles, but it is also a useful skill for helping friends and relatives get out of theirs. Too often, out of the best of intentions, we do the very thing guaranteed to make matters worse: We hector, lecture, bully, plead, or threaten. Anthony Pratkanis, a social psychologist who investigated how scammers prey on their elderly targets, collected heartbreaking stories of family members pleading with relatives who had been defrauded: "Can't you see the guy is a thief and the offer is a scam? You're being ripped off!" "Ironically, this natural tendency to lecture may be one of the worst things a family member or friend can do," Pratkanis says. "A lecture just makes the victim feel more defensive and pushes him or her further into the clutches of the fraud criminal." Anyone who understands dissonance knows why. Shouting "What were you *thinking?*" will backfire because it means "Boy, are you *stupid.*" Such accusations cause already embarrassed victims to withdraw further into themselves and clam up, refusing to tell anyone what they are doing. And what they are doing is investing more money, or buying more magazines, because now they really have an incentive to get the family savings back, show they are not stupid or senile, and prove that what they were thinking was perfectly sensible.[13]

Therefore, says Pratkanis, before a victim of a scam will inch back from the precipice, he or she needs to feel respected and supported.

Helpful relatives can encourage the person to talk about his or her values and how those values influenced what happened, while they listen uncritically. Instead of irritably asking "How could you possibly have believed that creep?" you say "Tell me what appealed to you about the guy that made you believe him." Con artists take advantage of people's best qualities—their kindness, politeness, and their desire to honor their commitments, reciprocate a gift, or help a friend. Praising the victim for having these worthy values, says Pratkanis, even if they got the person into hot water in this particular situation, will offset feelings of insecurity and incompetence. It's another form of Peres's third way: Articulate the cognitions and keep them separate. "When I, a decent, smart person, make a mistake, I remain a decent, smart person and the mistake remains a mistake. Now, how do I remedy what I did?"

So embedded is the link between mistakes and stupidity in American culture that it can be shocking to learn that not all cultures share the same phobia about them. In the 1970s, psychologists Harold Stevenson and James Stigler became interested in the math gap in performance between Asian and American schoolchildren: By the fifth grade, the lowest-scoring Japanese classroom was outperforming the highest-scoring American classroom. To find out why, Stevenson and Stigler spent the next decade comparing elementary classrooms in the U.S., China, and Japan. Their epiphany occurred as they watched a Japanese boy struggle with the assignment of drawing cubes in three dimensions on the blackboard. The boy kept at it for forty-five minutes, making repeated mistakes, as Stevenson and Stigler became increasingly anxious and embarrassed for him. Yet the boy himself was utterly unselfconscious, and the American observers wondered why they felt worse than he did. "Our culture exacts a great cost psychologically for making a mistake," Stigler recalled, "whereas in Japan, it doesn't seem to be that way. In Japan, mistakes, error, confusion [are] all just a natural part of the learning process."[14] (The boy eventually mastered the problem, to the cheers of his classmates.) The researchers also found that American parents, teachers, and children were far more likely than their Japanese and Chinese counterparts to believe that mathematical ability is innate; if you have it, you don't have to work hard, and if you don't have it, there's no point in trying. In contrast, most Asians regard math success, like achievement in any other domain, as a matter of persistence and plain hard work. Of course you will make mistakes as you go along; that's how you learn and improve. It doesn't mean you are stupid.

Making mistakes is central to the education of budding scientists and artists of all kinds, who must have the freedom to experiment, try this idea, flop, try another idea, take a risk, be willing to get the wrong answer. One classic example, once taught to American schoolchildren and still on many inspirational Web sites in various versions, is Thomas Edison's reply to his assistant (or to a reporter), who was lamenting Edison's ten thousand experimental failures in his effort to create the first incandescent light bulb. "I have not failed," he told the assistant (or reporter). "I successfully discovered 10,000 elements that don't work." Most American children, however, are denied the freedom to noodle around, experiment, and be wrong in ten ways, let alone ten thousand. The focus on constant testing, which grew out of the reasonable desire to measure and standardize children's accomplishments, has intensified their fear of failure. It is certainly important for children to learn to succeed; but it is just as important for them to learn not to fear failure. When children or adults fear failure, they fear risk. They can't afford to be wrong.

There is another powerful reason that American children fear being wrong: They worry that making mistakes reflects on their inherent abilities. In twenty years of research with American schoolchildren, psychologist Carol Dweck has pinpointed one of the major reasons for the cultural differences that Stevenson and Stigler observed. In her experiments, some children are praised for their efforts in mastering a new challenge. Others are praised for their intelligence and ability, the kind of thing many parents say when their children do well: "You're a natural math whiz, Johnny." Yet these simple messages to children have profoundly different consequences. Children who, like their Asian counterparts, are praised for their efforts, even when they don't "get it" at first, eventually perform better and like what they are learning more than children praised for their natural abilities. They are also more likely to regard mistakes and criticism as useful information that will help them improve. In contrast, children praised for their natural ability learn to care more about how competent they look to others than about what they are actually learning.[15] They become defensive about not doing well or about making mistakes, and this sets them up for a self-defeating cycle: If they don't do well, then to resolve the ensuing dissonance ("I'm smart and yet I screwed up"), they simply lose interest in what they are learning or studying ("I could do it if I wanted to, but I don't want to"). When these kids grow up, they will be the kind of adults who are afraid of making mistakes or taking responsibility for them, because that would be evidence that they are not naturally smart after all.

Dweck has found that these different approaches toward learning and the meaning of mistakes—are they evidence that you are stupid or evidence that you can improve?—are not ingrained personality traits. They are attitudes, and, as such, they can change. Dweck has been changing her students' attitudes toward learning and error for years, and her intervention is surprisingly simple: She teaches elementary-school children and college students alike that intelligence is not a fixed, inborn trait, like eye color, but rather a skill, like bike riding, that can be honed by hard work. This lesson is often stunning to American kids who have been hearing for years that intelligence is innate. When they accept Dweck's message, their motivation increases, they get better grades, they enjoy their studies more, and they don't beat themselves up when they have setbacks.

The moral of our story is easy to say, and difficult to execute. When you screw up, try saying this: "I made a mistake. I need to understand what went wrong. I don't want to make the same mistake again." Dweck's research is heartening because it suggests that at all ages, people can learn to see mistakes not as terrible personal failings to be denied or justified, but as inevitable aspects of life that help us grow, and grow up.

o   o   o

Our national pastime of baseball differs from the society that spawned it in one crucial way: The box score of every baseball game, from the Little League to the major leagues, consists of three tallies: runs, hits, and errors. Errors are not desirable, of course, but everyone understands that they are unavoidable. Errors are inherent in baseball, as they are in medicine, business, science, law, love, and life. But before we can deal with them, we must first acknowledge that we have made them.

A year and a half after the invasion of Iraq had begun, with deaths mounting, costs already running into the billions, an insurgency growing, and American troops bogged down in a war that George W. Bush had promised would be over quickly, a reporter asked the president for "three instances in which you came to realize you had made a wrong decision, and what you did to correct it." Bush replied: "[When people ask about mistakes] they're trying to say, 'Did you make a mistake going into Iraq?' And the answer is, 'Absolutely not.' It was the right decision. . . . Now, you asked what mistakes. I made some mistakes in appointing people, but I'm not going to name them. I don't want to hurt their feelings on national TV."[16]

In June 1944, Dwight Eisenhower, supreme commander of the Allied forces in Europe, had to make a crucial military decision. He knew the invasion of Normandy would be costly under the best of circumstances, and the circumstances were far from ideal. If the invasion failed, thousands of troops would have died in the effort, and the humiliation of defeat would have demoralized the Allies and heartened the Axis powers. Nonetheless, Eisenhower was prepared to assume full responsibility for the possibly catastrophic consequences of his decision to go forward. He wrote out a short speech he planned to release if the invasion had gone wrong. It read, in its entirety:

> Our landings in the Cherbourg-Havre area have failed to gain a satisfactory foothold and the troops have been withdrawn. My decision to attack at this time and place was based upon the best information available. The troops, the Air [Force] and the Navy did all that bravery and devotion to duty could do. If any blame or fault attaches to the attempt, it is mine alone.[17]

After writing this note, Eisenhower made one small but crucial change. He crossed out the end of the first sentence—"the troops have been withdrawn"—and replaced that passive construction with "and I have withdrawn the troops." How the eloquence of that "I" echoes down the decades.

In the final analysis, the test of a nation's character, and of an individual's integrity, does not depend on being error free. It depends on what we do after making the error. As the Chinese philosopher Lao Tzu ("Old Master") observed more than twenty-five-hundred years ago:

> A great nation is like a great man:
> When he makes a mistake, he realizes it.
> Having realized it, he admits it.
> Having admitted it, he corrects it.
> He considers those who point out his faults
>   as his most benevolent teachers.

AFTERWORD

o　　o　　o

We decided the order of authorship of this book by flipping a coin; it's that balanced a collaboration. However, from start to finish, each of us has firmly believed that he or she was working with the more talented coauthor. So, to begin with, we want to thank each other for making this project one of mutual encouragement and learning—and fun.

Our book has benefited from careful, critical readings by colleagues who are specialists in the areas of memory, law, couples therapy, business, and clinical research and practice. We would especially like to thank the following colleagues for their close evaluation of chapters in their fields of expertise, and for the many excellent suggestions they gave us: Andrew Christensen, Deborah Davis, Gerald Davison, Maryanne Garry, Bruce Hay, Brad Heil, Richard Leo, Scott Lilienfeld, Elizabeth Loftus, Andrew McClurg, Devon Polachek, Leonore Tiefer, and Donald Saposnek. In addition, we appreciate the comments, ideas, stories, research, and other information offered by J. J. Cohn, Joseph de Rivera, Ralph Haber, Robert Kardon, Saul

Kassin, Burt Nanus, Debra Poole, Anthony Pratkanis, Holly Stocking, and Michael Zagor. Our thanks also to Deborah Cady and Caryl McColly for their editorial help.

Our courtly agent and good friend Bob Lescher has been right there for us and with us from the first glimmer of a book proposal to the book's launch into the world. Bob's love of a good contract nearly matches his love of a good sentence, and we are grateful for his help with both. Moreover, Bob found our commissioning editor, Jane Isay, who has been a joy to work with. Jane has the grace, skill, and humor needed to let writers know what is wrong with their first drafts in a way that inspires us to revise—and revise, and revise—always bolstering our morale and helping us improve our prose. She is that rarity, a hands-on editor, and her stories and ideas infuse this book. We also thank our talented and supportive editor at Harcourt, Jenna Johnson, who shepherded our book from completion through production and beyond. Finally, we would like to thank managing editor David Hough, a man who loves everything about books (including authors), for making the production phase remarkably painless and educational, and Margaret Jones, for her exceptional skill in copyediting and fact checking.

Most of all, we give our thanks and love to our spouses, Ronan O'Casey and Vera Aronson. Mistakes were made by us in our lives, but not in our choice of a life partner.

—Carol Tavris and Elliot Aronson

ENDNOTES

o   o   o

Long before we became writers, we were readers. As readers, we often found notes an unwelcome intrusion in the flow of the story. It was usually a pain in the neck to be forever turning to the back of the book to learn what the author's source was for some persuasive (or preposterous) idea or research finding, but every so often there was candy—a personal comment, an interesting digression, a good story. We enjoyed assembling these notes, using the opportunity to reference and sometimes expand the points we make in the chapters. And there's some candy in here, too.

INTRODUCTION
Knaves, Fools, Villains, and Hypocrites:
How Do They Live with Themselves?

[1] "Spy Agencies Say Iraq War Worsens Terrorism Threat," *The New York Times,* September 24, 2006; the comment to conservative columnists was reported by one of them, Max Boot, in "No Room for Doubt in the Oval Office," the *Los Angeles Times* op-ed, September 20, 2006. For a detailed

accounting of George Bush's claims to the public regarding the war in Iraq, see Frank Rich (2006), *The Greatest Story Ever Sold: The Decline and Fall of Truth from 9/11 to Katrina*. New York: The Penguin Press. In his State of the Union address in January 2007, Bush acknowledged that "where mistakes were made" in a few tactics used in conducting the war, he was responsible for them. But he held firm that there would be no major changes in strategy: On the contrary, he would increase the number of troops and invest even more money in the war. As high-ranking members of Bush's administration left to write their memoirs, they have painted a portrait of Bush and his inner circle as people driven by certainty and "groupthink"; anyone who offered unwelcome facts was ignored, demoted, or fired. See, for example, Robert Draper (2007), *Dead Certain: The Presidency of George W. Bush*. New York: Free Press. See also Jack Goldsmith (2007), *The Terror Presidency: Law and Judgment Inside the Bush Administration*. New York: W. W. Norton.

[2] The American Presidency Project (online), www.presidency.ucsb.edu/ws/ index.php, provides documented examples of every instance of "mistakes were made" said by American presidents. It's a long list. Bill Clinton said that "mistakes were made" in the pursuit of Democratic campaign contributions, and later joked about the popularity of this phrase and its passive voice at a White House Press Correspondents dinner. Of all the presidents, Richard Nixon and Ronald Reagan used the phrase most, the former to minimize the illegal actions of the Watergate scandal, the latter to minimize the illegal actions of the Iran-Contra scandal. See also Charles Baxter's eloquent essay, "Dysfunctional Narratives: or: 'Mistakes were made,'" in Baxter (1997), *Burning Down the House: Essays on Fiction*. Saint Paul, MN: Graywolf Press.

[3] Gordon Marino (2004, February 20), "Before Teaching Ethics, Stop Kidding Yourself," in *The Chronicle of Higher Education*, p. B5.

[4] On the self-serving bias in memory (and the housework study in particular), see Michael Ross and Fiore Sicoly (1979), "Egocentric Biases in Availability and Attribution," *Journal of Personality and Social Psychology, 37*, pp. 322–336. See also Suzanne C. Thompson and Harold H. Kelley (1981), "Judgments of Responsibility for Activities in Close Relationships," *Journal of Personality and Social Psychology, 41*, pp. 469–477.

[5] John Dean, interviewed for *Playboy* by Barbara Cady, January 1975, pp. 65–80. Quote is on p. 78.

[6] Robert A. Caro (2002), *Master of the Senate: The Years of Lyndon Johnson*. New York: Knopf, p. 886.

[7] Katherine S. Mangan (2005, April 1), "A Brush With a New Life," *The Chronicle of Higher Education*, pp. A28–A30.

[8] See, for example, Sherwin Nuland (2003), *The Doctors' Plague: Germs, Childbed Fever, and the Strange Story of Ignac Semmelweiss*. New York: Norton/Atlas.

[9] Ferdinand Lundberg and Marynia F. Farnham (1947), *Modern Woman: The Lost Sex*. New York: Harper and Brothers, p. 11 (first quote), p. 120 (second quote).

[10] Edward Humes (1999), *Mean Justice*. New York: Pocket Books.

CHAPTER 1
Cognitive Dissonance: The Engine of Self-justification

[1] Press releases from Neal Chase, representing the religious group Baha'is Under the Provisions of the Covenant, in "The End Is Nearish," *Harper's*, February 1995, pp. 22, 24.

[2] Leon Festinger, Henry W. Riecken, and Stanley Schachter (1956), *When Prophecy Fails*. Minneapolis: University of Minnesota Press.

[3] Leon Festinger (1957), *A Theory of Cognitive Dissonance*. Stanford: Stanford University Press. See also Leon Festinger and Elliot Aronson (1960), "Arousal and Reduction of Dissonance in Social Contexts," in D. Cartwright and Z. Zander (eds.), *Group Dynamics* (third ed.), New York: Harper & Row, 1960–1; and Eddie Harmon-Jones and Judson Mills (eds.) (1999), *Cognitive Dissonance: Progress on a Pivotal Theory in Social Psychology*, Washington, DC: American Psychological Association.

[4] Elliot Aronson and Judson Mills (1959), "The Effect of Severity of Initiation on Liking for a Group," *Journal of Abnormal and Social Psychology, 59,* pp. 177–181.

[5] See, for example, Harold Gerard and Grover Mathewson (1966), "The Effects of Severity of Initiation on Liking for a Group: A Replication," *Journal of Experimental Social Psychology, 2,* pp. 278–287.

[6] For a good review of the research on this bias and its many applications, see Raymond S. Nickerson (1998), "Confirmation Bias: A Ubiquitous Phenomenon in Many Guises," *Review of General Psychology, 2,* pp. 175–220.

[7] Lenny Bruce (1966), *How to Talk Dirty and Influence People*. Chicago: Playboy Press and New York: Pocket Books, pp. 232–233.

[8] Steven Kull, director of the Program on International Policy Attitudes (PIPA) at the University of Maryland, commenting on the results of the

PIPA/Knowledge Networks poll, June 14, 2003, "Many Americans Unaware WMD Have Not Been Found."

[9] Drew Westen, Clint Kilts, Pavel Blagov, et al. (2006), "The Neural Basis of Motivated Reasoning: An fMRI Study of Emotional Constraints on Political Judgment During the U.S. Presidential Election of 2004," *Journal of Cognitive Neuroscience, 18*, pp. 1947–1958.

[10] Charles Lord, Lee Ross, and Mark Lepper (1979), "Biased Assimilation and Attitude Polarization: The Effects of Prior Theories on Subsequently Considered Evidence," *Journal of Personality and Social Psychology, 37*, pp. 2098–2109.

[11] Doris Kearns Goodwin (1994), *No Ordinary Time.* New York: Simon & Schuster/Touchstone, p. 321. (Emphasis in original.)

[12] In one of the earliest demonstrations of postdecision dissonance reduction, Jack Brehm, posing as a marketing researcher, showed a group of women eight different appliances (a toaster, a coffeemaker, a sandwich grill, and the like) and asked them to rate each item for its desirability. Brehm then told each woman that she could have one of the appliances as a gift, and gave her a choice between two of the products she had rated as being equally appealing. After she chose one, he wrapped it up and gave it to her. Later, the women rated the appliances again. This time, they increased their rating of the appliance they had chosen and decreased their rating of the appliance they had rejected. See Jack Brehm (1956), "Postdecision Changes in the Desirability of Alternatives," *Journal of Abnormal and Social Psychology, 52*, pp. 384–389.

[13] Daniel Gilbert (2006), *Stumbling on Happiness.* New York: Alfred A. Knopf.

[14] Robert E. Knox and James A. Inkster (1968), "Postdecision Dissonance at Post Time," *Journal of Personality and Social Psychology, 8*, pp. 319–323.

[15] Katherine S. Mangan (2005, April 1), "A Brush With a New Life," *The Chronicle of Higher Education*, pp. A28–A30.

[16] For example, see Brad J. Bushman (2002), "Does Venting Anger Feed or Extinguish the Flame? Catharsis, Rumination, Distraction, Anger, and Aggressive Responding," *Personality and Social Psychology Bulletin, 28*, pp. 724–731; Brad J. Bushman, Angelica M. Bonacci, William C. Pedersen, et al. (2005), "Chewing on It Can Chew You Up: Effects of Rumination on Triggered Displaced Aggression," *Journal of Personality and Social Psychology, 88*, pp. 969–983. The history of research disputing the assumption of catharsis is

summarized in Carol Tavris (1989), *Anger: The Misunderstood Emotion.* New York: Simon & Schuster/Touchstone.

[17] Michael Kahn's original study was "The Physiology of Catharsis," published in the *Journal of Personality and Social Psychology, 3,* pp. 278–298, in 1966. For another early classic, see Leonard Berkowitz, James A. Green, and Jacqueline R. Macaulay (1962), "Hostility Catharsis as the Reduction of Emotional Tension," *Psychiatry, 25,* pp. 23–31.

[18] Jon Jecker and David Landy (1969), "Liking a Person as a Function of Doing Him a Favor," *Human Relations, 22,* pp. 371–378.

[19] Benjamin Franklin (2004), *The Autobiography of Benjamin Franklin* (introduction by Lewis Leary). New York: Touchstone, pp. 83–84.

[20] Ruth Thibodeau and Elliot Aronson (1992), "Taking a Closer Look: Reasserting the Role of the Self-Concept in Dissonance Theory," *Personality and Social Psychology Bulletin, 18,* pp. 591–602.

[21] There is a large and lively research literature on the "self-serving bias," the tendency to believe the best of ourselves and explain away the worst. It is a remarkably consistent bias in human cognition, though there are interesting variations across cultures, ages, and genders. See Amy Mezulis, Lyn Y. Abramson, Janet S. Hyde, and Benjamin L. Hankin (2004), "Is There a Universal Positivity Bias in Attributions? A Meta-Analytic Review of Individual, Developmental, and Cultural Differences in the Self-serving Attributional Bias," *Psychological Bulletin, 130,* pp. 711–747.

[22] Philip E. Tetlock (2005), *Expert Political Judgment: How Good Is It? How Can We Know?* Princeton, NJ: Princeton University Press. In clinical psychology, the picture is the same: There is an extensive scientific literature showing that behavioral, statistical, and other objective measures of behavior are consistently superior to the clinical insight of experts and their clinical predictions and diagnoses. See Robin Dawes, David Faust, and Paul E. Meehl (1989), "Clinical Versus Actuarial Judgment," *Science, 243,* pp. 1668–1674; and W. M. Grove and Paul E. Meehl (1996), "Comparative Efficiency of Formal (Mechanical, Algorithmic) and Informal (Subjective, Impressionistic) Prediction Procedures: The Clinical/Statistical Controversy," *Psychology, Public Policy, and Law, 2,* pp. 293–323.

[23] Elliot Aronson and J. Merrill Carlsmith (1962), "Performance Expectancy as a Determinant of Actual Performance," *Journal of Abnormal and Social Psychology, 65,* pp. 178–182. See also William B. Swann Jr. (1990), "To Be Adored or

to Be Known? The Interplay of Self-Enhancement and Self-Verification," in R. M. Sorrentino & E. T. Higgins (eds.), *Motivation and Cognition,* New York: Guilford Press; and William B. Swann Jr., J. Gregory Hixon, and Chris de la Ronde (1992), "Embracing the Bitter 'Truth': Negative Self-Concepts and Marital Commitment," *Psychological Science, 3,* pp. 118–121.

[24] We are not idly speculating here. In a classic experiment conducted half a century ago, social psychologist Judson Mills measured the attitudes of sixth-grade children toward cheating. He then had them participate in a competitive exam with prizes offered to the winners. He arranged the situation so that it was almost impossible for a child to win without cheating, and also so that it was easy for the children to cheat, thinking they would not be detected. (He was secretly keeping an eye on them.) About half the kids cheated and half did not. The next day, Mills asked the children again how they felt about cheating and other misdemeanors. Those children who had cheated became more lenient toward cheating, and those who resisted the temptation adopted a harsher attitude. See Judson Mills (1958), "Changes in Moral Attitudes Following Temptation," *Journal of Personality, 26,* pp. 517–531.

[25] Jeb Stuart Magruder (1974), *An American Life: One Man's Road to Watergate.* New York: Atheneum. Haldeman's comments, p. 4; the golf-cart story, p. 7.

[26] Magruder, *An American Life.* Liddy's first proposal with the "mugging squads," p. 194 (the prostitutes would be "high-class," Liddy assured the group, "only the best," p. 195); "If [Liddy] had come to us at the outset . . . ," p. 214; "decisions that now seem insane . . . ," "We were past the point of halfway measures," p. 215.

[27] The number of total participants is an informed estimate from psychologist Thomas Blass, who has written extensively about the original Milgram experiment and its many successors. About 800 people participated in Milgram's own experiments; the rest were in replications or variations of the basic paradigm over a 25-year span.

[28] The original study is described in Stanley Milgram (1963), "Behavioral Study of Obedience," *Journal of Abnormal and Social Psychology, 67,* pp. 371–378. Milgram reported his study in greater detail and with additional supporting research, including many replications, in his subsequent (1974) book, *Obedience to Authority: An Experimental View.* New York: Harper & Row.

[29] William Safire, "Aesop's Fabled Fox," *The New York Times* op-ed, December 29, 2003.

CHAPTER 2
Pride and Prejudice . . . and Other Blind Spots

[1] James Bruggers, "Brain Damage Blamed on Solvent Use," *The* [Louisville] *Courier-Journal,* May 13, 2001; Bruggers, "Researchers' Ties to CSX Raise Concerns," *Courier-Journal,* October 20, 2001; Carol Tavris (2002, July/August), "The High Cost of Skepticism," *Skeptical Inquirer,* pp. 42–44; Stanley Berent (2002, November/December), "Response to 'The High Cost of Skepticism,'" *Skeptical Inquirer,* pp. 61, 63; his quote ("My research yielded important information . . .") is on p. 63; Carol Tavris's reply to Berent, same issue, pp. 64–65. On February 12, 2003, the Office for Human Research Protections wrote to the vice president for research at the University of Michigan, noting that the university's Institutional Review Board, of which Stanley Berent had been head, had "failed to document the specific criteria for waiver of informed consent" for Berent and Albers' research. The case of CSX, its arrangement with Stanley Berent and James Albers, and their conflict of interest is also described in depth in Sheldon Krimsky (2003), *Science in the Private Interest.* Lanham, MD: Rowman & Littlefield, pp. 152–153.

[2] Joyce Ehrlinger, Thomas Gilovich, and Lee Ross (2005), "Peering into the Bias Blind Spot: People's Assessments of Bias in Themselves and Others," *Personality and Social Psychology Bulletin, 31,* pp. 680–692; Emily Pronin, Daniel Y. Lin, and Lee Ross (2002), "The Bias Blind Spot: Perceptions of Bias in Self versus Others," *Personality and Social Psychology Bulletin, 28,* pp. 369–381. Our blind spots also allow us to see ourselves as being smarter and more competent than most people, which is why all of us, apparently, feel we are above average. See David Dunning, Kerri Johnson, Joyce Ehrlinger, and Justin Kruger (2003), "Why People Fail to Recognize Their Own Incompetence," *Current Directions in Psychological Science, 12,* pp. 83–87.

[3] Quoted in Eric Jaffe (2004, October), "Peace in the Middle East May Be Impossible: Lee D. Ross on Naive Realism and Conflict Resolution," American Psychological Society *Observer, 17,* pp. 9–11.

[4] Geoffrey L. Cohen (2003), "Party over Policy: The Dominating Impact of Group Influence on Political Beliefs," *Journal of Personality and Social Psychology, 85,* pp. 808–822. See also Donald Green, Bradley Palmquist, and Eric Schickler (2002), *Partisan Hearts and Minds: Political Parties and the Social Identities of Voters.* New Haven: Yale University Press. This book shows how

once people form a political identity, usually in young adulthood, the identity does their thinking for them. That is, most people do not choose a party because it reflects their views; rather, once they choose a party, its policies become their views.

[5] Emily Pronin, Thomas Gilovich, and Lee Ross (2004), "Objectivity in the Eye of the Beholder: Divergent Perceptions of Bias in Self versus Others," *Psychological Review, 111,* pp. 781–799.

[6] When privilege is a result of birth or another fluke of fortune, rather than merit, many of its possessors will justify it as providing benefits they earned. John Jost and his colleagues have been studying the processes of system justification, a psychological motive to defend and justify the status quo; see, for example, John Jost and Orsolya Hunyady (2005), "Antecedents and Consequences of System-Justifying Ideologies," *Current Directions in Psychological Science, 14,* pp. 260–265. One such system-justifying ideology is that the poor may be poor, but they are happier and more honest than the rich: Aaron C. Kay and John T. Jost (2003), "Complementary Justice: Effects of 'Poor But Happy' and 'Poor But Honest' Stereotype Exemplars on System Justification and Implicit Activation of the Justice Motive," *Journal of Personality and Social Psychology, 85,* pp. 823–837. See also Stephanie M. Wildman (ed.) (1996), *Privilege Revealed: How Invisible Preference Undermines America.* New York University Press.

[7] D. Michael Risinger and Jeffrey L. Loop (2002, November), "Three Card Monte, Monty Hall, Modus Operandi and 'Offender Profiling': Some Lessons of Modern Cognitive Science for the Law of Evidence," *Cardozo Law Review, 24,* p. 193.

[8] Dorothy Samuels, "Tripping Up on Trips: Judges Love Junkets as Much as Tom DeLay Does," *The New York Times* fourth editorial, January 20, 2006.

[9] Melody Petersen, "A Conversation with Sheldon Krimsky: Uncoupling Campus and Company," *The New York Times,* September 23, 2003. Krimsky also recounted the Jonas Salk remark.

[10] See Krimsky, *Science in the Private Interest,* note 1; Sheila Slaughter and Larry L. Leslie (1997), *Academic Capitalism,* Baltimore: The Johns Hopkins University Press; and Derek Bok (2003), *Universities in the Marketplace: The Commercialization of Higher Education,* Princeton, NJ: Princeton University Press; Marcia Angell (2004), *The Truth about the Drug Companies,* New York: Random House; and Jerome P. Kassirer (2005), *On the Take: How Medicine's Complicity with Big Business Can Endanger Your Health,* New York: Oxford University Press.

[11] National Institutes of Health Care Management Research and Educational Foundation (2003), "Changing Patterns of Pharmaceutical Innovation." Cited in Jason Dana and George Loewenstein (2003), "A Social Science Perspective on Gifts to Physicians from Industry," *Journal of the American Medical Association, 290,* 252–255.

[12] Investigative journalist David Willman won a Pulitzer Prize for his series on conflicts of interest in bringing new drugs to market; two of them include "Scientists Who Judged Pill Safety Received Fees," *Los Angeles Times,* October 29, 1999; and "The New FDA: How a New Policy Led to Seven Deadly Drugs," *Los Angeles Times,* December 20, 2000.

[13] Dan Fagin and Marianne Lavelle (1996), *Toxic Deception.* Secaucus, NJ: Carol Publishing.

[14] Richard A. Davidson (1986, May–June), "Source of Funding and Outcome of Clinical Trials," *Journal of General Internal Medicine, 1,* pp. 155–158.

[15] Lise L. Kjaergard and Bodil Als-Nielsen (2002, August 3), "Association between competing interests and authors' conclusions: Epidemiological study of randomised clinical trials published in *BMJ,*" *British Medical Journal, 325,* pp. 249–252. See also Krimsky, *Science in the Private Interest* (note 1), chapter 9, "A Question of Bias," for a review of these and other similar studies.

[16] Alex Berenson, Gardiner Harris, Barry Meier, and Andrew Pollack, "Dangerous Data: Despite Warnings, Drug Giant Took Long Path to Vioxx Recall," *The New York Times,* November 14, 2004.

[17] Richard Horton (2004), "The lessons of MMR," *The Lancet, 363,* pp. 747–749.

[18] Andrew J. Wakefield, Peter Harvey, and John Linnell (2004), "MMR—Responding to retraction," *The Lancet, 363,* pp. 1327–1328.

[19] Wikipedia, under the entry "Thimerosal," has an excellent, balanced review of the entire controversy surrounding this chemical (variously spelled thimerosol and thimerserol), used commonly since the 1930s as a preservative in vaccines and many household products, such as cosmetics and eye drops. In recent years, some consumer groups became concerned about the possibly toxic effects of mercury contained in this preservative, claiming it causes autism and other diseases. The Wikipedia entry represents their concerns fairly, but shows that their arguments have largely been based on anecdotes, exaggerated fears, unsupported claims, and the antivaccine research conducted by Mark Geier and David Geier, president of a company specializing in litigating on behalf of alleged vaccine injury claimants.

As for the research, in a study of all children born in Denmark between 1991 and 1998 (over half a million children), the incidence of autism in vaccinated children was actually a bit lower than in unvaccinated children: See Kreesten M. Madsen, Anders Hviid, Mogens Vestergaard, et al. (2002), "A Population-Based Study of Measles, Mumps, and Rubella Vaccination and Autism," *New England Journal of Medicine, 347,* pp. 1477–1482. Moreover, after vaccines containing thimerserol were removed from the market in Denmark, there was no subsequent decrease in the incidence of autism: See Kreesten M. Madsen et al. (2003), "Thimerserol and the Occurrence of Autism: Negative Ecological Evidence from Danish Population-Based Data," *Pediatrics, 112,* pp. 604–606. See also L. Smeeth, C. Cook, E. Fombonne, et al. (2004, September 11–17), "MMR vaccination and pervasive developmental disorders: A case-control study," *The Lancet, 364,* pp. 963–969.

The reaction of many parents of autistic children to this news is itself a story of dissonance. Having committed themselves to the belief that thimerserol is the agent responsible for their children's autism, they have rejected the conclusions of this research and statements in favor of vaccination from the Centers for Disease Control and Prevention, the Food and Drug Administration, the Institute of Medicine, the World Health Organization, and the American Academy of Pediatrics. Interestingly, as the Wikipedia entry points out, public resistance to vaccination programs began in 1853 and has remained active ever since, the thimerserol controversy simply being the latest addition.

[20] Dana and Loewenstein, "A Social Science Perspective on Gifts to Physicians from Industry," note 11.

[21] Robert B. Cialdini (1984/1993), *Influence: The Psychology of Persuasion* (rev. ed.). New York: William Morrow.

[22] Carl Elliott (2006, April), "The Drug Pushers," *The Atlantic Monthly,* pp. 82–93. Quote by his brother on p. 91.

[23] Carl Elliott (2001, September 24), "Pharma Buys a Conscience," *The American Prospect, 12,* archived as www.prospect.org/print/V12/17/elliott-c.html.

[24] C. Neil Macrae, Alan B. Milne, and Galen V. Bodenhausen (1994), "Stereotypes as Energy-Saving Devices: A Peek Inside the Cognitive Toolbox," *Journal of Personality and Social Psychology, 66,* pp. 37–47.

[25] Marilynn B. Brewer (1993), "Social Identity, Distinctiveness, and In-Group Homogeneity," *Social Cognition, 11,* pp. 150–164.

[26] Charles W. Perdue, John F. Dovidio, Michael B. Gurtman, and Richard B.

Tyler (1990), "Us and Them: Social Categorization and the Process of Intergroup Bias," *Journal of Personality and Social Psychology, 59,* pp. 475–486.

[27] Henri Tajfel, M. G. Billig, R. P. Bundy, and Claude Flament (1971), "Social categorization and intergroup behavior," *European Journal of Social Psychology, 1,* pp. 149–178.

[28] Nick Haslam, Paul Bain, Lauren Douge, Max Lee, and Brock Bastian (2005), "More Human Than You: Attributing Humanness to Self and Others," *Journal of Personality and Social Psychology, 89,* pp. 937–950.

[29] Gordon Allport (1954/1979), *The Nature of Prejudice.* Reading, MA: Addison-Wesley, pp. 13–14.

[30] Jeffrey W. Sherman, Steven J. Stroessner, Frederica R. Conrey, and Omar A. Azam (2005), "Prejudice and Stereotype Maintenance Processes: Attention, Attribution, and Individuation," *Journal of Personality and Social Psychology, 89,* pp. 607–622.

[31] Christian S. Crandall and Amy Eshelman (2003), "A Justification-Suppression Model of the Expression and Experience of Prejudice," *Psychological Bulletin, 129,* pp. 414–446, quote, p. 425. See also Benoît Monin and Dale T. Miller (2001), "Moral Credentials and the Expression of Prejudice," *Journal of Personality and Social Psychology, 81,* pp. 33–43. In their experiments, when people felt that their moral credentials as unprejudiced individuals were not in dispute—when they had been given a chance to disagree with blatantly sexist statements—they felt more justified in their subsequent vote to hire a man for a stereotypically male job.

[32] For the interracial experiment, see Ronald W. Rogers and Steven Prentice-Dunn (1981), "Deindividuation and Anger-Mediated Interracial Aggression: Unmasking Regressive Racism," *Journal of Personality and Social Psychology, 4,* pp. 63–73. For the English- and French-speaking Canadians, see James R. Meindl and Melvin J. Lerner (1985), "Exacerbation of Extreme Responses to an Out-Group," *Journal of Personality and Social Psychology, 47,* pp. 71–84. On the studies of behavior toward Jews and gay men, see Steven Fein and Steven J. Spencer (1997), "Prejudice as Self-Image Maintenance: Affirming the Self through Derogating Others," *Journal of Personality and Social Psychology, 73,* pp. 31–44.

[33] Paul Jacobs, Saul Landau, and Eve Pell (1971), *To Serve the Devil* (Vol. 2: *Colonials and Sojourners*). New York: Vintage Books. Quote by Charles Crocker, p. 81.

[34] Albert Speer (1970), *Inside the Third Reich: Memoirs.* New York: Simon & Schuster, p. 291.

[35] Doris Kearns Goodwin (2005), *Team of Rivals: The Political Genius of Abraham Lincoln.* New York: Simon & Schuster.

[36] Jeb Stuart Magruder (1974), *An American Life: One Man's Road to Watergate.* New York: Atheneum, p. 348.

CHAPTER 3
Memory, the Self-justifying Historian

[1] Quoted in George Plimpton (1997), *Truman Capote.* New York: Anchor/ Doubleday, p. 306. We are taking Vidal's version of this story on the grounds that he has never had compunctions about talking about either subject—politics or bisexuality—and therefore had no motivation to distort his memory.

[2] Anthony G. Greenwald (1980), "The Totalitarian Ego: Fabrication and Revision of Personal History," *American Psychologist, 35,* pp. 603–618.

[3] Edward Jones and Rika Kohler (1959), "The Effects of Plausibility on the Learning of Controversial Statements," *Journal of Abnormal and Social Psychology, 57,* pp. 315–320.

[4] See, for example, Michael Ross (1989), "Relation of Implicit Theories to the Construction of Personal Histories," *Psychological Review, 96,* pp. 341–357; Anne E. Wilson and Michael Ross (2001), "From Chump to Champ: People's Appraisals of Their Earlier and Present Selves," *Journal of Personality and Social Psychology, 80,* pp. 572–584; and Michael Ross and Anne E. Wilson (2003), "Autobiographical Memory and Conceptions of Self: Getting Better All the Time," *Current Directions in Psychological Science, 12,* pp. 66–69.

[5] Marcia K. Johnson, Shahin Hashtroudi, and D. Stephen Lindsay (1993), "Source Monitoring," *Psychological Bulletin, 114,* pp. 3–28; Karen J. Mitchell and Marcia K. Johnson (2000), "Source Monitoring: Attributing Mental Experiences," in E. Tulving & F. I. M. Craik (eds.), *The Oxford Handbook of Memory.* New York: Oxford University Press.

[6] Mary McCarthy (1957), *Memories of a Catholic Girlhood.* San Diego: Harcourt Brace & Co. "With the tin butterfly in his hand," p. 80; "I suddenly remembered," p. 82; "The most likely thing," p. 83.

[7] Barbara Tversky and Elizabeth J. Marsh (2000), "Biased Retellings of Events Yield Biased Memories," *Cognitive Psychology, 40,* pp. 1–38; see also Elizabeth

J. Marsh and Barbara Tversky (2004), "Spinning the Stories of Our Lives," *Applied Cognitive Psychology, 18,* pp. 491–503.

[8] Brooke C. Feeney and Jude Cassidy (2003), "Reconstructive Memory Related to Adolescent-Parent Conflict Interactions: The Influence of Attachment-Related Representations on Immediate Perceptions and Changes in Perceptions over Time," *Journal of Personality and Social Psychology, 85,* pp. 945–955.

[9] Daniel Offer, Marjorie Kaiz, Kenneth I. Howard, and Emily S. Bennett (2000), "The Altering of Reported Experiences," *Journal of the American Academy of Child and Adolescent Psychiatry, 39,* pp. 735–742. Several of the authors also wrote a book on this study. See Daniel Offer, Marjorie Kaiz Offer, and Eric Ostrov (2004), *Regular Guys: 34 Years Beyond Adolescence.* New York: Kluwer Academic/Plenum.

[10] On "mismemories" of sex, see Maryanne Garry, Stefanie J. Sharman, Julie Feldman, Gary A. Marlatt, and Elizabeth F. Loftus (2002), "Examining Memory for Heterosexual College Students' Sexual Experiences Using an Electronic Mail Diary," *Health Psychology, 21,* pp. 629–634. On the over-reporting of voting, see R. P. Abelson, Elizabeth D. Loftus, and Anthony G. Greenwald (1992), "Attempts to Improve the Accuracy of Self-Reports of Voting," in J. M. Tanur (ed.), *Questions About Questions: Inquiries into the Cognitive Bases of Surveys.* New York: Russell Sage. See also Robert F. Belli, Michael W. Traugott, Margaret Young, and Katherine A. McGonagle (1999), "Reducing Vote Overreporting in Surveys: Social Desirability, Memory Failure, and Source Monitoring," *Public Opinion Quarterly, 63,* pp. 90–108. On misremembering donating money, see Christopher D. B. Burt and Jennifer S. Popple (1998), "Memorial Distortions in Donation Data," *Journal of Social Psychology, 138,* pp. 724–733. College students' memories of their high-school grades are also distorted in a positive direction; see Harry P. Bahrick, Lynda K. Hall, and Stephanie A. Berger (1996), "Accuracy and Distortion in Memory for High School Grades," *Psychological Science, 7,* pp. 265–271.

[11] Lisa K. Libby and Richard P. Eibach (2002), "Looking Back in Time: Self-Concept Change Affects Visual Perspective in Autobiographical Memory," *Journal of Personality and Social Psychology, 82,* pp. 167–179. See also Lisa K. Libby, Richard P. Eibach, and Thomas Gilovich (2005), "Here's Looking at Me: The Effect of Memory Perspective on Assessments of Personal Change," *Journal of Personality and Social Psychology, 88,* pp. 50–62. The more consistent our memories are of ourselves in the present, the more accessible they are.

See Michael Ross (1989), "Relation of Implicit Theories to the Construction of Personal Histories," *Psychological Review, 96,* pp. 341–357.

[12] Michael Conway and Michael Ross (1984), "Getting What You Want by Revising What You Had," *Journal of Personality and Social Psychology, 47,* pp. 738–748. Memory distortions take many different paths, but most are in the service of preserving our self-concepts and feelings about ourselves as good and competent people.

[13] Anne E. Wilson and Michael Ross have shown how the self-justifying biases of memory help us move psychologically, in their words, from "chump to champ." We distance ourselves from our earlier "chumpier" incarnations if doing so allows us to feel better about how much we have grown, learned, and matured, but, like Haber, we feel close to earlier selves we thought were champs. Either way, we can't lose. See Wilson and Ross, "From Chump to Champ," note 4.

[14] The full text of *Fragments,* along with the true story of Wilkomirski's life, is in Stefan Maechler (2001), *The Wilkomirski Affair: A Study in Biographical Truth* (translated by John E. Woods). New York: Schocken. Maechler discusses the ways in which Wilkomirski drew on Kosinski's novel. For another investigation into Wilkomirski's life and the cultural issues of real and imagined memories, see Blake Eskin (2002), *A Life in Pieces: The Making and Unmaking of Binjamin Wilkomirski.* New York: W. W. Norton.

[15] The Will Andrews story is in Susan Clancy (2005), *Abducted: How People Come to Believe They Were Kidnapped by Aliens.* Cambridge, MA: Harvard University Press. On the psychology of belief in alien abduction, see also Donald P. Spence (1996), "Abduction Tales as Metaphors," *Psychological Inquiry, 7,* pp. 177–179. Spence interprets abduction memories as metaphors that have two powerful psychological functions: They encapsulate a set of free-floating concerns and anxieties that are widespread in today's political and cultural climate, anxieties that have no ready or easy remedy; and, by providing a shared identity for believers, they reduce the believers' feelings of alienation and powerlessness.

[16] Maechler, *The Wilkomirski Affair,* p. 273. See note 14.

[17] Maechler, *The Wilkomirski Affair,* p. 27.

[18] Maechler, *The Wilkomirski Affair,* p. 71. Wilkomirski accounted for having restless leg syndrome by telling a horrifying story: that when he was in Majdanek, he learned to keep his legs moving while he slept or otherwise "the rats would gnaw on them." But according to Tomasz Kranz, head of the research

department at the Majdanek Museum, there were lice and fleas at the camp, but not rats (unlike other camps, such as Birkenau). Maechler, p. 169.

[19] On the physical and psychological benefits of writing about previously undisclosed secrets and traumas, see James W. Pennebaker (1990), *Opening Up.* New York: William Morrow.

[20] On imagination inflation, see Elizabeth F. Loftus (2004), "Memories of Things Unseen," *Current Directions in Psychological Science, 13,* pp. 145–147; and Loftus (2001), "Imagining the Past," in *Psychologist, 14* (British Psychological Society), pp. 584–587; Maryanne Garry, Charles Manning, Elizabeth Loftus, and Steven J. Sherman (1996), "Imagination Inflation: Imagining a Childhood Event Inflates Confidence That It Occurred," *Psychonomic Bulletin and Review, 3,* pp. 208–214; Giuliana Mazzoni and Amina Memon (2003), "Imagination Can Create False Autobiographical Memories," *Psychological Science, 14,* pp. 186–188. On dreams, see Giuliana Mazzoni, Elizabeth F. Loftus, Aaron Seitz, and Steven J. Lynn (1999), "Changing Beliefs and Memories through Dream Interpretation," *Applied Cognitive Psychology, 2,* pp. 125–144.

[21] Brian Gonsalves, Paul J. Reber, Darren R. Gitelman, et al. (2004), "Neural Evidence that Vivid Imagining Can Lead to False Remembering," *Psychological Science, 15,* pp. 655–660. They found that the process of visually imagining a common object generates brain activity in regions of the cerebral cortex, which can lead to false memories of those imagined objects.

[22] Mazzoni and Memon, "Imagination Can Create False Autobiographical Memories," note 20.

[23] The effect is called "explanation inflation"; see Stefanie J. Sharman, Charles G. Manning, and Maryanne Garry (2005), "Explain This: Explaining Childhood Events Inflates Confidence for Those Events," *Applied Cognitive Psychology, 19,* pp. 67–74. Preverbal children do the visual equivalent of what adults do: They draw a picture of a completely implausible event, such as having a tea party in a hot-air balloon or swimming at the bottom of the ocean with a mermaid. After drawing these pictures, they often import them into their memories. A week later, they are far more likely than children who did not draw the pictures to say yes, that fanciful event really happened. See Deryn Strange, Maryanne Garry, and Rachel Sutherland (2003), "Drawing Out Children's False Memories," *Applied Cognitive Psychology, 17,* pp. 607–619.

[24] Maechler, *The Wilkomirski Affair,* p. 104. See note 14.

[25] Bernstein's letter: Maechler, *The Wilkomirski Affair,* p. 100; Matta's defense of Wilkomirski, p. 97; our emphasis.

[26] Richard J. McNally (2003), *Remembering Trauma.* Cambridge, MA: Harvard University Press, p. 233.

[27] Michael Shermer (2005, February), "Abducted!" *Scientific American,* pp. 33–34. Quotes on p. 33.

[28] Clancy, *Abducted,* p. 51. See note 15.

[29] "One night I woke up": Clancy, *Abducted,* p. 34; "I've been depressed," p. 34; baffling symptoms such as missing pajamas and unexpected nosebleeds, p. 33.

[30] For example, Giuliana Mazzoni and her colleagues showed in their laboratory how people can come to regard an impossible event (witnessing a demonic possession when they were children) as a plausible memory. One step in the process was reading about demonic possession, in passages that said it was much more common than most people realized, accompanied by testimonials. See Giuliana Mazzoni, Elizabeth F. Loftus, and Irving Kirsch (2001), "Changing Beliefs About Implausible Autobiographical Events: A Little Plausibility Goes a Long Way," *Journal of Experimental Psychology: Applied, 7,* pp. 51–59.

[31] "I couldn't be touched": Clancy, *Abducted,* p. 143. Will Andrews, "I was ready to just give up," and his wife's question, p. 2. See note 15.

[32] Clancy, *Abducted,* p. 50.

[33] Richard McNally, personal communication.

[34] Richard J. McNally, Natasha B. Lasko, Susan A. Clancy, et al. (2004), "Psychophysiologic Responding During Script-Driven Imagery in People Reporting Abduction by Space Aliens," *Psychological Science, 5,* pp. 493–497. See also Clancy, *Abducted* (note 15), and McNally, *Remembering Trauma* (note 26), for reviews of this and related research.

[35] It is interesting, nonetheless, that the autobiographies that once served as inspiring examples of a person's struggle to overcome racism, violence, disability, exile, or poverty seem today so out of fashion. Modern memoirs strive to outdo one another in the gruesome details of the writer's life. For an eloquent essay on this theme, see Francine Prose, "Outrageous Misfortune," her review of Jeannette Walls's *The Glass Castle: A Memoir* for *The New York Times Book Review,* March 13, 2005. Prose begins, "Memoirs are our modern fairy tales, the harrowing fables of the Brothers Grimm reimagined from the perspective of the plucky child who has, against all odds, evaded the fate of being chopped up, cooked and served to the family for dinner."

[36] Ellen Bass and Laura Davis (1988), *The Courage to Heal: A Guide for Women Survivors of Child Sexual Abuse.* New York: Harper & Row, p. 173. This statement remains in the revised and expanded third edition, 1994, on p. 183.

[37] For the best full account of this story, see Moira Johnston (1997), *Spectral Evidence: The Ramona Case: Incest, Memory, and Truth on Trial in Napa Valley.* Boston: Houghton Mifflin. Quote describing the charges, p. 160.
[38] Mary Karr, "His So-Called Life," *The New York Times* op-ed, January 15, 2006.

CHAPTER 4
Good Intentions, Bad Science: The Closed Loop of Clinical Judgment

[1] The story of Grace was told to us by psychologist Joseph de Rivera, who interviewed her and others in his research on the psychology of recanters. See, for example, Joseph de Rivera (1997), "The Construction of False Memory Syndrome: The Experience of Retractors," *Psychological Inquiry, 8,* pp. 271–292; and de Rivera (2000), "Understanding Persons Who Repudiate Memories Recovered in Therapy," *Professional Psychology: Research and Practice, 31,* pp. 378–386.
[2] The most comprehensive history of the recovered-memory epidemic remains Mark Pendergrast's 1996 *Victims of Memory* (second ed.). Hinesburg, VT: Upper Access Press; revised and expanded for a HarperCollins British edition, 1996. See also Richard J. Ofshe and Ethan Watters (1994), *Making Monsters: False Memory, Psychotherapy, and Sexual Hysteria,* New York: Scribners; Elizabeth Loftus and Katherine Ketcham (1994), *The Myth of Repressed Memory,* New York: St. Martin's Press; and Frederick Crews (ed.) (1998), *Unauthorized Freud: Doubters Confront a Legend,* New York: Viking. For an excellent sociology of hysterical epidemics and moral panics, see Philip Jenkins (1992), *Intimate Enemies: Moral Panics in Contemporary Great Britain.* Hawthorne, NY: Aldine de Gruyter.
     The specific example of the woman who claimed that her father molested her from the ages of five to twenty-three is known as Laura B., who sued her father, Joel Hungerford, in the state of New Hampshire in 1995. She lost.
[3] Two of the earliest and still best books on the day-care scandals and claims of widespread cults that were promoting ritual Satanic sexual abuse are Debbie Nathan and Michael Snedeker (1995), *Satan's Silence: Ritual Abuse and the Making of a Modern American Witch Hunt,* New York: Basic Books; and Stephen J. Ceci and Maggie Bruck (1995), *Jeopardy in the Courtroom: A Scientific Analysis of Children's Testimony,* Washington, DC: American Psychological

Association. Dorothy Rabinowitz, a *Wall Street Journal* editorial writer, was the first to publicly question the conviction of Kelly Michaels and get her case reopened; see also Rabinowitz (2003), *No Crueler Tyrannies: Accusation, False Witness, and Other Terrors of Our Times.* New York: Wall Street Press Books/ Free Press.

A related epidemic was the rise of alleged cases of multiple personality disorder, now called "dissociative identity disorder." Before 1980, there were only a handful of such cases; by the mid-1990s, by one estimate, there were some 40,000. When the MPD clinics were closed by successful lawsuits against psychiatrists who had been inducing the disorder in vulnerable patients, the disorder began to fade away, though not completely. See Joan Acocella (1999), *Creating Hysteria: Women and Multiple Personality Disorder.* San Francisco: Jossey-Bass. On hypnosis and other means of creating false memories of abduction, multiple personality disorder, and child abuse, see Nicholas P. Spanos (1996), *Multiple Identities and False Memories: A Sociocognitive Perspective.* Washington, DC: American Psychological Association.

[4] For example, in February, 2005, a Boston jury convicted a 74-year-old former priest, Paul Shanley, of sexually molesting twenty-seven-year-old Paul Busa when Busa was six. This claim followed upon the Church scandals that had revealed hundreds of documented cases of pedophile priests, so emotions understandably ran high against the priests and the Church's policy of covering up the accusations. Yet the *sole* evidence in Shanley's case was Busa's memories, which, Busa said, he recovered in vivid flashbacks after reading a Boston *Globe* article on Shanley. There was no corroborating evidence presented at the trial, and indeed much that disputed Busa's claims. See Jonathan Rauch, "Is Paul Shanley Guilty? If Paul Shanley Is a Monster, the State Didn't Prove It," *National Journal,* March 12, 2005, pp. 746–747; and JoAnn Wypijewski, "The Passion of Father Paul Shanley," *Legal Affairs,* September–October 2004. Other skeptical reporters included Daniel Lyons of *Forbes,* Robin Washington of *The Boston Herald,* and Michael Miner of the *Chicago Reader.*

[5] Some studies find that combined approaches—medication plus cognitive-behavior therapy (CBT)—are most effective; others find that CBT does as well. For a review of the issues and bibliography of research studies, see the American Psychological Association Presidential Task Force on Evidence-Based Practice (2006), "Evidence-Based Practice in Psychology," *American Psychologist, 61,* pp. 271–283. See also Dianne Chambless et al. (1998), "Update on Empirically Validated Therapies," *The Clinical Psychologist, 51,* pp.

3–16, and Steven D. Hollon, Michael E. Thase, and John C. Markowitz (2002), "Treatment and Prevention of Depression," *Psychological Science in the Public Interest, 3,* pp. 39–77. These articles contain excellent references regarding empirically validated forms of psychotherapy for different problems.

[6] Tanya M. Luhrmann (2000), *Of Two Minds: The Growing Disorder in American Psychiatry.* New York: Knopf. Her findings echo precisely what Jonas Robitscher described about his profession in 1980, in *The Powers of Psychiatry.* Boston: Houghton Mifflin.

[7] For an excellent review of the issues and the rise of pseudoscientific methods and practices in psychotherapy—including unvalidated assessment tests, treatments for autism and ADHD, and popular therapies—see Scott O. Lilienfeld, Steven Jay Lynn, and Jeffrey M. Lohr (eds.) (2003), *Science and Pseudoscience in Contemporary Clinical Psychology.* New York: Guilford. And for the other side of the story, articles on the most important contributions of clinical science, see Scott O. Lilienfeld and William T. O'Donohue (eds.) (2007), *The Great Ideas of Clinical Science.* New York: Routledge.

[8] On evidence that hypnosis is effective for a large number of acute and chronic pain conditions, see David R. Patterson and Mark P. Jensen (2003), "Hypnosis and Clinical Pain," *Psychological Bulletin, 29,* pp. 495–521. Hypnosis can also add to the effectiveness of cognitive-behavioral techniques for losing weight, quitting smoking, and other behavior problems; see Irving Kirsch, Guy Montgomery, and Guy Sapirstein (1995), "Hypnosis as an Adjunct to Cognitive-Behavioral Psychotherapy: A Meta-Analysis," *Journal of Consulting and Clinical Psychology, 2,* pp. 214–220. But the evidence is overwhelming that hypnosis is unreliable as a way of retrieving memories, which is why the American Psychological Association and the American Medical Association oppose the use of "hypnotically refreshed" testimony in courts of law. See Steven Jay Lynn, Timothy Lock, Elizabeth Loftus, Elisa Krackow, and Scott O. Lilienfeld (2003), "The Remembrance of Things Past: Problematic Memory Recovery Techniques in Psychotherapy," in Lilienfeld, Lohr, and Lynn, *Science and Pseudoscience in Contemporary Clinical Psychology* (note 7); and John F. Kihlstrom (1994), "Hypnosis, Delayed Recall, and the Principles of Memory," *International Journal of Experimental Hypnosis, 42,* pp. 337–345.

[9] Paul Meehl (1986, Summer), "Psychology: Does Our Heterogenous Subject Matter Have Any Unity?" *Minnesota Psychologist,* p. 4.

[10] Bessel van der Kolk's deposition was taken by attorney and psychologist R. Christopher Barden in van der Kolk's office in Boston, MA, December 27 and

28, 1996. This deposition was available online at the Web site of attorney Timothy Conlon, representing the plaintiffs. On Conlon's Web site, under "Deposition of Bessell [*sic*] van der Kolk," the psychiatrist is still described as "a leading authority on trauma and its effect on memory," and the dates of the deposition taken by Barden are noted; but the deposition itself has since been removed. http://www.tjcesq.com/CM/OnlineDocuments/OnlineDocuments19 .asp.

¹¹ John F. Kihlstrom (2004), "An Unbalanced Balancing Act: Blocked, Recovered, and False Memories in the Laboratory and Clinic," *Clinical Psychology: Science and Practice, 11.* He added that "if confidence were an adequate criterion for validity, Binjamin Wilkomirski might have gotten a Pulitzer Prize for history."

¹² Sigmund Freud (1924), "The Dissolution of the Oedipus Complex," in J. Strachey (ed.), *The Standard Edition of the Complete Psychological Works of Sigmund Freud* (Vol. 19). London: Hogarth.

¹³ Rosenzweig wrote: "On two separate occasions (1934 and 1937), first in gothic script and then in English, Freud made a similar negative response to any attempts to explore psychoanalytic theory by laboratory methods. This exchange clearly underscored Freud's distrust of, if not opposition to, experimental approaches to the validation of his clinically derived concepts. Freud consistently believed that the clinical validation of his theories, which were based originally and continuously on his self-analysis, left little to be desired from other sources of support." In Saul Rosenzweig (1997), "Letters by Freud on Experimental Psychodynamics," *American Psychologist, 52,* p. 571. See also Saul Rosenzweig (1985), "Freud and Experimental Psychology: The Emergence of Idio-Dynamics," in S. Koch and D. E. Leary (eds.), *A Century of Psychology as Science.* New York: McGraw-Hill. This book was reissued by the American Psychological Association in 1992.

¹⁴ See, for example, Lynn et al., "The Remembrance of Things Past," note 8.

¹⁵ Michael Nash offers one example in his 1994 article, "Memory Distortion and Sexual Trauma: The Problem of False Negatives and False Positives," *International Journal of Clinical and Experimental Hypnosis, 42,* pp. 346–362.

¹⁶ McNally, *Remembering Trauma,* p. 275.

¹⁷ The recovered-memory advocates in question are Daniel Brown, Alan W. Scheflin, and D. Corydon Hammond (1998), authors of *Memory, Trauma Treatment, and the Law,* New York: W. W. Norton; their rendering of the Camp Erika study, p. 156. For a review of this book that documents its authors' long association with the recovered-memory movement, their belief in

the prevalence of Satanic ritual-abuse cults, and their endorsement of the use of hypnosis to "recover" memories of abuse and generate multiple personalities, see Frederick Crews's "The Trauma Trap," *New York Review of Books, 51,* March 11, 2004. This essay has been reprinted, with other writings exposing the fallacies of the recovered-memory movement, in Frederick Crews (2006), *Follies of the Wise.* Emeryville, CA: Shoemaker & Hoard.

[18] Rosemary Basson, Rosemary McInnes, Mike D. Smith, Gemma Hodgson, and Nandan Koppiker (2002, May), "Efficacy and Safety of Sildenafil Citrate in Women with Sexual Dysfunction Associated with Female Sexual Arousal Disorder," *Journal of Women's Health & Gender-Based Medicine, 11,* pp. 367–377.

[19] Joan Kaufman and Edward Zigler (1987), "Do Abused Children Become Abusive Parents?" *American Journal of Orthopsychiatry, 57,* pp. 186–192. Ever since Freud, of course, there has been a widespread cultural assumption that childhood trauma always, inevitably, produces adult psychopathology. Research has shattered this assumption, too. Psychologist Ann Masten has observed that most people assume there is something special and rare about the children who recover from adversity. But "the great surprise" of the research, she concluded, is how ordinary resilience is. Most children are remarkably resilient, eventually overcoming even the effects of war, childhood illness, having abusive or alcoholic parents, early deprivation, or being sexually molested. See Ann Masten (2001), "Ordinary Magic: Resilience Processes in Development," *American Psychologist, 56,* pp. 227–238.

[20] For example, William Friedrich, Jennifer Fisher, Daniel Broughton, et al. (1988), "Normative Sexual Behavior in Children: A Contemporary Sample," *Pediatrics, 101,* pp. 1–8. See also www.pediatrics.org/cgi/content/full/101/4/e9. For an excellent review of the behavioral-genetics research on the stability of temperament regardless of a child's experiences, see Judith Rich Harris (1998), *The Nurture Assumption.* New York: The Free Press. That nonabused children often have nightmares and other symptoms of anxiety, see McNally, *Remembering Trauma,* note 16.

[21] Kathleen A. Kendall-Tackett, Linda M. Williams, and David Finkelhor (1993), "Impact of Sexual Abuse on Children: A Review and Synthesis of Recent Empirical Studies," *Psychological Bulletin, 113,* pp. 164–180; quote is from the article's abstract on p. 164. The researchers also found, not surprisingly, that the children's symptoms were related to the severity, duration, and frequency of the abuse, whether force had been used, the perpetrator's relationship to the

child, and degree of mother's support. In contrast to the predictions of recovered-memory therapists, about two-thirds of the victimized children recovered during the first twelve to eighteen months.

[22] In reviewing the research, Glenn Wolfner, David Faust, and Robyn Dawes concluded, "There is simply no scientific evidence available that would justify clinical or forensic diagnosis of abuse on the basis of doll play." Wolfner, Faust, and Dawes (1993), "The Use of Anatomically Detailed Dolls in Sexual Abuse Evaluations: The State of the Science," *Applied and Preventive Psychology, 2,* pp. 1–11.

[23] When the little girl was asked if this really happened, she said, "Yes, it did." When her father and the experimenter both tried to assure her by saying, "Your doctor doesn't do those things to little girls. You were just fooling. We know he didn't do those things," the child clung tenaciously to her claims. "Thus, repeated exposure to the doll, with minimal suggestions," the researchers cautioned, "resulted in highly sexualized play for this one child." Maggie Bruck, Stephen J. Ceci, Emmett Francoeur, and Ashley Renick (1995), "Anatomically Detailed Dolls Do Not Facilitate Preschoolers' Reports of a Pediatric Examination Involving Genital Touching," *Journal of Experimental Psychology: Applied, 1,* pp. 95–109.

[24] Thomas M. Horner, Melvin J. Guyer, and Neil M. Kalter (1993), "Clinical Expertise and the Assessment of Child Sexual Abuse," *Journal of the American Academy of Child and Adolescent Psychiatry, 32,* pp. 925–931; and Thomas M. Horner, Melvin J. Guyer, and Neil M. Kalter (1993), "The Biases of Child Sexual Abuse Experts: Believing Is Seeing," *Bulletin of the American Academy of Psychiatry and the Law, 21,* pp. 281–292.

[25] More than fifty years ago, Paul Meehl showed that relatively simple mathematical formulas outperformed clinicians' intuitive judgments in predicting patients' outcomes; see Paul E. Meehl (1954), *Clinical versus Statistical Prediction: A Theoretical Analysis and a Review of the Evidence,* Minneapolis: University of Minnesota Press; and Robyn Dawes, David Faust, and Paul E. Meehl (1989), "Clinical versus Actuarial Judgment," *Science, 243,* pp. 1668–1674. Meehl's findings have been repeatedly reconfirmed. See Howard Grob (1998), *Studying the Clinician: Judgment Research and Psychological Assessment.* Washington, DC: American Psychological Association.

[26] Our account of the Kelly Michaels case is based largely on Ceci and Bruck, *Jeopardy in the Courtroom* (note 3); and Pendergrast, *Victims of Memory* (note 2). See also Maggie Bruck and Stephen Ceci (1995), "Amicus Brief for the

Case of State of New Jersey v. Margaret Kelly Michaels, Presented by Committee of Concerned Social Scientists," *Psychology, Public Policy, & Law, 1(2)* [entire issue].

[27] Quoted in Pendergrast, *Victims of Memory*, p. 423; note 2.

[28] Jason J. Dickinson, Debra A. Poole, and R. L. Laimon (2005), "Children's Recall and Testimony," in N. Brewer & K. Williams (eds.), *Psychology and Law: An Empirical Perspective.* New York: Guilford. See also Debra A. Poole and D. Stephen Lindsay (1995), "Interviewing Preschoolers: Effects of Non-suggestive Techniques, Parental Coaching, and Leading Questions on Reports of Nonexperienced Events," *Journal of Experimental Child Psychology, 60,* pp. 129–154.

[29] Sena Garven, James M. Wood, Roy S. Malpass, and John S. Shaw, III (1998), "More Than Suggestion: The Effect of Interviewing Techniques from the McMartin Preschool Case," *Journal of Applied Psychology, 83,* pp. 347–359; and Sena Garven, James M. Wood, and Roy S. Malpass (2000), "Allegations of Wrongdoing: The Effects of Reinforcement on Children's Mundane and Fantastic Claims," *Journal of Applied Psychology, 85,* pp. 38–49.

[30] Gabrielle F. Principe, Tomoe Kanaya, Stephen J. Ceci, and Mona Singh (2006), "Believing Is Seeing: How Rumors Can Engender False Memories in Preschoolers," *Psychological Science, 17,* pp. 243–248.

[31] Debra A. Poole and Michael E. Lamb (1998), *Investigative Interviews of Children.* Washington, DC: American Psychological Association. Their work was the basis of the new protocols drafted by the State of Michigan Governor's Task Force on Children's Justice and Family Independence Agency (1998, 2004); see http://www.michigan.gov/documents/FIA-Pub779_13054_7.pdf. The National Institute of Child Health and Human Development (NICHD) also has prepared an investigative interview protocol that is widely used in research and assessment. For a good review, see Debra A. Poole and Jason J. Dickinson (2005), "The Future of the Protocol Movement" (invited commentary), *Child Abuse & Neglect, 29,* pp. 1197–1202.

[32] Ellen Bass and Laura Davis (1998), *The Courage to Heal: A Guide for Women Survivors of Child Sexual Abuse.* New York: Harper & Row, p. 18.

[33] In one study, researchers drew random samples of American clinical psychologists with Ph.D.s from names listed in the National Register of Health Service Providers in Psychology. They asked respondents how often they regularly used certain techniques specifically "to help clients recover memories of sexual abuse": hypnosis, age regression, dream interpretation, guided imagery

related to abuse situations, and interpreting physical symptoms as evidence of abuse. Slightly more than 40 percent said they used dream interpretation; about 30 percent said they used hypnosis; the fewest, but still about 20 percent, used age regression. About the same percentages disapproved of using these techniques; those in the middle apparently had no opinion. Debra A. Poole, D. Stephen Lindsay, Amina Memon, and Ray Bull (1995), "Psychotherapy and the Recovery of Memories of Childhood Sexual Abuse: U.S. and British Practitioners' Opinions, Practices, and Experiences," *Journal of Consulting and Clinical Psychology, 63,* pp. 426–437. More recent replications have found that the percentages have not changed appreciably.

[34] The notion that childhood sexual abuse is a leading cause of eating disorders has not been supported by empirical evidence, according to a meta-analysis of the leading studies. See Eric Stice (2002), "Risk and Maintenance Factors for Eating Pathology: A Meta-Analytic Review," *Psychological Bulletin, 128,* pp. 825–848.

[35] Richard J. McNally (2005), "Troubles in Traumatology," *The Canadian Journal of Psychiatry, 50,* pp. 815–816. His quote is on p. 815.

[36] John Briere made this statement at the 12th International Congress on Child Abuse and Neglect in 1998, in Auckland, New Zealand. These remarks were reported by the *New Zealand Herald,* September 9, 1998. The paper quoted Briere as saying that "missing memories of abuse are reasonably common, but evidence suggests that false memories of abuse are quite uncommon." See http://www.menz.org.nz/Casualties/1998%20newsletters/Oct%2098.htm.

[37] Quoted in Pendergrast, *Victims of Memory,* p. 567; note 2.

[38] Hammond made these remarks in his presentation, "Investigating False Memory for the Unmemorable: A Critique of Experimental Hypnosis and Memory Research," at the 14th International Congress of Hypnosis and Psychosomatic Medicine, San Diego, June 1997. Tapes of Hammond's talk have been offered by The Sound of Knowledge, Inc.

[39] For example, one group of psychiatrists and other clinical experts asked the United States Department of Justice to pass a law making it illegal to publish excerpts of children's testimony in the actual day-care cases. The DOJ refused. Basic Books was threatened with an injunction if it published Debbie Nathan and Michael Snedeker's *Satan's Silence,* an exposé of the day-care hysteria; Basic Books did not comply with their demands. The American Psychological Association was threatened with a lawsuit if it published Stephen Ceci and

Maggie Bruck's *Jeopardy in the Courtroom;* the APA delayed publication for several months. Our source is personal communications from the investigators involved.

⁴⁰ In the preface to the third edition of *The Courage to Heal* (p. 14), Bass and Davis responded to the scientific criticism directed at their book and attempted to justify their lack of professional training: "As authors, we have been criticized for our lack of academic credentials. But you do not have to have a Ph.D. to listen carefully and compassionately to another human being." That is true, but as we hope we have shown in this chapter, some training in science might prevent all those well-meaning, empathic listeners from leaping to unwarranted, implausible conclusions—especially when those conclusions can have tragic consequences. The authors did not attempt to correct any of the mistakes they made in the first edition, apart from making a few brief modifications and adding a self-protective caution that if your therapist pressures you to remember abuse, find another therapist. And oh, yes, for the third edition they talked with a "small number" of women who originally thought they might have been sexually molested but who instead found their pain stemmed from "emotional abuse" or other early trauma.

To our knowledge, neither Bass nor Davis has ever acknowledged that they were wrong in any of their basic claims about memory and trauma. According to her Web site, Laura Davis has moved on to the next trend, advocating reconciliation for families that have been broken apart by allegations of sexual abuse.
⁴¹ National Public Radio's *This American Life,* episode 215, aired June 16, 2002.

CHAPTER 5
Law and Disorder

¹ Timothy Sullivan (1992), *Unequal Verdicts: The Central Park Jogger Trials.* New York: American Lawyer Books/Simon & Schuster.
² Reyes confessed because, entirely by chance, he met one of the convicted defendants, Kharey Wise, in prison and apparently came to feel guilty about Wise's wrongful incarceration. Later he began telling prison officials that he had committed a crime for which others had been wrongly convicted, and a reinvestigation began. Steven A. Drizin and Richard A. Leo (2004), "The

Problem of False Confessions in the Post-DNA World," *North Carolina Law Review, 82,* pp. 891–1008; see p. 899.

[3] See www.innocenceproject.org and Barry Scheck, Peter Neufeld, and Jim Dwyer (2000), *Actual Innocence.* New York: Doubleday.

[4] Emphasis in original. Samuel R. Gross et al. (2004), "Exonerations in the United States, 1989 through 2003." http://www.mindfully.org/Reform/2004/Prison-Exonerations-Gross19apr04.htm. This research was subsequently published in a law journal: Samuel R. Gross, Kristen Jacoby, Daniel J. Matheson, Nicholas Montgomery, and Sujata Patil (2005), "Exonerations in the United States, 1989 through 2003," *Journal of Criminal Law and Criminology, 95,* pp. 523ff.

[5] Quoted in Richard Jerome, "Suspect Confessions," *The New York Times Magazine,* August 13, 1995, pp. 28–31; quote is on p. 31.

[6] Daniel S. Medwed (2004), "The Zeal Deal: Prosecutorial Resistance to Post-Conviction Claims of Innocence," *Boston University Law Review, 84,* p. 125. Medwed analyzes the institutional culture of many prosecutors' offices that makes it difficult for prosecutors to admit mistakes and correct them.

[7] Joshua Marquis, "The Innocent and the Shammed," *The New York Times* op-ed, January 26, 2006.

[8] *Harmful Error: Investigating America's Local Prosecutors,* published by the Center for Public Integrity, Summer 2003, reports on their analysis of 11,452 cases across the nation in which appellate court judges reviewed charges of prosecutorial misconduct. The center gave Marquis a chance to respond; "Those few cases," "The truth is that . . . ," p. 110. http://www.publicintegrity.org.

[9] Quoted in Mike Miner, "Why Can't They Admit They Were Wrong?" *Chicago Reader,* August 1, 2003.

[10] The main problem with the Voice Stress Analyzer is that the confirmation bias gets in the way. If you think the suspect is guilty, you interpret the microtremors as signs of lying, and if you think the suspect is innocent, you pay them no attention. For a bibliography and review of some of this research, see http://www.polygraph.org/voicestress.htm.

[11] Quoted in Paul E. Tracy (with the collaboration of Ralph Claytor and Chris McDonough) (2003), *Who Killed Stephanie Crowe?* Dallas, TX: Brown Books, p. 334.

[12] The account of Vic Caloca's involvement in the case, including the quotes by him, comes from a story written by investigative reporters John Wilkens and Mark Sauer, "A Badge of Courage: In the Crowe Case, This Cop Ignored the Politics while Pursuing Justice," *The San Diego Union-Tribune,* July 11,

2004. Druliner's quote is in Mark Sauer and John Wilkens, "Tuite Found Guilty of Manslaughter," *The San Diego Union-Tribune,* May 27, 2004.

[13] Deanna Kuhn, Michael Weinstock, and Robin Flaton (1994), "How Well Do Jurors Reason? Competence Dimensions of Individual Variation in a Juror Reasoning Task," *Psychological Science, 5,* pp. 289–296.

[14] Don DeNevi and John H. Campbell (2004), *Into the Minds of Madmen: How the FBI's Behavioral Science Unit Revolutionized Crime Investigation.* Amherst, NY: Prometheus Books, p. 33. This book is, unintentionally, a case study of the unscientific training of the FBI's Behavioral Science Unit.

[15] Quoted in Tracy, *Who Killed Stephanie Crowe?,* p. 184; note 11.

[16] Quoted on CBS's *Eye to Eye* with Connie Chung (1994).

[17] Introductory comments by Steven Drizin, "Prosecutors Won't Oppose Tankleff's Hearing," *The New York Times on the Web,* May 13, 2004.

[18] Edward Humes (1999), *Mean Justice.* New York: Pocket Books, p. 181.

[19] Andrew J. McClurg (1999), "Good Cop, Bad Cop: Using Cognitive Dissonance Theory to Reduce Police Lying," *U.C. Davis Law Review, 32,* pp. 389–453. First quote, p. 394; second, p. 429.

[20] This excuse is so common that it, too, has spawned a new term: "dropsy" testimony. David Heilbroner, a former New York assistant district attorney, wrote: "In dropsy cases, officers justify a search by the oldest of means: they lie about the facts. *As I was coming around the corner I saw the defendant drop the drugs on the sidewalk, so I arrested him.* It was an old line known to everyone in the justice system. One renowned federal judge many years ago complained that he had read the same testimony in too many cases for it to be believed any longer as a matter of law." David Heilbroner (1990), *Rough Justice: Days and Nights of a Young D.A.* New York: Pantheon, p. 29.

[21] McClurg, "Good Cop, Bad Cop," note 19, p. 391, quoting from the City of New York Commission to Investigate Allegations of Police Corruption and the Anti-Corruption Procedures of the Police Department: Commission Report 36 (1994), referred to as the Mollen Commission Report.

[22] Norm Stamper (2005), *Breaking Rank: A Top Cop's Exposé of the Dark Side of American Policing.* New York: Nation Books. See also "Let Those Dopers Be," Stamper's op-ed essay for the *Los Angeles Times,* October 16, 2005.

[23] Quoted in McClurg, "Good Cop, Bad Cop," note 19, pp. 413, 415.

[24] In Suffolk County, New York, in September 1988, homicide detective K. James McCready was summoned to a home where he found the body of Arlene Tankleff, who had been stabbed and beaten to death, and her husband, Seymour, who also

266 CAROL TAVRIS and ELLIOT ARONSON

had been brutally attacked. (He died a few weeks later.) Within hours, McCready declared that he had solved the case: The killer was the couple's son, Martin, age seventeen. During the interrogation, McCready repeatedly told Martin that he knew he had killed his parents because his father had briefly come out of his coma before dying and told police that Marty was his attacker. This was a lie. "I used trickery and deceit," McCready said. "I don't *think* he did it. I *know* he did it." The teenager finally confessed that he must have killed his parents while in a blackout. He immediately disavowed the confession and never signed it, but it was enough to get him sentenced to fifty years to life. In 2007, after Martin had spent twenty years in prison, his conviction was vacated, all charges were dropped, and he was released. Bruce Lambert, "Convicted of Killing His Parents, but Calling a Detective the Real Bad Guy," *The New York Times,* April 4, 2004.

[25] Quoted in Tracy, *Who Killed Stephanie Crowe?,* p. 175; note 11.

[26] Fred E. Inbau, John E. Reid, Joseph P. Buckley, and Brian C. Jayne (2001), *Criminal Interrogation and Confessions* (fourth ed.). Gaithersburg, MD: Aspen Publishers, p. 212.

[27] Inbau et al., p. 429.

[28] One of the most thorough dissections of the Reid Technique and the Inbau et al. manual is Deborah Davis and William T. O'Donohue (2004), "The Road to Perdition: 'Extreme Influence' Tactics in the Interrogation Room," in W. T. O'Donohue and E. Levensky (eds.), *Handbook of Forensic Psychology,* pp. 897–996. New York: Elsevier Academic Press.

[29] Louis C. Senese (2005), *Anatomy of Interrogation Themes: The Reid Technique of Interviewing.* Chicago: John E. Reid & Associates, p. 32.

[30] Quoted also in Saul Kassin (2005), "On the Psychology of Confessions: Does *Innocence* Put *Innocents* at Risk?" *American Psychologist, 60,* pp. 215–228.

[31] Saul M. Kassin and Christina T. Fong (1999), "I'm Innocent! Effects of Training on Judgments of Truth and Deception in the Interrogation Room," *Law and Human Behavior, 23,* pp. 499–516. In another study, Kassin and his colleagues recruited prison inmates who were instructed to give a full confession of their own crime and a made-up confession of a crime committed by another inmate. College students and police investigators judged the videotaped confessions. The overall accuracy rate did not exceed chance, but the police were more confident in their judgments. See Saul M. Kassin, Christian A. Meissner, and Rebecca J. Norwick (2005), "'I'd know a false confession if I saw one': A Comparative Study of College Students and Police Investigators," *Law and Human Behavior, 29,* pp. 211–227.

[32] This is why innocent people are more likely than guilty people to waive their Miranda rights to silence and to having a lawyer. In one of Saul Kassin's experiments, seventy-two participants who were guilty or innocent of stealing $100 were interrogated by a male detective whose demeanor was neutral, sympathetic, or hostile, and who then tried to get them to give up their Miranda rights. Those who were innocent were far more likely to sign a waiver than those who were guilty, and by a large margin—81 percent to 36 percent. Two thirds of the innocent suspects even signed the waiver when the detective adopted a hostile pose, shouting at them, "I know you did this and I don't want to hear any lies!" The reason they signed, they later said, was they thought that only guilty people need a lawyer, whereas they had done nothing wrong and had nothing to hide. "It appears," the experimenters concluded mournfully, "that people have a naïve faith in the power of their own innocence to set them free." Saul M. Kassin and Rebecca J. Norwick (2004), "Why People Waive Their Miranda Rights: The Power of Innocence," *Law and Human Behavior, 28,* pp. 211–221.

[33] Drizin and Leo, "The Problem of False Confessions in the Post-DNA World," p. 948; note 2.

[34] For example, one teenager, Kharey Wise, was told that the jogger was hit with a "very heavy object" and then was asked, "Was she hit with a stone or brick?" Wise said first that it was a rock; moments later, that it was a brick. He said one of the others had pulled out a knife and cut the jogger's shirt off, which wasn't true; there were no knife cuts. Saul Kassin, "False Confessions and the Jogger Case," *The New York Times* op-ed, November 1, 2002.

[35] New York v. Kharey Wise, Kevin Richardson, Antron McCray, Yusef Salaam, and Raymond Santana: Affirmation in response to motion to vacate judgment of conviction, Indictment No. 4762/89, by Assistant District Attorney Nancy Ryan, December 5, 2002. Quote on page 46.

[36] Adam Liptak, "Prosecutors Fight DNA Use for Exoneration," *The New York Times,* August 29, 2003. See also Daniel Medwed, "The Zeal Deal," for a review of the evidence of prosecutorial resistance to reopening DNA cases; note 6.

[37] Quoted in Sara Rimer, "Convict's DNA Sways Labs, Not a Determined Prosecutor," *The New York Times,* February 6, 2002.

[38] "The Case for Innocence," a *Frontline* special for PBS by Ofra Bikel, first aired October 31, 2000. Transcripts and information available from the PBS *Frontline* Web site at http://www.pbs.org/wgbh/pages/frontline/shows/case/etc/tapes.html.

[39] Drizin and Leo, "The Problem of False Confessions in the Post-DNA World," p. 928, note 200 on that page; note 2.

[40] In a famous case in North Carolina, where a victim identified the wrong man as the man who raped her, DNA was eventually traced to the true perpetrator; see James M. Doyle (2005), *True Witness: Cops, Courts, Science, and the Battle Against Misidentification.* New York: Palgrave Macmillan. Sometimes, too, a "cold case" is solved with DNA evidence. In Los Angeles in 2004, detectives working in the newly formed cold case unit got samples of semen from the body of a woman who had been raped and murdered years earlier, and checked them against the state's database of DNA from convicted violent felons. They got a match to Chester Turner, who was already in prison for rape. The detectives kept submitting DNA samples from other unsolved murders to the lab, and every month they got another match with Turner. Before long, they had linked him to twelve slayings of poor black prostitutes. Amidst the general exhilaration of catching a serial killer, District Attorney Steve Cooley quietly released David Jones, a retarded janitor with the mental age of a child, who had spent nine years in prison for three of the murders. If Turner had murdered only those three women, he would still be at large and Jones would still be in prison. But because Turner killed nine other women whose cases were unsolved, Jones was the lucky beneficiary of the efforts of the cold case unit. Justice, for him, was a byproduct of another investigation. No one, not even the cold case investigators, had any motivation to check Jones's DNA against the samples from the victims during those long nine years. But the new team of detectives had every motivation to solve old unsolved crimes, and that is the only reason that justice was served and Jones was released.

[41] Deborah Davis and Richard Leo (2006), "Strategies for Preventing False Confessions and their Consequences," in M. R. Kebbell and G. M. Davies (eds.), *Practical Psychology for Forensic Investigations and Prosecutions.* Chichester, England: Wiley, pp. 121–149. See also the essays in Saundra D. Westervelt and John A. Humphrey (eds.) (2001), *Wrongly Convicted: Perspectives on Failed Justice.* New Brunswick, NJ: Rutgers University Press.

[42] Quoted on the PBS show *Frontline,* "The Case for Innocence," October 31, 2000.

[43] D. Michael Risinger and Jeffrey L. Loop (2002, November), "Three Card Monte, Monty Hall, Modus Operandi and 'Offender Profiling': Some Lessons of Modern Cognitive Science for the Law of Evidence," *Cardozo Law Review, 24,* p. 193.

44 Davis and Leo, "Strategies for Preventing False Confessions . . . ," p. 145; note 41.

45 McClurg, "Good Cop, Bad Cop"; note 19. McClurg's own suggestions for using cognitive dissonance to reduce the risk of police lying are in this essay.

46 Saul M. Kassin and Gisli H. Gudjonsson (2004), "The Psychology of Confession Evidence: A Review of the Literature and Issues," especially the section on "Videotaping Interrogations: A Policy Whose Time Has Come," *Psychological Science in the Public Interest, 5,* pp. 33–67. See also Drizin and Leo, "The Problem of False Confessions . . . ," note 2; Davis and O'Donohue, "The Road to Perdition," note 28.

47 Quoted in Jerome, "Suspect Confessions," p. 31; note 5.

48 Thomas P. Sullivan (2004), "Police Experiences with Recording Custodial Interrogations." This study, with extensive references on the benefits of recordings, is posted on the Internet at http://www.law.northwestern.edu/ wrongfulconvictions/Causes/custodialInterrogations.htm. However, further research has shown that the camera angle can bias observers' judgments, especially if the camera is focused exclusively on the suspect and does not include the interviewer(s). G. Daniel Lassiter, Andrew L. Geers, Ian M. Handley, Paul E. Weiland, and Patrick J. Munhall (2002), "Videotaped Interrogations and Confessions: A Simple Change in Camera Perspective Alters Verdicts in Simulated Trials," *Journal of Applied Psychology, 87,* pp. 867–874.

49 Davis and Leo, "Strategies for Preventing False Confessions . . . ," p. 145; note 41. In Canada, the Federal/Provincial/Territorial Heads of Prosecutions Committee established a Working Group on the Prevention of Miscarriages of Justice. Their Report on the Prevention of Miscarriages of Justice, released January 2005, is available at http://canada.justice.gc.ca/en/ dept/pub/hop/.

50 Thomas Vanes, "Let DNA Close Door on Doubt in Murder Cases," the *Los Angeles Times* op-ed, July 28, 2003.

CHAPTER 6

Love's Assassin: Self-justification in Marriage

1 John Butler Yeats to his son William, November 5, 1917. In Richard J. Finneran, George M. Harper, and William M. Murphy (eds.), *Letters to W. B. Yeats, Vol. 2.* New York: Columbia University Press, p. 338.

² Andrew Christensen and Neil S. Jacobson (2000), *Reconcilable Differences.* New York: Guilford. We have taken excerpts from the story of Debra and Frank at the opening of chapter 1, pp. 1–7.

³ See Neil S. Jacobson and Andrew Christensen (1998), *Acceptance and Change in Couple Therapy: A Therapist's Guide to Transforming Relationships.* New York: W. W. Norton.

⁴ Christensen and Jacobson, *Reconcilable Differences,* p. 9; note 2.

⁵ There is a very large body of research on the way a couple's attributions about each other affect their feelings about each other and the course of their marriage. See, for example, Adam Davey, Frank D. Fincham, Steven R. H. Beach, and Gene H. Brody (2001), "Attributions in Marriage: Examining the Entailment Model in Dyadic Context," *Journal of Family Psychology, 15,* pp. 721–734; Thomas N. Bradbury and Frank D. Fincham (1992), "Attributions and Behavior in Marital Interaction," *Journal of Personality and Social Psychology, 63,* pp. 613–628; and Benjamin R. Karney and Thomas N. Bradbury (2000), "Attributions in Marriage: State or Trait? A Growth Curve Analysis," *Journal of Personality and Social Psychology, 78,* 295–309.

⁶ June P. Tangney, Patricia E. Wagner, Deborah Hill-Barlow, et al. (1996), "Relation of Shame and Guilt to Constructive versus Destructive Responses to Anger Across the Lifespan," *Journal of Personality and Social Psychology, 70,* 797–809.

⁷ John Gottman (1994), *Why Marriages Succeed or Fail.* New York: Simon & Schuster. Fred and Ingrid are on p. 69.

⁸ See, for example, Benjamin R. Karney and Thomas N. Bradbury (1995), "The Longitudinal Course of Marital Quality and Stability: A Review of Theory, Method, and Research," *Psychological Bulletin, 118,* pp. 3–34; and Frank D. Fincham, Gordon T. Harold, and Susan Gano-Phillips (2000), "The Longitudinal Relation between Attributions and Marital Satisfaction: Direction of Effects and Role of Efficacy Expectations," *Journal of Family Psychology, 14,* pp. 267–285.

⁹ Gottman, *Why Marriages Succeed or Fail,* p. 57; note 7.

¹⁰ Quoted in Ayala M. Pines (1986), "Marriage," in C. Tavris (ed.), *Every-Woman's Emotional Well-Being.* New York: Doubleday. Ellen's story is on p. 191; Donna and her "hate book" are on pp. 190–191.

¹¹ Julie Schwartz Gottman (ed.) (2004), *The Marriage Clinic Casebook.* New York: W. W. Norton. The story of this couple is in chapter 4, "Extramarital Affairs: The Pearl in the Oyster," by Julie Gottman, p. 50.

[12] John Gottman, *Why Marriages Succeed or Fail,* p. 127; for his description of the fifty-six couples, see p. 128; note 7.

[13] Donald T. Saposnek and Chip Rose (1990), "The Psychology of Divorce," in D. L. Crumbley and N. G. Apostolou (eds.), *Handbook of Financial Planning for Divorce and Separation.* New York: John Wiley. Their article is available online at http://www.mediate.com/articles/saporo.cfm. For a classic study of the ways that couples reconstruct their memories of their marriage and each other, see Janet R. Johnston and Linda E. Campbell (1988*), Impasses of Divorce: The Dynamics and Resolution of Family Conflict.* New York: Free Press.

[14] Jacobson and Christensen, *Acceptance and Change in Couple Therapy,* note 3, discuss new approaches to help partners accept each other rather than always trying to get the other to change.

[15] Vivian Gornick (2002), "What Independence Has Come to Mean to Me: The Pain of Solitude, the Pleasure of Self-Knowledge," in Cathi Hanauer (ed.), *The Bitch in the House.* New York: William Morrow, p. 259.

CHAPTER 7
Wounds, Rifts, and Wars

[1] Our portrayal of this couple is based on the story of Joe and Mary Louise in Andrew Christensen and Neil S. Jacobson (2000), *Reconcilable Differences,* New York: Guilford, p. 290.

[2] The story of the Schiavo family battle is drawn from news reports and the in-depth reporting by Abby Goodnough for *The New York Times,* "Behind Life-and-Death Fight, a Rift that Began Years Ago," March 26, 2005.

[3] Sukhwinder S. Shergill, Paul M. Bays, Chris D. Frith, and Daniel M. Wolpert (2003, July 11), "Two Eyes for an Eye: The Neuroscience of Force Escalation," *Science, 301,* p. 187.

[4] Roy F. Baumeister, Arlene Stillwell, and Sara R. Wotman (1990), "Victim and Perpetrator Accounts of Interpersonal Conflict: Autobiographical Narratives about Anger," *Journal of Personality and Social Psychology, 59,* pp. 994–1005. The examples of typical remarks are ours, not the researchers'.

[5] Luc Sante, "Tourists and Torturers," *The New York Times* op-ed, May 11, 2004.

[6] Amos Oz, "The Devil in the Details," the *Los Angeles Times* op-ed, October 10, 2005.

7 Keith Davis and Edward E. Jones (1960), "Changes in Interpersonal Perception as a Means of Reducing Cognitive Dissonance," *Journal of Abnormal and Social Psychology, 61,* pp. 402–410; see also Frederick X. Gibbons and Sue B. McCoy (1991), "Self-Esteem, Similarity, and Reactions to Active versus Passive Downward Comparison," *Journal of Personality and Social Psychology, 60,* pp. 414–424.

8 David Glass (1964), "Changes in Liking as a Means of Reducing Cognitive Discrepancies between Self-Esteem and Aggression," *Journal of Personality, 32,* pp. 531–549. See also Richard M. Sorrentino and Robert G. Boutilier (1974), "Evaluation of a Victim as a Function of Fate Similarity/Dissimilarity," *Journal of Experimental Social Psychology, 10,* pp. 84–93; and Richard M. Sorrentino and Jack E. Hardy (1974), "Religiousness and Derogation of an Innocent Victim," *Journal of Personality, 42,* pp. 372–382.

9 Yes, he really said it. See Derrick Z. Jackson, "The Westmoreland Mind-Set," *Boston Globe,* July 20, 2005. Westmoreland made these remarks in the 1974 Vietnam documentary *Hearts and Minds.* According to Jackson, "The quote so stunned director Peter Davis that he gave Westmoreland a chance to clean it up." He didn't.

10 Ellen Berscheid, David Boye, and Elaine Walster (Hatfield) (1968), "Retaliation as a Means of Restoring Equity," *Journal of Personality and Social Psychology, 10,* pp. 370–376.

11 Stanley Milgram (1974), *Obedience to Authority.* New York: Harper & Row, p. 10.

12 On demonizing the perpetrator as a way of restoring consonance and maintaining a belief that the world is just, see John H. Ellard, Christina D. Miller, Terri-Lynne Baumle, and James Olson (2002), "Just World Processes in Demonizing," in M. Ross and D. T. Miller (eds.), *The Justice Motive in Everyday Life.* New York: Cambridge University Press.

13 John Conroy (2000), *Unspeakable Acts, Ordinary People.* New York: Knopf, p. 112.

14 Bush made his remark on November 7, 2005, after news that detainees were being held in secret "terror jails" and the abuses at Abu Ghraib prison had been exposed. Inhofe made his comments on May 11, 2004, during the Senate Armed Services Committee hearings regarding abuses of Iraqi prisoners at Abu Ghraib prison. In February 2004, the International Committee of the Red Cross had issued its findings, "Report of the International Committee of the Red Cross (ICRC) on the Treatment by the Coalition Forces of Prisoners

of War and Other Protected Persons by the Geneva Conventions in Iraq during Arrest, Internment and Interrogation." This document is available at
http://www.globalsecurity.org/military/library/report/2004/icrc_report_iraq_
feb2004.htm. Under #1, "Treatment During Arrest," see point 7: "Certain
CF [Coalition Forces] military intelligence officers told the ICRC that in their
estimate between 70% and 90% of the persons deprived of their liberty in
Iraq had been arrested by mistake."

[15] Charles Krauthammer made the case for the limited use of torture in "The
Truth about Torture: It's time to be honest about doing terrible things," in *The
Weekly Standard,* December 5, 2005.

[16] Remarks of Condoleezza Rice at Andrews Air Force Base, December 5,
2005, as she was departing for a state visit to Europe.

[17] William Schulz, "An Israeli Interrogator, and a Tale of Torture," letter to *The
New York Times,* December 27, 2004. A year later, the *Times* reported the case
of Ibn al-Shaykh al-Libi, a former Al Qaeda leader, who was captured in Pak-
istan by American forces and sent for "questioning" to Egypt. The Egyptians
sent him back to the American authorities when he finally confessed that Al
Qaeda members had received chemical weapons training in Iraq—information the Americans wanted to hear. Later, Libi said he made the story up to
appease the Egyptians, who were torturing him (with American approval). A
Times editorial in the aftermath of this story (December 10, 2005) noted that
"torture is a terrible way to do the very thing that the administration uses to
excuse it—getting accurate information. Centuries of experience show that
people will tell their tormenters what they want to hear, whether it's confessing to witchcraft in Salem, admitting to counterrevolutionary tendencies in
Soviet Russia or concocting stories about Iraq and Al Qaeda."

[18] An anonymous sergeant describing the handling of detainees in Iraq in a
Human Rights Watch report, September 2005; reprinted with other commentary in "Under Control," *Harper's,* December 2005, pp. 23–24.

[19] Riccardo Orizio (2003), *Talk of the Devil: Encounters with Seven Dictators.*
New York: Walker & Company.

[20] Louis Menand, "The Devil's Disciples: Can You Force People to Love Freedom?," *New Yorker,* July 28, 2003.

[21] Timothy Garton Ash, "Europe's Bloody Hands," the *Los Angeles Times,* July
27, 2006.

[22] Christensen and Jacobson, *Reconcilable Differences,* p. 291; note 1.

[23] For a thoughtful analysis of the social and personal costs of forgiveness that

is uncritical and premature, letting perpetrators off the hook of responsibility and accountability for the harm they caused, see Sharon Lamb (1996), *The Trouble with Blame: Victims, Perpetrators, and Responsibility.* Cambridge, MA: Harvard University Press.

²⁴ Solomon Schimmel (2002), *Wounds Not Healed by Time: The Power of Repentance and Forgiveness.* Oxford, England: Oxford University Press, p. 226. Psychologist Ervin Staub, himself a Holocaust survivor, has been studying the origins and dynamics of genocide for many years, and most recently has devoted himself to the project of reconciliation between the Tutsi and Hutu in Rwanda. See Ervin Staub and Laurie A. Pearlman (2006), "Advancing Healing and Reconciliation in Rwanda and Other Post-conflict Settings," in L. Barbanel and R. Sternberg (eds.), *Psychological Interventions in Times of Crisis,* New York: Springer-Verlag; and Daniel Goleman (2006), *Social Intelligence,* New York: Bantam Books.

²⁵ Broyles told this story in a 1987 PBS documentary, "Faces of the Enemy," based on the book of the same title by Sam Keen. It is still available on VHS and DVD from PBS.

CHAPTER 8
Letting Go and Owning Up

¹ All quotations are taken from the transcript of Oprah's show, January 26, 2006.

² "Wayne Hale's Insider's Guide to NASA," by Nell Boyce. NPR *Morning Edition,* June 30, 2006. The full text of Hale's e-mail to colleagues is available online.

³ Reagan's defense started out well—"First, let me say I take full responsibility for my own actions and for those of my administration"—but then he added a series of "but they did it"s: "As angry as I may be about activities undertaken without my knowledge, I am still accountable for those activities. As disappointed as I may be in some who served me, I'm still the one who must answer to the American people for this behavior. And as personally distasteful as I find secret bank accounts and diverted funds—well, as the Navy would say, this happened on my watch." And this is how he took "full responsibility" for breaking the law: "A few months ago I told the American people I did

not trade arms for hostages. My heart and my best intentions still tell me that's true, but the facts and the evidence tell me it is not."

[4] Daniel Yankelovich and Isabella Furth (2005, September 16), "The Role of Colleges in an Era of Mistrust," *The Chronicle of Higher Education,* pp. B8–B11. Quote on p. B11.

[5] Posted on the Web site of an advocacy group called The Sorry Works!, a coalition of physicians, hospital administrators, insurers, patients, and others concerned with the medical malpractice crisis. At Mount Sinai School of Medicine in New York and several other medical schools, residents are learning how to acknowledge mistakes and apologize for them, as well as how to distinguish a bad outcome that is not their fault from one that is. See Katherine Mangan, "Acting Sick," *The Chronicle of Higher Education,* September 15, 2006.

[6] Richard A. Friedman, "Learning Words They Rarely Teach in Medical School: 'I'm Sorry,'" *The New York Times* Science section, July 26, 2005.

[7] *Harmful Error: Investigating America's Local Prosecutors,* published by the Center for Public Integrity, Summer 2003. http://www.publicintegrity.org.

[8] Faced with a wave of verified wrongful convictions, Great Britain has adopted a number of reforms. For example, the government established the Criminal Cases Review Commission, an independent council to investigate allegations of misconduct and suppression or falsification of evidence. In 1984, in response to several high-profile wrongful convictions that proved to have been based on coerced confessions, England and Wales passed the Police and Criminal Evidence Act, which made it illegal for police interrogators to lie about evidence to induce confessions and required all interrogations to be recorded. According to Richard Leo, although British interrogation today is more conversational and designed to get information rather than confession, the confession rate has not declined since passage of this act. See Richard Leo (2007), *Police Interrogation and American Justice.* Cambridge, MA: Harvard University Press.

[9] Warren G. Bennis and Burt Nanus (1995), *Leaders: Strategies for Taking Charge* (rev. ed.). New York: HarperCollins, p. 70.

[10] Quote from Shimon Peres in Dennis Prager's *Ultimate Issues,* Summer 1985, p. 11.

[11] This message was posted on the listserv Teaching in the Psychological Sciences, May 1, 2003.

[12] Quoted in Charles Baxter (1997), "Dysfunctional Narratives: or: 'Mistakes Were Made,'" in *Burning Down the House: Essays on Fiction.* Saint Paul, MN: Graywolf Press, p. 5. There is some dispute about the second sentence of Lee's remarks, but not about his assuming responsibility for his disastrous actions.

[13] Anthony Pratkanis and Doug Shadel (2005), *Weapons of Fraud: A Source Book for Fraud Fighters.* This book is available free from the AARP; for more information, go to www.aarp.org/wa.

[14] Stigler recalled this story in an obituary for Harold Stevenson, the *Los Angeles Times,* July 22, 2005. For their research, see Harold W. Stevenson and James W. Stigler (1992), *The Learning Gap,* New York: Summit; and Harold W. Stevenson, Chuansheng Chen, and Shin-ying Lee (1993, January 1), "Mathematics Achievement of Chinese, Japanese, and American Schoolchildren: Ten Years Later," *Science, 259,* pp. 53–58.

[15] Carol S. Dweck (1992), "The Study of Goals in Psychology," *Psychological Science, 3,* pp. 165–167; Carol S. Dweck and Lisa Sorich (1999), "Mastery-Oriented Thinking," in C. R. Snyder (ed.), *Coping: The Psychology of What Works.* New York: Oxford University Press; Claudia M. Mueller and Carol S. Dweck (1998), "Praise for Intelligence Can Undermine Children's Motivation and Performance," *Journal of Personality and Social Psychology, 75,* pp. 33–52. Dweck has also written a book for general audiences: Carol S. Dweck (2006), *Mindset: The New Psychology of Success.* New York: Random House.

[16] Bush's response was made at the second presidential candidates' debate with John Kerry, October 8, 2004.

[17] Eisenhower's handwritten document is available at http://www.archives.gov/education/lessons/d-day-message/. See also Michael Korda (2007), *Ike: An American Hero.* New York: HarperCollins. On the *Charlie Rose* show on November 16, 2007, Korda said of Eisenhower: "When things went right, he praised his subordinates and made sure they got the praise; and when things went wrong, he took the blame. Not many presidents have done that, and very few generals."

INDEX

○   ○   ○